Housing America's Poor

*Urban and Regional Policy
and Development Studies*

Michael A. Stegman, Series Editor

Housing America's Poor

Edited by Peter D. Salins

The University of North Carolina Press
Chapel Hill and London

© 1987 The University of North Carolina Press

Manufactured in the United States of America

Library of Congress Cataloging-in-Publication Data

Housing America's poor.

  (Urban and regional policy and development studies)
  Includes index.
  1. Poor—Housing—United States.   2. Housing policy—
United States.   3. Public housing—United States.
I. Salins, Peter D.   II. Series.
HD7287.96.U5H68   1987   363.5′8   86-40449
ISBN 0-8078-1738-4
ISBN 0-8078-4181-1 (pbk.)

Contents

Preface

National housing policy, especially as it affects the poor, is in a state of flux. From 1965 to 1980 successive national administrations experimented with a series of housing programs. Each new program was launched with high hopes and a great deal of fanfare, only to be scaled back or canceled a few years later. Each administration beginning with President Lyndon Johnson's Great Society had a different theory about the nature of the country's housing problems and a different set of approaches to cure them. For better or worse, the merry-go-round of housing policy innovation has now largely drawn to a halt. The present administration in Washington is unsympathetic to both the ends and means of earlier housing programs. And as important, the traditional champions of housing subsidies and housing reform have grown weary of the battle and offer only weak arguments against government's tendency to withdraw from the housing arena.

This does not mean, of course, that we have seen the end of government intervention in the housing market. It does mean, however, that this is a time to take stock of what we can and should do about housing policy. Past approaches to improving housing for low-income Americans must be reappraised. New approaches must be designed. Above all, the goals of a national housing program must be clearly articulated. And the means to implement such a program must be proportionate both to the goals and to the resources available, given realistic political and economic constraints.

It was to promote just such a rethinking of national low-income housing policy options that the Lavanburg Foundation, a New York City institution founded in 1927 to promote better housing conditions for the poor, sponsored this book and the conference that preceded it. I was charged by the foundation to find a set of contributors for the book who would be able to define the housing needs of low-income Americans, look carefully and critically at the impact of earlier public housing policies and programs, and evaluate newer approaches, current and proposed.

In choosing the contributors, and as I worked with them on the scope of their respective chapters, I was concerned that we keep sight of the larger economic, social, and political context in which government-sponsored housing policies operate. As such, the first five chapters represent attempts to answer a series of broad-gauge conceptual questions. Why has housing for the poor been such an apparently intractable problem? How effective have past housing programs been and how well have they met contemporary goals? What has been the role of the private sector in improving housing conditions? Who, among the poor, are in the greatest need of housing assistance, and why? Where, in our urban areas, should housing for the poor be located, or should this question even be asked? The next three chapters examine various current and proposed approaches to housing policy and evaluate their feasibility. Can we salvage and recycle blighted urban neighborhoods of older housing? To what extent are the most effective housing subsidies not really part of housing programs at all but built into the tax code and the banking system? Should we combine two disparate approaches—tax subsidies and housing vouchers—into a comprehensive housing panacea? My concluding essay reviews the various arguments that emerge in the book and offers speculations as to the ingredients of an effective and politically acceptable national low-income housing policy.

This book was an intensely collaborative effort. I was indeed fortunate to be able to enlist as authors some of the nation's most highly respected housing policy specialists: George Sternlieb and David Listokin, John Weicher, William Apgar, Ira (Jack) Lowry, Howard Sumka, Kevin Villani, and Elizabeth Roistacher. Happily, both in temperament and expertise, the group was well balanced, reflecting different conceptual viewpoints and differing niches of analysis and experience.

There were some very important contributors to this book who do not appear as chapter authors. The entire project was, to a large extent, the brainchild of Roger Starr, whose encouragement and support were crucial from the initial conceptualization through the final editing of the manuscript. Louis Winnick was a constant guide (and goad) in shaping the book's intellectual content. A distinguished panel of discussants was involved in critiquing the chapters when they first were delivered as conference papers: Jameson Doig, Cushing Dolbeare, Grace Milgram, Edgar Olsen, Eugenie Birch, Philip Clay, Feather O'Connor, Margaret Drury, Kathryn Wylde, Thomas Osterman, Michael Lappin, Julia Vitullo-Martin, Wilhemina Leigh, Brian Comerford, Sue Marshall, James Carr, Donald Sullivan, and John Kain.

Finally, I am deeply indebted to the Lavanburg Foundation and especially its president, Oscar Straus, for the generous funding of this enterprise and for the high level of moral support offered during all stages of the effort.

The road traveled in completing this book was a long one. The project was first launched in the summer of 1983. I believe the time and effort were well worth it. Both in my interaction with the many contributors and the opportunity the project gave me to immerse myself so deeply in the housing policy field, I found this to be one of the most intellectually stimulating and rewarding experiences of my academic career.

Peter D. Salins
New York, New York
October 1986

Housing America's Poor

America's Permanent Housing Problem

Peter D. Salins

High on the list of America's permanent problems is housing for the poor. From the beginning of the industrial revolution to the present day, social reformers have been decrying the foul housing conditions in the worst neighborhoods of our cities. Today, after a century of irregular but steadily advancing national affluence coupled with increased government intervention has assured that most other basic needs of most Americans are being met, there is a nagging perception among both scholars and lay people that a significant number of the nation's households are not adequately housed.

The apparent permanence of the phenomenon which in housing policy jargon is called "substandard" housing is not the result of lack of interest in the problem by the country's opinion or leadership elites. Not only has there been periodic reform activity in private and public housing dating back to the turn of the century, but since 1949 the promise of decent housing for all Americans has been enshrined as a high national priority. The Housing Act of 1949 specifically seeks to achieve "a decent home and a suitable living environment for *every American family*" (emphasis added). In pursuit of this objective, since the housing act was passed, the national government has subsidized the construction of 1.2 million new apartments for the poor, eight hundred thousand new apartments for moderate-income families, and seven hundred thousand new apartments for the elderly. It has also underwritten as many as 1.5 million rent supplements per year and offered housing assistance to tens of thousands of households under other subsidy rubrics. Altogether it is estimated that more than 5 million subsidized housing units have been built or rehabilitated since 1950, embodying an aggregate federal contribution of $35 billion, the equivalent of more than $110 billion in 1986. These figures do not include the indirect benefits accruing to the entire housing sector through various features of the taxation and banking laws.

The foregoing statistics represent only the national effort. Virtually every U.S. state and most of the larger cities have agencies dedicated to the improvement of housing conditions for the poor. Some of them act merely as conduits for federal assistance, but many supplement such efforts with local resources. At least five hundred thousand families today live in housing subsidized primarily by states and localities. In addition, the local welfare assistance programs, aid to families with dependent children (AFDC) in particular, underwrite a large portion of the rents paid by their clients.

Why, then, is housing for the poor still so problematical? After all, we have largely eliminated hunger (through general affluence supplemented by food stamps); we have nearly universalized access to health care (through employer-financed insurance plans supplemented by Medicaid and Medicare); and everyone appears to be reasonably well dressed. Even luxury consumer goods reach the lowest-income households. Why should housing stand out as an area in which the welfare state has failed after decades of costly government intervention?

The answer, of course, is that we have not really failed. Never before have so many been so well housed. The correct question is, why do so many thoughtful people think we have failed? The answer lies in our inability to agree on two issues: what constitutes acceptable housing, and who deserves housing assistance.

The Moving Target

The inability to define consistent housing standards and goals is what I call the problem of the "moving target." One reason that substandard or inadequate housing remains, no matter how much money we throw at the problem, is that we keep redefining and raising the standards of what can be considered decent housing. For example, in the first half of the century one of the most critical dimensions of housing inadequacy was overcrowding. Not only was overcrowding seen as degrading, it was associated with such health problems as tuberculosis. Fifty years ago overcrowding meant that more than 1.5 persons in a household were sharing a room. In 1950 the standard was set at more than 1.0 persons per room. At that time more than 16 percent of all homes were "overcrowded." By 1970 overcrowding had abated to the extent that fewer than 8 percent of all dwelling units had an occupancy of more than 1 person per room. Rather than rejoice in this accomplishment, housing experts concluded that overcrowding was not such an important test of housing adequacy after all. Progress on this front continues nonetheless. Today fewer than 4 percent of all U.S. households exceed the 1 person per room standard, and only a negligible fraction exceed the earlier 1.5 person standard.

Another moving target among housing conditions concerned plumbing facilities. When a great many houses and apartments lacked full indoor plumbing, meaning that many families had to share kitchens and bathrooms with others, this was considered an essential shortcoming of the nation's housing stock. In 1940 nearly 45 percent of all dwellings lacked some private plumbing components. By 1970 fewer than 10 percent of all homes suffered from such deficiencies, and that criterion too no longer seemed important.

Having nearly wiped out overcrowding and lack of plumbing, in the 1960s we went after "dilapidation." Dilapidation refers to the visibly unsatisfactory physical conditions that characterize rundown houses or apartments. Dilapidation is another housing objective we have largely conquered. We no longer gather official data on dilapidation, but even in 1970, the latest year in which the Census Bureau counted dilapidated dwellings, only 3.7 percent of the housing stock met the definition, one-fifth the 1940 rate of 18 percent (for an explanation of changing definitions of dilapidation, see Chapter 3). Dilapidation, as an unsatisfactory objective condition, is with us still and has not quite disappeared as a housing criterion. But because so much dilapidation can be remedied with sweat equity (people painting their apartments, glazing their broken window panes, unstopping their toilets) or minor rehabilitation and repair expenditures, it is fading fast as an object of reformers' concern. Attention has now shifted to neighborhood quality and "affordability."

Today advocates of housing reform argue that even when dwelling units occupied by the poor are not overcrowded, contain their own kitchens and bathrooms, and may even be in somewhat decent repair, they are set in a dismal environment. They are surrounded by abandoned buildings, on streets that are unsafe and littered with trash (see Chapter 4). Deterioration of neighborhoods is, of course, a highly subjective condition. For example, the *Annual Housing Survey (AHS)* of 1983 tried to define the problem by eliciting the incidence of a host of arguably "unsatisfactory neighborhood conditions." It found that one or another such conditions was present near the homes of 64 percent of the respondents. Only 37 percent of the survey households, however, found any of the conditions "bothersome," and fewer than 10 percent thought they were serious enough to consider moving.

Another moving target emerges when the point is pressed that even the minority of poor families whose homes suffer from none of these deficiencies are paying too high a proportion of their income for rent. This is the problem of "affordability," which has emerged as today's favorite edition of the moving target. A household faces an affordability problem, it is maintained, if it must pay more than 25 or 30 percent of its income in rent. The affordability criterion is especially slippery. The ratio-busting rent level numerator is as likely to reflect the owner's (or society's) preference for higher-quality dwellings as it is to indicate exorbitant rent inflation. The insufficient income of the affordability ratio's denominator often does not reflect noncash public assistance (such as food stamps and Medicaid) or off-the-books income. The affordability concept is most inappropriately applied to well-housed middle-income families who deliberately choose to devote a high proportion of their budget to shelter. I do not wish to belabor the issue of whether housing today is indeed more or less affordable than in the past. I merely cite this criterion as the latest in a long, and possibly endless, line of problematical housing targets which are discovered as earlier ones fade away to sustain the permanency of America's housing problem.

Not only do we constantly change the criteria for assessing housing inadequacy, but the criteria have evolved in a direction away from specific intolerable, measurable, and remediable conditions such as density of occupancy and availability of plumbing facilities toward more subjective, and therefore often insoluble, conditions. The identification of housing problems has been moving steadily toward conditions that defy consistent description or measurement, conditions that many analysts—or the tenant sufferers—do not find unacceptable, and conditions that are more descriptive of the tenants and their behavior than of the housing stock. Obviously, such housing conditions can never be eliminated.

The impact on policy of the problem of the moving target can be seen clearly in the varying analyses and prescriptions offered by contributors to this book. For example, much of the difference of viewpoint separating John C. Weicher (Chapter 3), who thinks the housing problem has been largely solved through the private market-induced upgrading of the entire housing stock, and William C. Apgar, Jr. (Chapter 5), who sees a large quotient of disadvantage remaining, rests on sharply varying applications of criteria of housing quality.

The Broadened Target

A second reason for the persistent perception that housing is a problem arises from the tendency of the housing policy community to expand the definition of the eligible population over time. The earliest reformers were intent on eliminating the stock of clearly wretched housing, the "slums" as they were (and still are) popularly termed, regardless of the characteristics of the slum dwellers. When so much of the nation's housing was distinctly inferior, helping the housing rather than the housed was a perfectly reasonable approach, given the unlikelihood that any sizable number of nonpoor would inadvertently benefit. With the Great Society programs of the 1960s and since, the potential beneficiary class began to expand under a variety of rubrics and justifications. We heard increasingly about the need to help low- and moderate-income families, with "moderate" income often defined as a threshold near or even above the national median. The consequence of this target broadening is that today more than one-third of families receiving housing assistance belong to the moderate-income group. It was argued that we needed to broaden the reach of the housing agenda because (1) moderate-income families fell between the cracks of the housing market, too rich for subsidized housing but too poor to enter the private housing market without assistance; (2) subsidized housing projects or neighborhoods of subsidized housing would be "stabilized" if they were not entirely income-segregated, so middle- and lower-middle-class families had to be bribed to live in such areas to lend balance and provide behavioral norms for the poor; and (3) many poor families eventually emerge from poverty to cross the eligibility threshold and should not be required to move when that happens.

None of these justifications is entirely without merit. Nevertheless, the expansion of the beneficiary class eligible for housing assistance has undermined efforts to help the poor. Translating the concept into operational programs has meant spreading an inevitably limited dollar amount of assistance more thinly across a larger target population. Such programs displace potential poor beneficiary households with more affluent ones and result in the underwriting of fewer, but more expensive, dwelling units. They also disrupt the fragile private market for lower-priced housing by putting discount-priced publicly assisted housing in competition with that of private owners and developers, often triggering the wholesale deterioration of neighborhoods that now looms as an important criterion of housing inadequacy. Such programs tempt upwardly mobile lower-middle-class families into neighborhoods of great social instability, possibly blighting their hard-won prosperity. Finally, broadening the eligibility base has confused the general public and the housing policy establishment alike. When government housing assistance is viewed as an entitlement reaching well into the middle class, it raises expectations that can never be fulfilled, adding to the apparent permanency of the housing problem. That such programs inevitably help families (or elderly individuals) who are not presently "housing disadvantaged" appears inequitable to spokespersons on both ends of the ideological spectrum. Advocates for the poor see housing as yet another area of public policy whose programs for the poor have been preempted by the middle class. Conservatives perceive that housing is yet another field in which the government needlessly preempts the private market.

A Lack of Equity

In addition to attacking a moving target and serving a broadened beneficiary base, housing policy has always been profoundly inequitable. The inequity has many dimensions and is very pervasive. One dimension involves quality. Among one hundred poor households potentially eligible for housing assistance, eighty-five will receive no help, and of the fifteen that are helped three may receive a luxurious new apartment in an excellent neighborhood, four may get a modest unit in a deteriorating area, and eight may end up only with a rehabilitated older apartment or a slight reduction in rent. Housing assistance, unlike, for example, public assistance in nutrition or health care, is a lottery. Any eligible family has only a small chance of winning at all, and like all lotteries, the prizes vary enormously in value.

Another dimension of inequity involves the relations among the assisted and the unassisted populations. Especially as the income standards for eligibility are broadened, many families receiving housing assistance will have higher incomes than those that do not receive assistance. Many assisted families will not only be occupying better housing than eligible families that lose out in the housing lottery but also occupying better housing than families that are purportedly too well off to be eligible.

Nor is there any assurance that assisted families will have necessarily been badly housed before they receive help. Many well-housed families move to subsidized housing and many of the occupants of— by current definition—substandard housing are passed over.

Defining the Problem

However open to criticism the legacy of housing policy might be because of its constantly shifting standards, its continuously broadening constituency base, and its deeply ingrained inequity, it would be difficult to argue that there is not a genuine residuum of housing need. But to speak of a housing *crisis* is not only hyperbolic, it is downright untrue. Much of the case of the crisis-mongers rests on the increasingly publicized plight of the "homeless." Homelessness, however, is far more symptomatic of the growing number of uncared-for mentally and socially dysfunctional people to be found in our center cities than it is of a housing emergency.

Clearly, housing conditions in the United States have improved steadily over the years, and the vast majority of American families and individuals are well housed by any historical or cross-national standard. Therefore the remaining housing need must be viewed in the context of a recognition that the economy and housing market of the nation have performed remarkably well in providing decent shelter for most Americans.

The issues that must be addressed in fashioning housing policy for the poor might be best understood by touring the conceptual landscape while seeking answers to a series of hypothetical questions.

Who among the poor are likely to require housing assistance today? Housing reformers have used the blanket rubric of "housing disadvantage" to characterize all households that live in overcrowded or dilapidated dwellings, or whose homes are in "deteriorated" neighborhoods, or who devote more than 30 percent of their (cash) income to rent. The largest cohort of such households consists of families with children headed by women, many of whom are on welfare. Approximately 25 percent of all housing-disadvantaged poor families are female-headed, and nearly 50 percent of all female-headed households are housing disadvantaged. This group accounts for only 7 percent of the nation's households but represents 15 percent of the population of large cities. Female-headed families are, of course, at the core of all poverty-related problems of our society. Housing is only one of their more conspicuous needs.

Other housing-disadvantaged cohorts among the poor include young, single, unemployed males not living with their parents and the functionally impaired. Both groups, like the female-headed families, depend heavily on public assistance, and members of these groups constitute a disproportionate part of the growing "homeless" population.

The elderly are everyone's favorite needy group, in housing as in other areas, but as a class they have actually been doing quite well. More than 60 percent own their own homes, and a variety of private and public programs allow elderly homeowners to cash in their equity to help meet their monthly bills. As long-term residents of rental housing the elderly are often vested in relative housing bargains. Finally, the incomes of the elderly are rising more rapidly than those of the rest of the population because of the broadened scope and inflation-indexed benefit levels of social security.

One group decidedly *not* among the housing disadvantaged by any objective standard is young married couples, with or without children. Such families are often cited in popular stories about the growing housing crisis, especially if they are in the market as first-time home buyers. This group is also most likely to benefit from the broadening of the eligibility base for housing assistance. Young couples, however, are generally among the best rather than the worst-housed sectors of the population.

How bad are housing conditions for the housing-disadvantaged poor? This question gets to the heart of the issue of the moving target raised earlier. By objective historical or international standards, even the housing of our poorest families is not so bad. Of the 37 million households classified as "lower income" (meaning they receive less than 80 percent of the median income), fewer than 4 percent live in homes that are overcrowded, only 5 percent lack internal kitchens or bathrooms, and only 10 percent live in dwellings that are deteriorated. As indicated earlier, the main contemporary concerns of housing reformers are the badly deteriorated neighborhoods in which the disadvantaged groups live and/or the share of their income that goes for housing. These concerns must be seen in the context of the observations that many of the stigmata of "deteriorated neighborhoods" are supplied by their residents, and the rent/income ratios do not always reflect the upgrading of housing quality or the dollar value of noncash public assistance or off-the-books income.

If we consider the residual American housing problem in absolute rather than proportional terms, a great many people are involved. More than 17 million households suffer from some housing disadvantage. Nearly 6 million live in "physically inadequate" housing (dilapidated units or otherwise deteriorated structures and neighborhoods), slightly over 1 million are overcrowded (more than one person per room), and nearly 11 million pay more than 30 percent of their income in rent. The short answer to this question is that many of the poor live in fairly decent dwellings in rotten neighborhoods, and they have little money left over after they pay their rent. In addition, we must reckon with the housing conditions of the totally dysfunctional, who spend their nights in the streets or public shelters because of an inability to find, maintain, or pay for any housing at all.

How much have past and present government programs helped improve housing conditions for the poor? This is an enormously contentious question, of course, but my brief answer would be, not much. To begin with, as George Sternlieb and David Listokin indicate in Chapter 2, national and state housing programs have reached only a fraction of the families that are nominally eligible for housing assistance. This is because housing assistance, unlike food stamps or Medicaid, never was viewed as an open-ended entitlement for the eligible population. In some years a great deal of public money went into housing, in others very little. Many housing dollars were "wasted" (from the viewpoint of helping the maximum number of ill-housed poor secure decent housing) by building a small number of new expensive apartments rather than many cheap ones or fixing up an even greater number of old ones and by helping a very large number of families that were neither poor nor badly housed. This negative evaluation becomes even bleaker if one believes the conclusions of several studies (cited by Weicher in Chapter 3), which argue that the public inventory of housing construction displaced rather than added to the stock built by the private sector.

If government programs have not helped that much, how does one account for the improvement of housing conditions? The most convincing explanation is that rising incomes and high rates of private housing production have so expanded the supply of, and demand for, good housing that the worst dwellings were simply knocked out of the inventory. In addition, the upgrading of housing owes something to the "push" of old housing demolition, which has reinforced the "pull" of voluntary moves to better housing on the part of those families who had high enough incomes and new homes to beckon them. Federally subsidized urban redevelopment, for example, has been an important factor in speeding the demolition of the stock of substandard housing in center cities (see Chapter 5). Although urban redevelopment did not enlarge the stock of low- or moderate-cost housing (because it was meant to revive "blighted" downtown areas with upscale commercial activity and high-rent apartments), the "federal bulldozer" did sweep away many long-standing slums.

If housing conditions have so dramatically improved, why do we still see so many abysmally deteriorated neighborhoods? That is the sixty-four-dollar question of current housing policy. Why, indeed? There are several theories, none standing without challenge. One view, which I will call the "musical chairs" paradigm, blames the very success of the housing market in producing so much new housing. The argument is as follows. Housing conditions at the level of the individual dwelling unit improve when the average rate of new housing production over a period of time exceeds the rate of new family formation. This situation permits families to "trade up" in housing quality, even if they must pay more for their new homes than the ones they leave are worth. Something has to happen to the dwellings that are left behind. Usually they are passed down to successively lower-income households until the poorest of contemporary families are brought into the process. But even the poorest households will leave their former dwellings behind. It is this stock of unwanted housing that, in a complicated process, results in neighborhood deterioration. If all the poor traded up together, entire neighborhoods would be abandoned and sooner or later demolished. For a while, urban redevelopment forced this process to happen. Usually, however, moves out of older neighborhoods are random and irregular, leaving pockets of vacancies. These pockets create high vacancy rates in many buildings, causing their owners first to neglect them, later to abandon them. The cancer of random vacancies spread over broad sections of the lower-income precincts of cities shows up as massive visible physical decay.

Eventually, however, the resulting large decline in the inventory of low-cost housing may overtake the slack demand, causing rents to rise and displacing the poorest or most irresponsible tenants. The local community then faces a no-win dilemma. If slack elsewhere in the community can absorb the displaced households, the cycle of decay will resume in a new location. If, however, the local housing market is tight, the most disorganized families or individuals may wind up as wards of the municipality in temporary shelters—becoming members of the official "homeless" class.

An alternative theory of neighborhood deterioration places primary emphasis on the social characteristics of the poor rather than on the dynamics of the housing market. This argument stresses changes that have taken place in the nature of poverty and the people who are likely to be poor. As general affluence increased and an increasing percentage of all families had incomes high enough to afford decent private market housing, those families who remained poor were increasingly likely to be deviant. The teenage mother of young children, in particular, is not likely to function well as a caretaker of a house or apartment, or as the custodian of her children to make sure that they behave respectfully toward their own or their neighbors' physical surroundings. When the hard-core poor inherit formerly satisfactory housing in the hand-me-down process, they often cause it to run down rapidly. The presence of many such families in an area drives out the remaining respectable middle- and moderate-income families. The result is physical deterioration, high vacancies, and abandonment.

A third explanation blames the owners of rental properties and/or the banks that are expected to provide housing financing. This view assumes that as property owners see their buildings occupied by poorer (especially minority) families they reduce expenditures for repair and maintenance. A conspiratorial version of this view blames the disinvestment on the owners' desire to exploit the vulnerability of their tenants to secure windfall profits. A more generous version acknowledges that low-income families cannot afford to pay rents high enough to permit landlords to maintain their buildings properly. Property owners are not alone in the disinvestment process. They are complemented by the local banks that refuse to renew mortgages when they come due or to finance properties when they are sold to new owners. This "redlining" (based on the notion that banks circle undesirable neighborhoods in red pencil on their city maps) starves low-income neighborhoods of necessary funds for maintenance and upgrading even where the housing stock is initially in good condition.

Which version of this Rashomon-like explanation of neighborhood deterioration is correct? I personally lean toward a synthesis of the "musical chairs" and the "social characteristics" paradigms, although disinvestment undoubtedly plays an important part in the scenario of neighborhood decline. Proof of any one theory must rest on circumstantial evidence and inductive reasoning. For example, we have had considerable experience with policies that attempted to remedy neighborhood deterioration presumably based on landlord and bank disinvestment. Studies have shown that when there were no changes in the population composition of such areas, the infusion of public subsidies to reverse disinvestment has not been notably successful (see Chapter 6). We also have had considerable experience with providing housing for poor families in entire developments of well-maintained, publicly owned or assisted housing. In such cases neither disinvestment nor random vacancies and abandonment can occur. Nonetheless, when the population of these developments has been made up largely of female-headed households with young and teenaged children, the projects suffer from serious physical deterioration, as well as crime, vandalism, and abuse of the public environment.

Does this mean that neighborhood deterioration is an insoluble problem? Not necessarily, but it does mean that solving the housing problem for the poor no longer requires simply a bricks-and-mortar effort. We must recognize that sheltering today's poor—who have personal social and economic problems much more severe than yesterday's poor—according to contemporary housing standards that are considerably more demanding than those of the past poses a great challenge. Furthermore, this daunting task must be pursued with slender resources. The public housing failures of the past, the retrenchment of the public sector, the public refusal to engage heavily in social amelioration or income redistribution all add up to an environment for housing reform which demands that we must rely primarily on the private market and that we make sure that the housing-subsidy dollars that are made available stretch further.

Above all, a realistic view of the housing problems of the poor, especially the ubiquitous spectacle in cities from coast to coast of neighborhood squalor, demands that we fit our policies and programs to a candid assessment of the constraints posed by the social and behavioral characteristics of the families we wish to help. We must recognize the role these characteristics play in causing dwelling and neighborhood deterioration and reject the simplistic charge that such recognition means we are "blaming the victim." We must also recognize the legitimate wishes of the poor themselves, who may interpret their needs quite differently from the physical and aesthetic meliorism of middle-class planners. They may not even want their meager allotment of subsidy crumbs from the public banquet table to take the form of housing assistance.

The Rest of the Book

This brief introduction just scratches the surface of the conundrum of how properly to assist America's poor in their quest for decent housing. The various questions raised in this chapter will be addressed, often in contradictory ways, in the chapters that follow. The next four will analyze and define the problem from a variety of perspectives—historical, descriptive, normative, and spatial. The four succeeding chapters will address a variety of potential solutions. I cannot promise the reader that the book will settle, once and for all, the issue of housing for the poor. The problem is complex not only in its hard, substantive dimensions but in its "soft," subjective elements as well. Even armed with the same data, different analysts can come to varying—even opposing—conclusions because of differences in values and expectations. This book should, however, clarify the terms of the debate over housing policy. The reader, like the contributors, must choose from among varying views about the nature and the severity of America's housing problem. And the reader, like the contributors, must choose from among the various remedies discussed, extant and proposed. I hope, however, that even among this diversity of views and viewpoints, one message will emerge loud and clear. That is that if we have a sincere interest in improving American housing conditions we must be brutally honest with ourselves in defining the problem, setting objectives, and evaluating solutions.

References

Aaron, Henry J. 1972. *Shelter and Subsidies.* Washington, D.C.: Brookings Institution.

Congressional Research Service. 1983. *Housing: A Reader.* Washington, D.C.: U.S. Government Printing Office.

Grigsby, W., M. Baratz, and D. Maclennan. 1983. *Shelter Subsidies for Low Income Households.* Philadelphia: Research Reports, Department of City and Regional Planning, University of Pennsylvania.

Grigsby, W., and L. Rosenburg. 1975. *Urban Housing Policy.* New York: APS Publications and Center for Urban Policy Research, Rutgers University.

McKenna, W. F., and C. A. Hills. 1982. *The Report of the President's Commission on Housing.* Washington, D.C.: U.S. Government Printing Office.

Solomon, A. P. 1974. *Housing the Urban Poor: A Critical Evaluation of Federal Housing Policy.* Cambridge, Mass.: MIT Press.

U.S. Department of Commerce, Bureau of the Census. *Annual Housing Survey: 1980, United States and Regions.* Part A.

———. *1950 Census of Housing,* vol. 1, sec. 1.

———. *1960 Census of Housing,* vol. 2, sec. 1.

———. *1970 Census of Housing: Components of Inventory Change.* HD(4)–1.

———. *Sixteenth Census of the United States: 1940, Housing,* vol. 2, sec. 1.

Weicher, John. 1980. *Housing: Federal Policies and Programs.* Washington, D.C.: American Enterprise Institute.

2

A Review of National Housing Policy

George Sternlieb and
David Listokin

Housing Past and Future

It is nearly a hundred years since the pioneering 1892 congressional study commission report on slum conditions in America's larger cities; more than eighty years since President Franklin D. Roosevelt's housing commission recommended federal intervention in the cause of improving shelter; a half century since the Great Depression brought the federal government front and center into the era of housing; and we are more than a generation beyond the crest of the wave of enthusiasm for urban renewal and the infinite perfectibility of central cities. Gone from the memories of all but scholars and historians is the vision of building 26 million housing units in a decade with a fifth of them to be allocated to low- and moderate-income families—a goal enunciated by the 1968 Housing Act.

The casting off of old initiatives, the emptying of the pipelines of programs that accompanied the housing slump in the first two years of the Reagan administration provides a breathing space; the abrupt change from the housing policies and priorities of post–World War II America provides a necessity for a reevaluation. What lessons can we learn from the past? The evolving rules of the game, as well as knowledge of what has worked and not worked and why, are crucial to understand the issues of today and to serve as a matrix in planning policy for the future. This chapter, in an attempt to provide some partitions for a relatively seamless, if disorderly, web, begins with a broad chronological review of the evolution of federal housing concerns and involvement and concludes with an evaluation of conceptual approaches and issues of program development.

Early Twentieth Century: The Limited Role of Government

It is difficult in this era of 3 million federal employees, of near trillion-dollar budgets, to step back in time to the turn of the century, when practically all of the central cabinet staff was compressed into the old Executive Office Building. Its gingerbreaded, calm exterior encapsulated all but a very few of the executive branch agencies. The federal government was actively pursuing the Indians, debating the future of public lands, conducting international affairs—and at least from current perspectives, doing remarkably little else.

Housing as an official member of the cabinet family would have to wait for two-thirds of a century to be admitted into the sacred portals. The *Statistical Abstract*, which has just celebrated its hundredth year, was still counting teepees and wigwams and attempting to define rental multifamily housing as something other than tenements.[1]

This is not to suggest that there was a lack of awareness of America's housing issues. Pioneered by New York, for nearly half a century investigations and, increasingly, legislation had attempted to govern the harsh inadequacy of central city tenements.[2] Thus a legislative report of 1857 spoke of the "hideous squalor and deadly effluvia; the dim, undrained courts oozing with pollution; the dark, narrow stairways, decayed with age, reeking with filth, overrun with vermin; the rotted floors, ceilings begrimed, and often too low to permit you to stand upright; the windows stuffed with rags—the gaunt, shivering forms and wild ghastly faces in these black and beetling abodes."[3]

But half a century later, Jacob Riis's *The Battle with the Slums* sadly enough reported the same conditions.[4] Government groups and concerned individuals hoping to effect reform were faced with population increases that make those of current Central America or Africa seem relatively mild, as Europe decanted its landless peasantry and urban slum dwellers into the New World. Tenement laws were passed, but their effects were limited in application as well as design.[5] Those of goodwill were armed with a sense of outrage but little conviction about the role of government. Government in the fashion that we know it today had yet to be invented in the United States. As late as the beginning of the 1930s, with one exception, there was no state legislature that met annually; typically they met biennially.

The very concept of a federal role, in what were viewed as local problems, was foreign to the American political geist. Theodore Roosevelt, based on his exposure to reform movements in New York and the realities of the slum conditions familiar to him from his tenure as police commissioner (described so effectively in Lincoln Steffens's *Autobiography*),[6] impounded a Senate commission on the topic. The report that resulted in 1902 suggested the taking of unsanitary housing and its purchase or improvement financed by government. Its recommendation that "all unsanitary and unsightly property should be condemned and purchased by the government, improved in a uniform manner and inexpensive and healthful habitation erected for the poor, who could rent or purchase their homes on installment plans at low rates of interest,"[7] was completely incongruous with the limited nature of the federal mandate of the time. It would be more than fifty years before a significant approach along the lines envisioned by the task force at the turn of the century would begin to be implemented.

World War I provided both incentives and political backing for new federal government incursions into all spheres of economic life. Principal among them were actions in housing. The enormous increases in industrial production for the war and resulting concentrations of population generated a need for housing. The federal government authorized housing loans for shipyard employees, and though the action was somewhat belated and the pipeline relatively slow, more than ten thousand units were produced under this mandate. Perhaps even more consequential was the unprecedented organization of the U.S. Housing Corporation to build and manage housing for defense workers.[8] Under its aegis, more than five thousand units were produced.

Following the war, the productive and supervisory structures generated to fulfill these needs were dismantled (the housing units were quickly sold to the private sector) but the concepts and, to a certain degree, the precedent remained. They were to serve in the next great era of national emergency.

Between these periods, however, was one of the great boom times in America's housing. The wealth accumulated in the prosperity of the war which survived the sharp recession of 1919 triggered a housing boom. The physical volume of residential construction nearly quadrupled from 1920 through 1925, despite the primitive nature of the available financing system (see Figure 2.1). Loans typically were open-ended, with no provision for amortization, and written for relatively short terms. Not uncommonly, first mortgages were available for only 30 to 50 percent of the value of the property; a flourishing second, indeed third mortgage market was the consequence.

In the years of the 1920s, migration off the land substantially alleviated many of the housing problems of rural America and housing in urban areas tended to improve, in part as a function of reform movements. New York City led the reform thrust through the 1902 Tenement House Act and was followed by many of America's urban areas.[9] Perhaps even more important, advances in rail and road car transit mechanisms permitted and fostered a wave of suburbanization, accelerating the filtering-down process for rural immigrants.

By today's standards, much of urban America's housing in the 1920s would be considered dreadful, but by contemporary standards, for most of its inhabitants, the new housing represented a great improvement. And for America's burgeoning middle class, it had few parallels in the rest of the world.

The Depression Era: The Dawn of Housing Policies

The 1920s ended with a proverbial bang. Black Monday and Black Thursday on the 1929 stock market were shortly followed by the resounding failure of the housing market and, not coincidentally, of practically all of America's industry as well. By 1931, nearly a thousand home mortgages were being foreclosed daily.[10]

It is striking to note in Figure 2.1 that the decline in residential construction preceded the great crash and the fall in industrial production followed. The precipitousness of the decline has no parallel in current times. We moved from the peak of nearly a million hous-

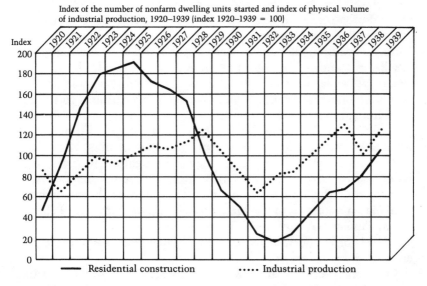

Figure 2.1. *Housing and Industrial Production, 1920–1939*

Source: National Housing Agency, reprinted from Mel Scott, *American City Planning since 1890* (Berkeley and Los Angeles: University of California Press, 1971), p. 279.

ing units constructed in 1925 to less than a tenth of that number in 1933. By that year on-site construction throughout the country employed only 150,000 persons.

The clash between old institutions and the new exigencies was highlighted by President Herbert Hoover's Conference on Homebuilding and Homeownership of 1931.[11] In language that was to be repeated over the years by subsequent presidential committees, task forces, and the like, the inadequacies of the housing industry, the diseconomies of the building cycle, the limitations of financial institutions, and the constraints of land use controls (barely a half dozen years after cities had first experimented with zoning) are documented.[12]

But the grim diagnosis was accompanied by weak medicine: a plea to private industry and local government to respond to the worsening housing and mortgage situation by exhibiting greater sympathy for the millions of families in danger of losing their homes. This recommendation made little sense in the face of a near-revolutionary situation, with lynch mobs attacking the courts in the Midwest in efforts to stop foreclosure proceedings.

The arrival of the New Deal resulted in mechanisms that, though blunted by court injunctions and a measure of political backlash, were to serve as precedents for much of the post–World War II housing and urban renewal initiatives. The Reconstruction Finance Corporation (RFC) was authorized in 1932 to make loans to low-income/slum redevelopment housing corporations,[13] one of the foundation blocks, in somewhat different form, of urban renewal. The 1933 National Industrial Recovery Act authorized federal financing of low-rent/slum-clearance housing and indeed financed almost forty thousand housing units before its use of eminent domain was declared unconstitutional.[14] In the face of the virtual collapse of the nation's financial institutions and structures, the Homeowners' Loan Act of 1933 and the 1934 National Housing Act brought the federal government and its entities directly into the mortgage market with a reinvention of thrift institutions, now dedicated to the financing of housing on a long-term, regulated base.[15] Major elements of the National Housing Act of 1934 in its multiple titles (summarized in Table 2.1) have continued with minor conceptual shifts to the present day.

Amid this activity there were warning signals in congressional hearings and public statements of the administration that indicated the limitations on housing as a priority. Although President Roosevelt spoke forcefully of a nation, one-third of which was ill-housed, the basic legislation was passed only on the grounds of fostering jobs and economic recovery. Thus Harry L. Hopkins spoke first of unemployment in endorsing the 1934 act:

> The building trades in America represent by all odds the largest single unit of our unemployment. Probably more than one-third of all the unemployed are identified, directly and indirectly, with the building trades. . . . Now, a purpose of this bill, a fundamental purpose of this bill, is an effort to get these people back to work. . . . There has been no repair work done on housing since 1929. . . . And finally, we believe it is essential that we unloose private credit rather than public funds in the repairing of those houses and the building of new houses.[16]

The objective of alleviating housing conditions was far from hidden, but it was necessary to build a broader constituency primarily interested in jobs and economic reinvigoration. Even the 1937 Housing Act, which authorized the public housing program, basically was sold under the same rubric of job stimulation and economic growth.[17]

Table 2.1.
A Century of Federal Housing Programs and Actions

Date	Legislation/Other	Activity/Authorization
I. *Early Studies*		
1892	Congressional study commission (Pub. Res. 52-22)	Investigate slum conditions in cities over 200,000 population
1902	President's (Theodore Roosevelt) Housing Commission	Recommended condemnation of unsanitary housing and purchase, improvement, and loan financing by government
II. *World War I Responses*		
1918	Loans for shipyard workers (P.L. 65-102)	Federal loans authorized for housing for shipyard employees; more than 10,000 units produced
1918	U.S. Housing Corporation (P.L. 149-164)	Build, organize, and manage housing for defense workers; more than 5,000 units produced

Table 2.1 *continued*

Date	Legislation/Other	Activity/Authorization

III. *Depression Era Responses*

1931	President's (Herbert Hoover) Conference on Home Building and Home Ownership	Document inadequacies in the housing industry (e.g., financing, land use controls)
1932	Reconstruction Finance Corporation (RFC) authorized by Emergency Relief and Construction Act of 1932 (P.L. 72-302)	RFC authorized to make loans to low-income/slum redevelopment housing corporations; $8 million advanced to Knickerbocker Village in New York City, $15 million for Kansas rural housing
1933	Homeowners' Loan Act of 1933 (P.L. 73-43)	(a) FHLBB authorized to create Home Owners' Loan Corporation (HOLC); HOLC refinanced distressed mortgages with long-term, amortized loans (more than one million loans were refinanced) (b) FHLBB authorized to provide for the organization, operation, and regulation of federal savings and loan associations, which were extended tax and other benefits in return for focusing on local home financing
1933	National Industrial Recovery Act (P.L. 73-67)	Authorized federal financing of low-rent, slum-clearance housing; financed more than 40,000 housing units; NIRA use of eminent domain declared unconstitutional
1934	National Housing Act (P.L. 74-486)	Federal Housing Administration (FHA) created and given numerous powers: *Title I:* FHA insures home improvement loans *Title II*, Section 203: FHA insures long-term, amortized, high loan-to-value ratio, one-to-four family home loans *Title III:* Authorizes establishment of national mortgage association (Fed-

		eral National Mortgage Association [FNMA] chartered 1938) *Title IV:* Federal Savings and Loan Insurance Corporation created to insure savings accounts
1937	Bankhead-Jones Farm Tenant Act (P.L. 75-210)	Authorized secretary of agriculture to make long-term, low-cost loans for purchasing, refinancing, and/or repairing farm properties
1937	Housing Act (P.L. 75-412)	Authorized public housing program/ U.S. Housing Authority; the latter could make loans or capital grants to local public housing agencies (PHAs)

IV. *World War II Responses*

1940	Defense Homes Corporation (DHC) (P.L. 588 and 611)	DHC authorized to provide housing in Washington, D.C., and other defense locations
1940	Landham Act (P.L. 76-849)	Authorized provision of public war housing accommodations; almost 1 million units ultimately provided
1941	National Housing Act (P.L. 77-24)	Title VI added to provide insurance for mortgages on one-to-four-family homes in critical defense locations (Section 603); more than 350,000 units insured
1942	Emergency Price Control Act (P.L. 77-421)	Authorized federal rent controls
1942	National Housing Act (P.L. 77-559)	Section 608 added to Title VI of the National Housing Act to provide mortgage insurance for multifamily rental housing for defense workers (Section 608 was extended after the war for non-defense purposes)
1944	Serviceman's Re-adjustment Act (P.L. 78-346)	Veterans' Administration authorized to guarantee liberal mortgages made to veterans

V. *Early Postwar Responses*

1949	Housing Act (P.L. 83-560)	*National Housing Policy and Goal:* Declared importance of providing

Table 2.1 *continued*

Date	Legislation/Other	Activity/Authorization
		sound housing and realization of that goal through private enterprise *Title I:* Authorized $1 billion in loans and $500 million in grants to aid local slum clearance programs *Title II:* Increase in Title II Federal Housing Administration (FHA) mortgage insurance authorized *Title III:* Increase in public housing (to 800,000 units) authorized *Title IV:* Secretary of agriculture authorized to establish programs to improve farm housing
1953	Advisory Committee on Government Policies and Programs (E.O. 10486)	Committee recommends that government expand efforts to deter housing deterioration and foster rehabilitation
1954	Housing Act (P.L. 83-560)	Among other changes (e.g., restrictions on Section 608 to curb abuses), the Housing Act introduced programs to encourage rehabilitation/upgrading in urban renewal areas. A "workable program" requirement was introduced to foster planning, which would now be assisted by Section 701 grants. Section 220 authorized FHA insurance for one-to-four-family dwellings in urban renewal neighborhoods; Section 221 insured mortgages on sister multifamily projects. To foster a secondary market for these new mortgages, Federal National Mortgage Administration (FNMA) was authorized to provide "special assistance functions (purchases)." (These special assistance functions ultimately became the responsibility of the Government National Mortgage Association [GNMA] when GNMA was split from FNMA in 1968.)

| 1959 | Housing Act (P.L. 372) | Section 202 authorized direct low-cost loans for rental housing for the elderly |

VI. *New Frontier–Great Society Responses*

1961	Housing Act (P.L. 70)	Section 221 program broadened to include low- and moderate-income, not just displaced families; Section 221(d)(3) program authorized to provide below-market-rate mortgages for rental housing; new home improvement loan programs—Section 220(h) and 203(k)—authorized in urban renewal areas
1964	Housing Act (P.L. 88-560)	Section 312 low-cost loans authorized for rehabilitation
1965	Housing Act (P.L. 89-117)	Rent supplements for privately owned housing authorized. The supplement would pay the difference between the fair market rent and one-fourth of the tenant's income. Section 23 also authorized public housing authorities to lease private units.
1966	Demonstration Cities and Metropolitan Development Act (P.L. 89-754)	Authorized demonstration programs for upgrading inner-city neighborhoods
1967	National Commission on Urban Problems (Douglas Commission)	National commission appointed by President Lyndon Johnson
1968	Housing Act (P.L. 90-448)	The act authorized many new housing programs and established a ten-year housing production goal of 26 million units with about one-fifth allocated to low- to moderate-income families. Section 235 subsidized low-income rental projects; Section 236, multifamily. Both programs provided mortgages with interest rates as low as 1 percent. The existing FNMA was partitioned into two separate corporations—FNMA, which would continue market operations, and GNMA, which would focus

Table 2.1 *continued*

Date	Legislation/Other	Activity/Authorization
		on special assistance functions. In addition, the Housing Act authorized a National Housing Partnership, riot insurance, and flood insurance, and guarantees of obligations issued by new community developers.
1969	Housing Act (P.L. 91-152)	Rent in public housing limited to one-fourth of tenant income (Brooke Amendment)
1970	Emergency Home Finance Act of 1970 (P.L. 91-432)	Purchase authority of FNMA extended to conventional mortgages; new secondary market institutions—Federal Home Loan Mortgage Corporation (FHLMC)—created
1970	Housing Act (P.L. 91-609)	Secretary of the Department of Housing and Urban Development (HUD) authorized to conduct experimental housing allowance programs

VII. *Reappraisal and New Directions*

Date	Legislation/Other	Activity/Authorization
1973	Impoundment of housing subsidy and community development funds	Effective January 1973, a moratorium on housing/community development assistance was imposed
1973	*Housing in the Seventies* study	HUD report criticized equity and cost of existing housing subsidies. (This report was critiqued by the Congressional Research Service.)
1974	Housing Act (P.L. 93-383)	Title I replaced many categorical housing/community development programs with Community Development Block Grants. A new Section 8 program replaced the Section 23 leasing subsidy. Section 8 provided payments equal to the difference between the fair market rent and the amount affordable by low- to moderate-income families (first 25, then increased to 30 percent of gross in-

		come). Section 8 could be applied for new, existing, and rehabilitated housing.
1977	Housing Act	Urban Development Action Grants (UDAG) authorized communities in "distress" to submit applications and compete for UDAG awards; UDAG can be used for both residential and nonresidential purposes
1983	Housing Act (P.L. 91-181)	Section 8 voucher demonstration program authorized as well as Rental Rehabilitation Grants and Housing Development Grants (new construction and substantial rehabilitation)

Sources: U.S. Congress, House of Representatives, Committee on Banking, Currency and Housing, Subcommittee on Housing and Community Development, *Evolution of the Role of the Federal Government in Housing and Community Development: A Chronology of Legislative and Selected Executive Actions, 1892–1974* (Washington, D.C.: U.S. Government Printing Office, 1975); Barry G. Jacobs et al., *Guide to Federal Housing Programs* (Washington, D.C.: Bureau of National Affairs, 1982).

Housing: A Second Wartime Emergency

Housing production benefited greatly from the defense buildup that finally moved the nation out of the Depression doldrums by 1940. Even as late as 1938, the physical volume of housing was barely half that of the 1920 peak (see Figure 2.1), but the shift of war workers and the mobilization that followed the institution of selective service generated increased demand for housing. Under wartime pressures, the federal government tried to meet the demand.

The initial responses were merely elaboration of those pioneered in the World War I period. The scale, however, was much more substantial: the number of units produced moved into the seven-figure area. The mortgage insurance programs pioneered in the 1930s were revived and focused on critical defense locations to facilitate financing of multifamily rental housing for defense workers.[18] They were extended after the war and served as progenitors for many similar programs.

Not least among the federal activities was the implementation of emergency price controls, which put in place rent controls and certified them as an appropriate act of government in the face of emergencies.[19] Although New York had first introduced rent control immediately after World War I, this was the rest of the nation's first taste of an institution which real estate developers viewed as insidious poison but consumers saw as a certification of housing as an essential good.

The Early Postwar Responses

After the war, the nation agreed that Americans were housing-short and that "something should be done" for our older cities, with the federal government taking direct responsibility to solve the problem. The resulting legislation contained something for everyone.

Perhaps the most influential of the postwar housing responses was the pioneering effort in 1944 to assure returning veterans access to low-interest, low-down-payment, long-term mortgages through Veterans' Administration mortgage guarantees and Federal Housing Administration mortgage insurance.[20] Although the concept of providing housing and/or land for returning veterans dates back to the classical era (those who have visited Blenheim Palace can see the rewards of a nation grateful to the Duke of Marlboro for his success several hundred years ago), the motivating element was not merely gratitude but the fear of a resumption of economic malaise once the wartime stimulus was over. The specter of the Depression was still fresh in the minds of political leaders.

The first omnibus housing act of the post–World War II period, that of 1949,[21] set in place a particularly striking initiative in response to downtown merchants and real estate entrepreneurs of the central city, who were vaguely disquieted by the beginnings of suburbanization and even more troubled by the increasing shabbiness of their central business districts after the long period of underinvestment that dated back to the 1920s. Title I of the 1949 act authorized $1 billion in loans and $500 million in grants to purchase downtown land and sell it at a discount to private developers for "slum clearance." The program assumed that the economic centrality of major cities and their basic vigor were unimpaired and all that was required was cosmetic cleanup—sometimes viewed as moving the poor and increasingly the blacks to less obtrusive locations.

Finally, public housing, which had established its credibility in the late 1930s, was substantially augmented with authorization for eight hundred thousand units in a program that received surprising backing from both sides of the political spectrum.[22]

It is instructive to review those programs that were proposed but not legislated in the postwar era. Specifically rejected after much discussion, for example, was a program of rent supplements to needy families. This proposal was endorsed by the real estate boards of the time but was viewed as being too open-ended in cost and counter-productive with respect to improving housing quality:

> It has been argued before the subcommittee that such families should be assisted by rent certificates just as grocery stamps have been furnished to needy families. The number of families entitled to rent certificates upon any such basis would be infi-nitely larger than those requiring other relief. It is not at all cer-tain that such a plan would bring about improvement in the bad housing accommodations that now exist. In fact, the scheme might work to maintain the profitability of slum areas and con-sequently, to retard their elimination. It would certainly require a detailed regulation of private rental quarters both as to condi-tion and rent.[23]

The issues of regulating both the costs and the quality of accom-modations subject to rent subsidies echo to the present day. Leasing private facilities for the needy was also rejected as posing too great a risk. The basic housing assistance mix, therefore, consisted of aid to the poor through public housing, mortgage insurance to increase the total supply of housing for the new middle class, and urban renewal to revitalize the urban core.

The increased scope of federal housing intervention brought to the fore a basic conflict between the cities and the national government as to the objectives of housing and development policy. The cities have to the present day been concerned with regeneration and resto-ration of the dominance of the middle class. The national govern-ment and its bureaucracy have acted as advocates for the poor and needy, attempting to ensure that some significant portion of federal funding would solve their needs.

This conflict of objectives lay behind arguments promoting hous-ing subsidies only for the needy and underhoused (by the conven-tional wisdom of sanitary standards and the like) as against the pro-vision of more luxurious, better-sited housing for the more affluent.[24]

The 1960s: The Acts of Contrition

The sweeping housing development initiatives of the immediate postwar period gave way to lesser ameliorative efforts. The Section 221 program lowered the cost of financing for housing, first to rectify the sins of urban renewal by housing those displaced, later broadened to help all low- and moderate-income families.[25] Section 312 was introduced to provide low-cost loans for rehabilitation. Section 23 permitted public housing authorities to lease private apartments (see Table 2.1).[26]

Then came the era of urban riots, the tragedy of Martin Luther King's martyrdom, and the exercise of Lyndon Johnson's political skills. In combination these events produced an explosion of new programmatic activity in the second half of the 1960s. Notable examples include the Demonstration Cities and Metropolitan Act of 1966 and the Housing Act of 1968,[27] which added programs offering below-market interest rates to the older device of mortgage insurance. Such programs had existed for specialized purposes earlier in the decade (Sections 202 and 221 (d)(3); see Table 2.1) but were universalized and stretched to offer interest rates as low as 1 percent. Section 236 offered low-rate financing for construction of multifamily units, and Section 235 provided low-cost financing to promote low-income homeownership. Sections 235 and 236 also stretched out mortgage amortization to forty years. A secondary mortgage market was created through the partitioning of "Fannie Mae" (Federal National Mortgage Administration) to sustain the flood of financing generated by the construction of 26 million housing units in the decade, a large share of them subsidized.

Events of the 1960s marked an end to the belief that housing was the key to resolving social issues and the beginning of the dissolution of the old alliance of housing reformers and homebuilders. The stresses of race, complicated by class conflict and the growing awareness of the cost of housing programs began to splinter the former coalition. The last policy product of the 1960s, the Housing Act of 1970,[28] introduced the experimental housing allowance program, which was to test the use of vouchers, hitherto a forbidden topic.

The 1970s and Beyond: America's Midlife Housing Crisis

The housing initiatives of the 1950s and 1960s were victims of their own success. Aided by the variety of financing mechanisms that the national government put in place, new housing starts peaked in 1972 at 2.4 million units, nearly four hundred thousand of which resulted from programs subsidized by the Department of Housing and Urban Development (HUD) (see Table 2.2). If rehabilitated units are added, the total federally subsidized production volume reached almost five hundred thousand by the early 1970s (see Table 2.2).

Table 2.2.

Total and Subsidized New Housing Production:
1950–1985 (estimated)

Year[a]	Total new housing units started (in thousands)	Total subsidized new housing units started (in thousands)	Total new subsidized units as percent of total new units
1950	1,952	44	2.2
1951	1,491	71	4.8
1952	1,505	59	3.9
1953	1,438	35	2.4
1954	1,550	19	1.2
1955	1,646	19	1.2
1956	1,346	21	1.6
1957	1,222	47	3.9
1958	1,376	62	4.5
1959	1,529	34	2.2
1960	1,272	42	3.3
1961	1,365	36	2.6
1962	1,492	39	2.6
1963	1,635	48	2.9
1964	1,561	55	3.5
1965	1,510	64	4.2
1966	1,196	72	6.0
1967	1,322	91	6.9
1968	1,546	163	10.5
1969	1,500	197	13.1
1970	1,469	431	29.3
1971	2,085	441 (483)[b]	21.2
1972	2,379	388 (430)	16.3
1973	2,057	290 (332)	14.1
1974	1,353	142 (172)	10.5
1975	1,171	111 (129)	9.5
1976	1,548	118 (138)	7.6
1977	2,002	191 (217)	9.5
1978	2,036	232 (265)	11.4
1979	1,760	237 (277)	13.5
1980	1,313	208 (266)	15.8
1981	1,100	178 (211)	16.2
1982	1,072	178 (204)	16.6
1983	1,713	124 (143)	7.2
1984	1,756	99 (114)	5.6
1985	1,745	70 (78)	4.0

Table 2.2 *continued*

Sources: Data on total new housing starts derived from U.S. Department of Commerce, Bureau of the Census, *Historical Statistics of the United States, Colonial Times to 1970* (Washington, D.C.: U.S. Government Printing Office, 1975); U.S. Department of Commerce, Bureau of the Census, *Statistical Abstract of the United States, 1982–83* (Washington, D.C.: U.S. Government Printing Office, 1982); U.S. Department of Commerce, Bureau of the Census, "Housing Starts December 1983 Construction Reports C20-83-12," January 1984. Data on subsidized new housing starts were derived from different sources: 1950 to 1970 data obtained from Anthony Downs, *Federal Housing Subsidies: How Are They Working* (Lexington, Mass.: D. C. Heath, 1973); 1971 to 1982 data from U.S. Department of Housing and Urban Development, *1980 and 1982 National Housing Production Report* (Washington, D.C.: U.S. Government Printing Office, 1983); 1983 to 1985 data from estimates provided by HUD, Office of Economic Analysis.

[a]Subsidized new housing starts from 1971 onward are shown by fiscal, not calendar year. (Total new housing starts are always shown by calendar year.)

[b]Data in parentheses indicate total subsidized housing production (new construction and rehabilitation).

But a number of countervailing forces were at work which were to make these data the high-water mark of government-assisted activity. In January 1973, newly reelected President Richard Nixon imposed a moratorium on housing and community development assistance and called for formal reevaluation of housing and urban programs. The intriguing phenomenon is not Nixon's act but the limited amount of protest it engendered. The homebuilders, once strong advocates of federal housing programs, particularly in central cities, were present at the hearings—but did not complain. The thrift institutions, increasingly involved with suburban housing using private mortgage insurance, no longer were dependent upon Washington. And the disenchantment with the housing programs of the previous years was widespread. HUD had become one of the nation's leading owners of housing through default, generating exaggerated fears of foreclosure and scandal in the subsidized housing sector. In a radical change of emphasis, Congress introduced the Section 8 program, which involved a major shift from the long-term policy of direct supply subsidies to one of promoting increases in effective demand through rent subsidies.

This was merely part of the revolution implicit in the Housing Act of 1974, which replaced categorical programs with Community Development Block Grants (CDBG)[29] and mortgage subsidy programs with ones enhancing the housing buying power of the needy. It was to take another decade for the federal government to move more completely from the supply side of the housing equation to the demand side by giving vouchers.

This shift commemorated the drastic decline of housing as a broad-based, politically popular government activity. Inflation, foreign affairs, and the economy took central stage in the 1970s. Middle America had achieved its housing goals. Federal government housing programs, which in the 1950s had developed a constituency by giving something to everybody, had by the 1970s been reduced to serving the interests and necessities of a small, and not particularly favored, group of the poor. The government housing sector could not survive this attrition of its political base.

The Current Nostrum: The Housing Voucher

In 1974, with the introduction of the Section 8 program, federal housing policy was purportedly oriented to enhancing the purchasing power of those in need of housing assistance. In reality, for much of the next decade Section 8 was applied as one of the most potent housing-supply subsidies of all time. The Section 8 commitments were given mostly to developers of new housing rather than to tenants.

The Reagan administration, which came to power in 1981, however, has been attempting to make the housing voucher—that is, a pure demand-side subsidy—functional reality. Although funding for Section 8, both new and substantially rehabilitated housing, has been nearly terminated, the administration's support for vouchers has remained steadfast. The Housing Act of 1983 brings vouchers from a demonstration experiment to operating program status. What has been wrought?

The housing voucher program has antecedents going back at least fifty years to the debates at the beginning of the New Deal. Its most direct ancestor is the Section 23 leasing program of 1965, which allowed local public housing agencies to lease and rent out to their client households privately owned and operated housing units.

The Section 8 program of 1974 brought federal housing one step closer to the voucher concept. The federally funded agency defined appropriate cost constraints as well as quality standards; but the assisted consumer, within these parameters of cost and quality, acted as a relatively independent shopper.

Section 8, however, very quickly disappointed the hopes and expectations of its formulators. It was originally envisioned as a program to assimilate the poor into the broad spectrum of society and shelter, to be implemented by limiting Section 8 subsidized apartments to 20 percent of a project total. This restriction proved impossible to enforce—or perhaps was not tried hard enough or long enough. Instead, the Section 8 program rapidly became a relief measure to rescue financially insecure projects under earlier programs, notably Section 236 and those state agency-sponsored efforts to finance housing that could not achieve break-even rent levels.

The voucher concept raises complex issues. In our opinion, principal among them is one that has bedeviled all social welfare programs: Is a poor person, plus government cash assistance, really equivalent to a moderate-income consumer with equivalent purchasing power? Or is there something uniquely different, either in the poor person's competence or the receptivity of society, that requires structured guidance?

A housing voucher program raises many questions. Is there enough adequate low-cost housing available? Can the low-income consumer find it without assistance? Will landlords accept such individuals and households? Will new low-cost housing continue to be built? Will the new purchasing power of the poor person engender the rehabilitation and repair of heretofore unsatisfactory dwellings to bring them up to satisfactory conditions? Even the Experimental Housing Allowance Program of 1972–79 (EHAP),[30] one of the largest social science experiments in our history, and its voluminous critiques[31] have not been able to answer all of these questions.

The alternative of housing projects subsidized by the federal government is a very expensive and very wasteful process. Therefore, housing vouchers must play a role, but they may not be able to handle the job exclusively.

It is also important that housing is not always a high priority in the personal and household budget of the low-income individual. Nathan Glazer's seminal article in *Public Interest* challenged the assumption that the poor value improvements in shelter above all other goods.[32] Some critics of the housing voucher program suggest that the issue is not the shelter allowance per se and accuse voucher supporters of trying to sneak in a back-door income subsidy.

Nevertheless, the housing voucher, in one form or another, is now a central feature of housing policy. But the debate over the proper format for housing subsidies will continue. Given the evolution of housing subsidies over the past half century, it may be instructive to turn from the mechanics of their operation to an evaluation of what has been accomplished and an assessment of emerging themes and influences.

Old Ends, New Beginnings

The old saw that "man is what he eats" can be paraphrased (with equal lack of precision) by an equivalent—"countries are what they subsidize" (see Table 2.2). Much has been made by housing task forces (the Douglas and Kaiser commissions[33] in particular come to mind) of the erratic, cyclical nature of total housing starts in the United States; peaks to troughs regularly show differences of 50 percent and more. But these sways are relatively modest when compared with the erratic levels of subsidized new housing starts. From 1950 through 1967, subsidized starts remained consistently below one hundred thousand, with the value relative to all housing construction rarely moving above 5 percent until the mid-1960s.

In the Great Society era the picture was drastically altered. From nearly 200,000 subsidized new housing starts in the late 1960s (about one-seventh of total new production), the pace rose rapidly to a peak of almost 450,000 new subsidized units, about one-fifth of total production, by the early 1970s (see Table 2.2).

Then came the 1973 subsidized housing moratorium. By the mid-1970s, subsidized production dropped back to a low of one hundred thousand units, a quarter of the volume achieved in the early part of the decade. With the advent of the Carter administration in 1977, federally subsidized new housing starts again increased, reaching about two hundred thousand units in 1980 (some one-sixth of the total new production, but in a very bad housing year). Even the recent high point of subsidized production was little more than half that of the earlier peak.

The roller coaster took another dip with the coming into power of the Reagan administration in 1981. The magnitude of change is evident in Table 2.2. Subsidized new housing starts dropped to about 180,000 in 1981–82, 125,000 in 1983, and continued to fall to 100,000 in 1984 and 70,000 in 1985. The latter figure represents a return to the modest level of subsidized production volume of the mid-1960s.

What is most striking is the "successful failure" of the Reagan administration. Faced with a housing industry driven back to levels of production not seen for two generations, it did not subscribe to the conventional wisdom of using housing as a key countercyclical tool. Instead, the brakes on housing subsidies were sharply applied (with little Democratic outcry).

The coalition devoted to the old political magic of direct subsidies to housing has been shattered. The Great Society era in shelter, at least as viewed from Washington, was over. The new federal housing orientation of the Nixon administration's second term was barely interrupted by the post-Watergate Carter interregnum.

This is not to belittle the local efforts of the last dozen years aimed at reducing housing costs through a variety of interventions. The federally funded Community Development Block Grants, a Nixon-era successor to urban renewal, provided a stimulus for local communities to build or, more likely, rehabilitate low-cost housing.

Although local standards vary enormously, the growth in CDBG-financed housing activity has been impressive. In fiscal year 1976, CDBG funding was responsible for the rehabilitation of approximately 28,000 units; by 1982, for 225,000.[34] Similarly, the mechanism of tax-exempt financing of low- and moderate-cost housing through the issuance of state mortgage bonds has been exploited with such vigor as to prompt a congressional backlash scaling it back. It is noteworthy that the Ullman Amendment, which called for the elimination of state mortgage banks, was sponsored not by the Republicans but by the newly fiscally conscious Democrats. Notwithstanding these and other local initiatives (undertaken, as always, with federal money), the cessation of a national commitment to subsidized housing for poor or moderate-income households is obvious.

Much to the amazement of housing analysts, however, this has not meant the end of the world. After an initial period of shock, such devices as the variable-rate mortgage and the construction of privately developed modest-scale housing have served to undermine the premise that only the government can build houses for the average American. Thus many of the players in the old public sector housing coalition are too busy making money in the private sector to form a new alliance for low-cost housing for the poor.

This is a field, however, in which prosperity has often been short-lived. In the happy breathing space that is now available, it may be worthwhile to recite some lessons of the past and some potential themes for the future.

Past Policies and Future Directions

The following basic generalizations regarding a half century of fitful federal housing policy can be made.

Calibration. Recent studies by the Center for Urban Policy Research indicate that there is a three-to-five-year gap between the time a decision is made to build one-family housing developments and the time the units are ready for occupancy; in multifamily housing, the time span can be substantially greater. Therefore, to use public housing programs, with their mandated locational, cost, configurational, and tenantry limitations, as a countercyclical fiscal tool is questionable. The subsidy mechanism is generally conceived at the depths of a recession yet the housing comes into being just as the economic cycle is reaching its peak. Some fiscal calming is in order. The result is that housing intervention, rather than being countercyclical, serves as a disturbing cyclical accelerator.

Longevity. The federal government has focused on new conventionally built housing, which is enormously expensive. For such programs to make any economic sense, the housing units must last at least forty years. Housing is not an appropriate good to offer families in short-term need. It should rest on a demand base of stable and responsible long-term usage. Unfortunately, this requirement has frequently been lacking.

Thus a number of major housing projects, located in central cities which have been losing population rapidly, now suffer from the same abandonment as their private neighbors. Even private units built with public subsidy may reflect the political exigency attending their construction rather than the demographic underpinnings that would maintain their long-range economic viability.

Costs. In general, the costs of government-subsidized housing have been vastly understated. The use of nominal off-the-balance-sheet financing can represent a raid on the federal treasury much larger than the nominal price tag put on a program by its advocates. The political temptation to avoid large onetime lump-sum costs has tended to generate extraordinary long-term assaults on the public fisc.

Subsidized housing has also been less efficient than comparable private housing. For example, the Section 8 program, as well as earlier predecessors similarly dependent for their success on a depreciation tax cover, have created incentives to maximize costs—and therefore the tax write-off capacity of a project—and every disincentive to be efficient.

Developers interviewed by the Center for Urban Policy Research admitted that rehabilitation jobs that could be done for their own account at a cost of $15,000 cost more than $40,000 under Section 8.

Equally consequential, though perhaps less often noted, is the price of economic failure. The abandoned public housing projects are paralleled by failures in the programs providing below-market interest rates. More than a quarter of all of the structures subsidized by the Section 236 below-market interest rate program for multifamily housing have gone through at least one renegotiation of mortgage. Many have gone through several. Each renegotiation has resulted in much greater costs to the federal pocketbook than were anticipated at the time of the passage of the original enabling legislation. Write-downs of 50 percent or more of the value of government-insured mortgages have been accompanied by interest moratoriums and new project subsidies that make a mockery of nominal accounting procedures.

The very nature of federal legislation and political realities tends to maximize the unit costs and minimize the "bang for the buck." For example, the Davis-Bacon Act raises labor costs on government projects substantially above those in the private sector and accelerates inflation for the entire construction industry.

Targeting. The concepts of vertical equity (subsidized housing programs should treat people differently depending upon their income) and horizontal equity (equal treatment for those who have approximately equal income), though easily subscribed to, have never been implemented. As indicated in Chapter 1, low-income housing efforts by the federal government have constituted a lottery, with a minority of the eligible getting a payoff and the majority being left out.

The political necessity of securing a broad supportive coalition and the flows of funds, subsidies, profits, and tax covers that emerge from housing programs suggest the analogy of feeding sparrows by assuring oats for the horses.

Inclusionary Zoning

A multitude of new conceptual approaches have been spawned in the vacuum left by direct government subsidy.[35] Inclusionary zoning and development charges are two prominent local measures to foster the production of lower-cost housing.

Inclusionary zoning is a feature of the cross-subsidization of internal projects that has been described as "a process intended to set aside a portion of the total number of units in a development at below-market prices in order to expand housing available to low- and moderate-income persons."[36] A share, usually 10 to 25 percent, of the total new housing production within a development is to be sold or rented at below-market prices. To encourage a developer to comply, many inclusionary programs offer inducements such as a density bonus, a reduction in the subdivision, parking, or setback requirements, or lower-cost financing.

Inclusionary programs in the United States date from the early 1970s. In 1971, Fairfax County, Virginia, required builders of fifty or more units to commit at least 15 percent of the units to low- and moderate-income families.[37] And in response to the *Degroff*[38] decision, which declared inclusionary requirements as unconstitutional taking, Fairfax amended its requirement in 1973 to provide for a density bonus.[39] In 1973, Arlington County, Virginia, enacted a 10 percent inclusionary goal, which, if realized, would result in a 10 percent density bonus.[40] The same year, Montgomery County, Maryland, adopted a mandatory inclusionary requirement for builders of fifty or more units that they set aside 15 percent of their production for moderate-income families.[41] To facilitate compliance, the county authorized up to a 20 percent density bonus. In some cases, the purview of inclusionary zoning ordinances has been broader. For instance, the California Coastal Commission required a hotel developer in Marina del Rey to provide a youth hostel, moderate-cost coffee shop, and special weekend discount rates for low- to moderate-income families.[42]

The inclusionary spirit soon swept the country. In 1973, Lakewood, Colorado, required that 10 to 15 percent of the units in housing projects of fifty or more homes be offered at below-market prices.[43] Shortly thereafter, Boulder, Colorado, passed a similar provision.[44] It was in California, however, that inclusionary mechanisms became most common. As a result of a series of state statutory requirements relating to expanded housing opportunities (for example, mandating that local governments "make adequate provision for the housing needs of all economic segments of the community," requiring municipalities to provide "regulatory concessions and incentives" to foster such housing, and preparing model local inclusionary ordinances), scores of California municipalities adopted inclusionary provisions. In 1973, Palo Alto required that developers of twenty or more units set aside one in five as low- or moderate-cost units.[45] Other cities followed suit.

The most extensive California inclusionary program, in housing affected, is in Orange County.[46] It requires that 25 percent of all units in developments of five or more houses in most areas of the county (locations already fulfilling their inclusionary mandate are exempt) be affordable by families earning below 80 percent of the median, another 10 percent for households earning between 80 and 100 percent of the median, and a final 5 percent for households earning between 100 and 120 percent of the median. Developers can satisfy their inclusionary requirement by building the one-quarter share in each project; building more than a 25 percent share of affordable units in one of their developments and then transferring the "credit" to a project that is under quota; buying "credits" from other builders; and land donations or in-lieu cash payments to the county. However it is satisfied, the inclusionary requirement is costly to builders. As compensation, the county offers developers density bonuses, modifications to subdivision requirements, accelerated processing, and tax-exempt financing.

Orange County's inclusionary program has resulted in the planning and production of a considerable amount of affordable housing. As of 1982, there were commitments to build more than five thousand units; eight hundred were already built and occupied,[47] mostly low-cost developments. More affluent developments subsidized them by buying their fair-share obligation off-site.

Orange County has recently rescinded its inclusionary housing provision. Although this decision represents a setback, inclusionary zoning received a strong affirmation in the 1983 New Jersey State Supreme Court decision, *Southern Burlington County NAACP* v. *The Township of Mount Laurel* (commonly referred to as *Mount Laurel II.)*[48] According to the New Jersey decision, "every municipality's land use regulations . . . must provide a realistic opportunity for decent housing for its indigenous poor . . . [and] for a fair share of the region's present and prospective low- and moderate-income housing need."[49] The state supreme court declared that inclusionary zoning was one affirmative measure to meet the Mount Laurel mandate. This declaration has spurred numerous municipalities in the state to adopt inclusionary requirements.

Development Charges

Inclusionary zoning requires residential builders to contribute to the general welfare by providing low-cost housing. Should the obligation be extended to nonresidential developers? Some municipalities have decided that they do also have a housing responsibility. San Francisco has taken the lead in this approach. In 1981, the city created an Office/Housing Production Program (OHPP) under which developers of at least 50,000 square feet of office space must build, or cause to be built, .9 housing units (640 square feet) for every 1,000 square feet of office space.[50] The results of the program can be summarized thus: Developers gain "housing credits" by contributing directly to a housing trust fund, building the housing themselves, or aiding other residential developers to build or rehabilitate housing units. By late last year (1983), the program had produced twenty-six hundred dwelling units and exacted $19 million in contributions from twenty-seven office developers. Of this amount, $4.88 million was contributed into the program's Home Mortgage Assistance Trust Fund, which has subsidized the mortgages of seventy-six low- and moderate-income families buying existing homes. Funds from the trust also will help finance the construction of new condominium and cooperative units and subsidize mortgage payments for their low- to moderate-income buyers.

Other cities are considering similar provisions. A proposed "linkage program" in Boston would require developers of over one hundred thousand square feet of office space to contribute a "neighborhood impact excise" of $5 a square foot over a twelve-year period to a neighborhood housing trust.[51] New York City is evaluating a similar approach, which would combine contributions by developers with a potpourri of other funds so as to capitalize a housing financing pool.[52] Office developers would contribute directly to the housing fund, and residential developers have the option of setting aside units for lower-income tenants. Of the cash contributions, 25 percent would be used within the same neighborhood, and more in poorer areas. Joel Werth notes:

> What's particularly interesting about this proposal is that the $200 million trust fund would come not from one but over a dozen sources: developer contributions ($30 to $60 million a year); the city's share of state mortgage recording fees ($22 million); repayments of UDAG and CDBG loans and sale of city-owned property ($17.5 million); higher building permit fees ($5 million); registration fees for real estate syndications and interest earned on escrow accounts set up to hold security deposits ($17.5 million); filing fees by newly formed cooperatives and condominiums ($7.5 million); revenues generated by tax increment financing districts ($7.5 million); taxes on major real estate transfers ($15 million); the city's capital budget appropriations ($20 million); state budget appropriations ($20 million); inclusionary zoning payments made in lieu of providing on-site units ($20 million); annual repayment of loans made by the housing trust fund ($11 million).[53]

It is important to place the inclusionary requirements and development charges in perspective. These new techniques have offset to some extent the decline in federal support for low-cost housing, but they do not fully compensate. Municipalities are in the position of attempting to make bricks without straw. Those that have strong demand for development may succeed in doing so by increasing taxes and earmarking the new revenues for housing. In the long run, the economic and political viability of this process is questionable. In any case, although for most of this century the federal government dominated the provision of lower-cost and subsidized housing, for today and the likely future the housing cast of characters is much broader, including federal, state, and local players.

Notes

1. U.S. Department of Commerce, Bureau of the Census (1975).

2. See, for example, Friedman and Spector (1975:41); Ford et al. (1936); Lubove (1963); and Veiller (1910).

3. Quoted in Friedman (1969:28).

4. Riis (1895).

5. See Friedman (1969).

6. Steffens (1968).

7. See Jacobs et al. (1982:3).

8. See U.S. Congress, House of Representatives, Committee on Banking, Currency and Housing, Subcommittee on Housing and Community Development (1975:1).

9. See Listokin (1984).

10. See Semer et al. (1976a:3, 82); Scott (1971:316).

11. *Proceedings and Report of the President's Commission on Homebuilding and Homeownership* (1931).

12. See Scott (1971:194—95).

13. Public Law 72-302, July 21, 1932; see Scott (1971:318).

14. Public Law 73-67, June 16, 1933.

15. Public Law 73-43, June 13, 1933; Public Law 73-470, June 27, 1934.

16. Quoted in Semer et al. (1976a:9).

17. Public Law 75-412, September 1, 1937.

18. Public Law 77-59, May 26, 1942.

19. Public Law 77-421, January 30, 1942.

20. Public Law 78-346, June 22, 1944.

21. Housing Act of 1949, Public Law 81-171, July 15, 1949.

22. Meyerson and Banfield (1955).

23. Semer et al. (1976b:114).

24. Wheaton (1954).

25. Housing Act of 1954, Public Law 83-560, August 2, 1954.

26. Housing Act of 1961, Public Law 70-87, June 30, 1961.

27. Demonstration Cities and Metropolitan Development Act of 1966, Public Law 89-754, November 4, 1966; Housing and Urban Development Act of 1968, Public Law 90-448, August 1, 1968.

28. Housing and Urban Development Act of 1970, Public Law 91-609, December 31, 1970.

29. Housing and Community Development Act of 1974, Public Law 93-383, August 22, 1974.

30. See U.S. Department of Housing and Urban Development (1980); Carlson and Heinberg (1978); Abt Associates (1973); McDowell (1979); and Goedert (1978).

31. Bradbury and Downs (1981).

32. Glazer (1967).

33. See National Commission on Urban Problems (1969).

34. See Listokin (1983:15).

35. U.S. Advisory Commission on Intergovernmental Relations (1982).

36. State of Connecticut, Department of Housing (1974:9).

37. Fairfax County, Va., Code Ch. 30 (1961), as amended by Amendment 156 (1971).

38. *Board of Supervisors* v. *Degroff Enterprises*, 214, Va. 235, 198, S.E. 2d 600 (1973).

39. Fairfax County, Va., Code Ch. 30 (1961), as amended by Amendment 249 (1975).

40. Arlington County, Va., Resolution of Developer Provision of Moderate-Income Housing (February 22, 1972).

41. Montgomery County Council, Bill 372, Code 25A, Montgomery County, Md. (1974).

42. Ellickson (1981:1172); also see Goedert (1976:1015); Franklin et al. (1974).

43. Lakewood, Colorado, Planning Commission Policy, No. 15 (1973).

44. Boulder, Colorado City Council Resolution 115 (1977).

45. California Government Code, Section 65 302(c), cited in Schwartz and Johnston (1983:20).

46. Los Angeles, Calif., Municipal Code 12.03, 12.39, 13.04, as amended by Ordinance No. 145. 927 (1974).

47. Schwartz and Johnston (1983:13).

48. *Southern Burlington County NAACP* v. *The Township of Mount Laurel*, 67 N.J. 151, 336 A. 2d 713, appeal dismissed and cert. denied, 423 U.S. 808 (1975) *(Mount Laurel I)*; *Southern Burlington County NAACP* v. *The Township of Mount Laurel*, 92 N.J. 158, 456 A. 2d 390 (1983) *(Mount Laurel II)*.

49. Kayden and Zan (1983).

50. Werth (1984:22).

51. Ibid.:23.

52. Citizens Housing and Planning Council, "Memorandum" (1984).

53. Werth (1984:22).

References

Abt Associates. 1973. *Experimental Design and Analysis Plan of the Demand Experiment.* Cambridge, Mass.: Abt Associates.

Arlington County, Va., Resolution of Developer Provision of Moderate-Income Housing. February 22, 1972.

Board of Supervisors v. *Degroff Enterprises*, 214, Va. 235, 198, S.E. 2d 600 (1973).

Boulder, Colorado. 1977. City Council Resolution 115.

Bradbury, Katherine, and Anthony Downs. 1981. *Do Housing Allowances Work?* Washington, D.C.: Brookings Institution.

Carlson, David B., and John D. Heinberg. 1978. *How Housing Allowances Work: Integrated Findings from the Experimental Allowance Program.* Washington, D.C.: Urban Institute.

Citizens Housing and Planning Council. "Memorandum." 1984.

Demonstration Cities and Metropolitan Development Act of 1966, Public Law 89-754. November 4, 1966.

Ellickson, Robert C. 1981. "The Irony of Inclusionary Zoning." *Southern California Law Review* 54(6):1172.

Fairfax County, Va., Code Ch. 30 (1961), as amended by Amendment 156 (1971), cited in *Hastings Constitutional Law Journal* (Fall 1976):1053.

Fairfax County, Va., Code Ch. 30 (1961), as amended by Amendment 249 (1975).

Ford, James, et al. 1936. *Slums and Housing.* Cambridge, Mass.: Harvard University Press.

Franklin, Herbert M., et al. 1974. *In-Zoning—A Guide for Policymakers on Inclusionary Land Use Programs.* Washington, D.C.: Potomac Institute.

Friedman, Lawrence M. 1969. *Government and Slum Housing: A Century of Frustration.* Chicago: Rand McNally, p. 28.

Friedman, Lawrence M., and Michael Spector. 1975. "Tenement Housing Legislation in Wisconsin: Reform and Reaction." *American Journal of Legal History.* Chapter 908, 9:41.

Glazer, Nathan. 1967. "Housing Problems and Housing Policies." *Public Interest.* 7:21–51.

Goedert, Jean E. 1976. "Density Bonus Zoning to Provide Low- and Moderate-Cost Housing." *Hastings Constitutional Law Journal* 3(4):1015.

———. 1978. *Generalizing from the Experimental Housing Allowance: An Assessment of Site Characteristics.* Washington, D.C.: Urban Institute.

Housing Act of 1949, Public Law 81-171, July 15, 1949.

Housing Act of 1954, Public Law 83-560, August 2, 1954.

Housing Act of 1961, Public Law 70-87, June 30, 1961.

Housing and Community Development Act of 1974, Public Law 93-383, August 22, 1974.

Housing and Urban Development Act of 1968, Public Law 90-448, August 1, 1968.

Housing and Urban Development Act of 1970, Public Law 91-609, December 31, 1970.

Public Law, 72-302, July 21, 1932.

Public Law 73-43, June 13, 1933.

Public Law 73-67, June 16, 1933.

Public Law 73-470, June 27, 1934.

Public Law 75-412, September 1, 1937.

Public Law 77-59, May 26, 1942.

Public Law 77-421, January 30, 1942.

Public Law 78-346, June 22, 1944.

Jacobs, Barry G., et al. 1982. *Guide to Federal Housing Programs.* Washington, D.C.: Bureau of National Affairs, p. 3.

Kayden, Jerold S., and Leonard A. Zan. 1983. "Mount Laurel II: Landmark Decision in Zoning and Low Income Housing Holds Lessons for Nation." *Zoning and Planning Law Report* 6:3.

Lakewood, Colorado. 1973. Planning Commission Policy, No. 15.

Listokin, David. 1983. *Housing Rehabilitation: Economic, Social and Policy Perspectives.* New Brunswick, N.J.: Rutgers University, Center for Urban Policy Research, p. 15.

————. 1984. *Housing Receivership: Self-Help Neighborhood Revitalization.* New Brunswick, N.J.: Rutgers University, Center for Urban Policy Research.

Los Angeles, Calif., Municipal Code 12.03, 12.39, 13.04, as amended by Ordinance No. 145.927. 1974.

Lubove, Roy. 1963. *The Progressives and the Slums: Tenement House Reform in New York City, 1890–1917.* Pittsburgh: University of Pittsburgh Press.

McDowell, James L. 1979. *Housing Allowances and Housing Improvement: Early Findings.* Santa Monica: Rand Corporation. Rand Report-N-1198-HUD.

Meyerson, Martin, and Edward G. Banfield. 1955. *Politics, Planning and the Public Interest.* New York: Free Press.

Montgomery County Council, Bill 372, Code 25A, Montgomery County, Md. 1974.

National Commission on Urban Problems. 1969. *National Commission on National Problems: Building the American City.* New York: Praeger.

Proceedings and Report of the President's Commission on Homebuilding and Homeownership, December 19, 1931.

Riis, Jacob. 1895. *The Battle with the Slums.* New York: Macmillan.

Schwartz, Seymour I., and Robert A. Johnston. 1983. "Inclusionary Housing Programs." *Journal of the American Planning Associates* 49(1):13–20.

Scott, Mel. 1971. *American City Planning since 1890.* Berkeley and Los Angeles: University of California Press, pp. 194–95, 316–18.

Semer, Milton P., et al. 1976a. "Evolution of Federal Legislation Policy in Housing: Housing Credits." In *Housing in the Seventies, Working Paper I.* U.S. Department of Housing and Urban Development, Washington, D.C.: U.S. Government Printing Office, p. 3.

————. 1976b. "A Review of Federal Subsidized Housing Programs." In *Housing in the Seventies, Working Paper I.* U.S. Department of Housing and Urban Development, Washington, D.C.: U.S. Government Printing Office, pp. 82–114.

Southern Burlington County NAACP v. *The Township of Mount Laurel,* 67 N.J. 151, 336 A. 2d 713, appeal dismissed and cert. denied, 423 U.S. 808 (1975) *(Mount Laurel I).*

Southern Burlington County NAACP v. *The Township of Mount Laurel,* 92 N.J. 158, 456 A. 2d 390 (1983) *(Mount Laurel II).*

State of Connecticut, Department of Housing. 1974. *Housing and Land Use: Community Options for Lowering Housing Costs.* Hartford: Department of Housing, p. 9.

Steffens, Lincoln. 1968. *Autobiography.* New York: Harcourt Brace.

U.S. Advisory Commission on Intergovernmental Relations. 1982. *Significant Features of Fiscal Federalism, 1981–82.* Washington, D.C.: U.S. Government Printing Office.

U.S. Congress, House of Representatives, Committee on Banking, Currency and Housing, Subcommittee on Housing and Community Development. 1975. *Evolution of the Role of the Federal Government in Housing and Community Development: A Chronology of Legislative and Selected Executive Actions, 1892–1974.* Washington, D.C.: U.S. Government Printing Office, p. 1.

U.S. Department of Commerce, Bureau of the Census. 1975. *Historical Statistics of the United States from Colonial Times to 1970.* Washington, D.C.: U.S. Government Printing Office. Housing Document: 93-78, 93d Cong., 1st sess.

U.S. Department of Housing and Urban Development. 1980. *The Experimental Housing Allowance Program: Conclusions, the 1980 Report.* Washington, D.C.: U.S. Government Printing Office.

Veiller, Lawrence. 1910. *Housing Reform.* New York: Russell Sage Foundation.

Werth, Joel. 1984. "Tapping Developer." *Planning* 50(4):22–23.

Wheaton, William. 1954. "The Evolution of Federal Housing Programs." Ph.D. dissertation, University of Chicago.

3

Private Production
Has the Rising Tide
Lifted All Boats?
John C. Weicher

Housing Quality: Lifting the Boats

The United States has enjoyed a steady improvement in the quality of housing throughout the postwar period. By every available measure, the nation has far fewer inadequate housing units than at any previous time and is close to achieving the goal of a "decent home" originally conceived in the late 1940s.[1]

This improvement in housing quality has been partly obscured by the problems of defining and measuring the overall physical condition of a unit. From 1940 to 1960, the U.S. Census Bureau asked its enumerators to evaluate the housing units they visited. In an attempt to minimize subjectivity in the enumeration, the bureau provided criteria for classifying a unit as substandard, including pictures of typical "dilapidated" houses and apartments. Despite these efforts, an evaluation of the *1960 Census of Housing* showed a high incidence of classification error, with enumerators and evaluators disagreeing over which units were dilapidated.[2]

The gravity of this classification problem is open to dispute. After examining the census evaluation, Frank Kristof reported that the errors resulted in an underestimate of substandard units by only 1.2 percent of the total stock and concluded that the issue was "a tempest in a teapot."[3] Such a level of error would clearly not affect the overall pattern of improvement (see Table 3.1). The bureau decided to discontinue the measurement of overall housing conditions, but after significant objections from city governments that used the data for planning purposes, the bureau partially reversed its decision and began providing estimates of dilapidated housing, but using a different method. It surveyed a smaller number of units, correlated the incidence of dilapidation with that for other characteristics, then inferred the total number of dilapidated units in the country and in individual cities. Numbers for 1970, however, are probably less reliable than for earlier years. They are also the last to be compiled for the "traditional" (original census) definition of substandard housing.

Since 1973, different information about housing quality has been

1 %

Table 3.1.

Measures of Substandard Housing, 1940–1980
(percentage of all occupied housing)

Problem	1940	1950	1960	1970	1980
Substandard	48.6	35.4	16.0	8.4	N.a.
Lacking complete plumbing	44.6	34.0	14.7	5.5	2.2
Dilapidated	18.1 [a]	9.1	4.6	3.7	N.a.
Crowding (more than 1.0 persons per room)	20.2	15.8	11.5	8.8	4.2
Severe crowding (more than 1.5 persons per room)	9.0	6.2	3.8	2.0	1.0

Sources: Data are from the following U.S. Bureau of the Census sources: *Sixteenth Census of the United States: 1940, Housing,* vol. 2, pt. 1; *1950 Census of Housing,* vol. 1, pt. 1; *1960 Census of Housing,* vol. 2, pt. 1; *1970 Census of Housing: Components of Inventory Change,* HD(4)-1; *Annual Housing Survey: 1980, United States and Regions,* pt. A.

N.a. = not available.

[a] "Needing major repairs" in 1940.

collected as part of the *Annual* [now American] *Housing Survey.* This survey contains information on thirty different categories of housing deficiencies for a one-in-a-thousand sample of the U.S. housing stock: the presence and working order of plumbing, heating, electrical, and other major systems and the existence of specific structural defects such as leaky roofs and basements, holes in floors, walls, or ceilings, and missing stairs or rails in apartment buildings. Several analysts, mostly within government agencies, have used the AHS data to develop new measures of housing inadequacy.

The new measures are much more complex than the traditional ones. Often they group characteristics into categories such as "plumbing" or "maintenance" and formulate a criterion of adequacy for each category. A typical measure, developed by John Simonson and Richard Clemmer of the U.S. Department of Housing and Urban Development (see Table 3.2), indicates that the quantity of inadequate housing has continued to decline during the 1970s, as shown in Table 3.3. Comparison of Table 3.1, which is based on the traditional definition, and Table 3.3, based on Simonson and Clemmer's definition, however, demonstrates that the new measure cannot be viewed as a substitute for the old. Table 3.1 indicates that in 1970, 8.4 percent of the occupied stock was "substandard"; Table 3.3 shows

Table 3.2.

*Deficiencies That Cause a Housing Unit to Be
Judged Physically Inadequate*

Type	Description
Plumbing	*Lacks or shares some or all plumbing facilities.* The unit must have hot and cold piped water, a flush toilet, and a bathtub or shower—all inside the structure and for the exclusive use of the unit.
	Lacks adequate provision for sewage disposal. The unit must be connected to a public sewer, septic tank, cesspool, or chemical toilet. (Units with this deficiency almost invariably have a plumbing deficiency as well.)
	Had breakdown of flush toilet for six consecutive hours or longer three or more times during last ninety days.
Kitchen	*Lacks or shares some or all kitchen facilities.* The unit must have an installed sink with piped water, a range or cookstove, and a mechanical refrigerator—all inside the unit and for exclusive use of the unit.
Physical structure	*Has three or more of six structural problems:* leaking roof; open cracks or holes in interior walls or ceiling; holes in interior floors; peeling paint or broken plaster over one square foot in an interior wall or ceiling; evidence of rats or mice in the last ninety days; leaks in basement.
Common areas	*Has three or more of four common area problems:* no light fixtures (or no working light fixture) in common hallway; loose, broken, or missing steps on common stairways; loose or missing stair railings; no elevator in building (for units two or more floors from the main building entrance in buildings four or more stories high).
Heating	*Has unvented room heaters that burn oil or gas.* If the unit is heated mainly by room heaters burning gas, oil, or kerosene, the heaters must have a flue or vent.
	Had breakdown of heating equipment for six consecutive hours or longer three or more times during the past winter.

Table 3.2. *continued*

Type	Description
Electrical	*Lacks electricity.*
	Has three out of three signs of electrical inadequacy: one or more rooms without a working wall outlet; fuses blown or circuit breakers tripped three or more times during the last ninety days; exposed wiring in the unit.

Source: Richard B. Clemmer and John C. Simonson, "Trends in Substandard Housing, 1940–1980," *AREUEA Journal* 10 (Winter 1983): Exhibit 5.

that in 1973, 11.8 percent was "physically inadequate." There is no reason to believe that housing quality deteriorated in those three years and some reason to believe that it kept improving; this was a period of rising incomes and record levels of private and subsidized production. Clemmer and Simonson, recognizing the discrepancy, have attempted to produce a time series for the traditional definition of substandard housing which extends past 1970. The series, shown in Table 3.4, indicates continued progress since 1970. Probably as good an estimate of the changing incidence of low-quality housing on a consistent basis as possible, it surely is sufficient to demonstrate the trend of continuing improvement.

Quality Changes for Special Groups

All these data are aggregate figures. Improvements also have occurred in the housing of various groups that have frequently received special attention in housing policy, although there are numerous gaps in the data available. The best data are presented in Table 3.5 for five major population groups: blacks, Hispanics, residents of rural areas, and two measures of poverty—the bottom quarter of the income distribution and households with real incomes of $10,000 or less in 1980 dollars. The table includes only the two traditional criteria for which there are data in 1980: units lacking complete plumbing and crowding (units with more than one person per room). For the former, disaggregated data are available for blacks and rural residents from 1940 but for income groups only from 1950; for crowding, there are not full data for ethnic groups and income classes until

Table 3.3.

Housing Inadequacy, 1973–1980
(percentage of occupied units)

Year	Percentage inadequate
1973	11.8
1974	11.0
1975	10.7
1976	10.2
1977	10.2
1978	10.1
1979	9.8
1980	9.6

Source: Calculated by the author from numbers in Clemmer and Simonson, "Trends in Substandard Housing," Exhibit 7, and U.S. Bureau of the Census and U.S. Department of Housing and Urban Development, *Annual Housing Survey*, Part A, 1973 to 1980.

Table 3.4.

Estimated Substandard Housing, 1940–1980
(percentage of occupied units)

Year	Percentage substandard
1940	48.6
1950	35.4
1960	16.0
1970	8.4
1973	7.5
1974	7.1
1975	6.9
1976	6.6
1977	6.6
1978	6.5
1979	6.3
1980	6.2

Source: Clemmer and Simonson, "Trends in Substandard Housing," Exhibit 8.

Table 3.5.

Substandard Housing for Special Groups, 1940–1980
(percentage of occupied units)

	Panel A: Lacking Complete Plumbing				
Group	1940	1950	1960	1970	1980
Blacks[a]	79.6	70.9	41.9	16.3	6.1
Hispanics	N.a.	N.a.	N.a.	6.6	2.4
Rural residents	74.8	61.6	31.5	13.8	4.8
Lowest quarter of income distribution	N.a.	60.1	33.9[b]	7.9	5.0
Real income below $10,000 in 1980 dollars	N.a.	51.6	30.0[c]	13.0	5.0

	Panel B: Crowding		
Group	1960	1970	1980
Blacks[a]	28.3	19.2	9.1
Hispanics	N.a.	25.7	19.2
Rural residents	20.6	9.9	4.7
Lowest quarter of income distribution	12.1	7.1	4.3
Real income below $10,000 in 1980 dollars	12.7	8.5	4.3

Sources: Same as Table 3.1.
N.a. = not available.
[a]Nonwhites in 1940 and 1950.
[b]Estimated; correct percentage lies between 31.2 and 35.2.
[c]Estimated; correct percentage lies between 27.4 and 31.1.

1960.[4] But the data that are available confirm the pattern of improvement for these groups: from 1940 to 1970, these groups experienced a reduction in the incidence of dilapidated and substandard housing.

Reported changes in some of the most serious defects reported in the *Annual Housing Survey* further indicate physical improvement in housing for these groups. These figures, published annually since 1973 for blacks and Hispanics but only since 1978 for income classes, are reported in Table 6 for the two ethnic groups. In seven of the eight measures, the incidence of a defect declined between 1973 and 1980; the exception, for blacks and Hispanics, is the presence of rats or mice.

Table 3.6.

*Incidence of Housing Defects, Black and Hispanic Households,
1973 and 1983 (percentages)*

	Blacks		Hispanics	
Defect	1973	1983	1973	1983
Shared or no bathroom	11.0	5.3	5.0	2.6
Shared or no kitchen	7.9	2.8	2.5	1.5
Presence of rats or mice	26.0	26.6	19.9	19.3
Exposed wiring	6.2	4.0	4.7	4.1
Lacking working out- lets in some rooms	12.6	5.8	6.4	4.3
Leaky roof	15.6	12.2	9.9	10.7
Interior wall or ceiling cracks	16.0	15.3	13.0	11.5
Holes in floors	7.2	6.3	4.4	4.3

Source: Annual Housing Survey, Part B, 1973 and 1983.

The incompleteness of the data for these and other groups do not invalidate the pattern of improvement. Housing for these major groups remains worse than for the nation as a whole. The reason for the higher incidence of housing inadequacy may be that these groups, like many other groups of interest in housing policy, are disproportionately poor. But the incidence of inadequacy is declining rapidly, indicating that housing quality is improving for the disadvantaged in general.

Explaining the Improvement:
What Is Lifting the Boats?

There are four common explanations for the postwar improvement in housing quality: rising real incomes for American families including the poor; a falling relative price for housing;[5] a high rate of new private housing production, predominantly for upper-income households, which ultimately results in better housing available to the poor ("filtering"); and government programs to clear slums and subsidize new housing production specifically for the poor.

All of these phenomena have occurred during the postwar period, concurrently with the downward trend in substandard housing (see Table 3.7). It is clear from Table 3.7 that subsidized production pro-

Table 3.7.

Trends in Income, Housing Costs, and Construction, 1950–1980

	1950s	1960s	1970s
Median real income (percentage change over decade):			
Families	+37.5	+33.9	+ 0.8
Unrelated males	+30.2	+39.4	+13.5
Unrelated females	+31.6	+37.3	+26.9
Real housing costs (percentage change over decade):			
Rent (CPI)	+ 5.9	− 8.4	−18.0
Homeownership (CPI)[a]	+ 3.9[b]	+13.6	+15.1
Homeownership (Hendershott and Shilling)	+15.4[c]	−27.1	22.6
New construction (millions of units):			
Total units	16.24	16.48	20.52
Total units/net household form	1.59	1.58	1.23
Private units	15.96	15.99	19.45
Subsidized new low-income units	0.29	0.49	1.07
Subsidized existing units	0	0.10	0.77

Sources: U.S. Bureau of the Census, *Statistical Abstract of the United States,* various editions, for income, CPI housing costs, total new construction, and household formation; Patric H. Hendershott and James D. Shilling, "The Economics of Tenure Choice, 1955–1979," in C. F. Sirmans, ed., *Research in Real Estate,* vol. 1 (Greenwich, Conn.: JAI Press, 1982), for Hendershott and Shilling measure of homeownership cost; U.S. Department of Housing and Urban Development, *HUD Statistical Yearbook,* various years, for subsidized units.

[a] The sharp rise in the CPI homeownership index after 1960 is now generally recognized to misrepresent the situation confronting homebuyers: when inflation and the tax treatment of owner-occupied housing are considered, ownership became an increasingly profitable investment after 1965. These factors are omitted in the CPI. The measure developed by Hendershott and Shilling is one of several recent efforts to construct a more appropriate cost index; it is used here because it is available for the longest period.

[b] Covers 1953–60 period only.

[c] Covers 1955–60 period only.

grams by themselves were not directly responsible for all or even most of the improvement that occurred. At best, they may have contributed to a looser housing market, reducing the demand for lower-quality housing, thereby making it possible for the poor to afford better housing.

The Concept of Filtering

This chapter is concerned with how the housing quality and economic well-being of the poor may be affected by housing policy and changes in the housing market. Therefore, the relevant question is, does the price of the modest but decent housing fall when new construction occurs? If it does, then poor people are better off in a strict economic sense; their housing costs less, and they can buy better housing, more of other goods and services, or both.

The process by which new housing production for the well-to-do results in improvement in housing quality for the poor has been called "filtering."[6] As new housing is built, some families move into it and leave their old housing vacant. The demand for the type of housing they formerly occupied decreases, reducing its price and permitting families with somewhat lower incomes to buy or rent it. In turn, these families move out of housing that is somewhat lower in quality, reducing the demand for that type of housing and enabling families of still lower income to move in. At the bottom of the quality distribution, some households move from substandard to standard housing, and some are able to move out of the worst housing, which then drops out of the stock.

Not all new construction expedites the filtering process. Filtering occurs if there is a reduction in construction costs (because of technological progress or reduced regulation) or if there is an increase in income among the well-to-do. But units built simply to meet growth in a locality do not necessarily make the market looser; there must be construction in excess of net household formation. Also, government subsidy of the price or interest rate is not likely to cause filtering unless the subsidy induces construction that would not otherwise have occurred, using resources that would have been unemployed. This might occur during a recession. But if the resources would have been used in other economic activity, the subsidy is basically an income transfer to the new home buyers (or new apartment renters) from the rest of society, including the families who would move up. Their incomes are lower, so even if the price of better housing is lower, they may not be able to take advantage of it.

It is important to distinguish the filtering concept from general economic growth. Filtering is hypothesized to occur when the incomes of the rich increase, even if the incomes of the poor do not. Economic growth, particularly in this country, results in higher incomes throughout the population. The notion of the "rising tide" usually refers to economic growth in general; an increase in income for the rich alone is more akin to a locomotive pulling the economy. In fact, both may have been occurring recently. During the postwar period, the income distribution seems to have become slightly more equal, then after 1967 slightly more unequal, but the changes are small. Throughout the period, the poor have increasingly lived in better housing, whether or not filtering has been happening.

It is also important to identify other phenomena that are distinct from the filtering process. First is the process whereby a series of individual households replace each other in a sequence of housing moves. Several studies have identified and interviewed in sequence the specific households that moved, starting with the buyers of new houses, to see whether their housing improved. There is a "chain of moves," continuing until the chain ends, when the last family moves to its new home. The best known of these studies is by John Lansing, Charles Clifton, and James C. Morgan, written in 1969.

Second is the process whereby individual housing units deteriorate over time. Vintage models of the housing stock, such as Richard F. Muth's 1973 study, incorporate this basic assumption and trace out its implications. There is also a small but growing body of literature on housing maintenance.

Third is the process whereby even well-maintained older housing units become less desirable relative to the rest of the housing stock as they age and new units are built. Thus a given house, even if reasonably well maintained, is likely to be occupied over time by households that are farther down in the income distribution.

Fourth are the processes that operate at the neighborhood level and help to explain patterns of neighborhood change and succession, by income and race. Studies by Charles Leven, James Little, Hugh Nourse, and Richard Read in 1976 and by Kerry E. Vandell in 1981 exemplify this literature.

The Economic Argument

There has been some controversy among economists as to whether the rising tide can lift all boats in the long run. This theory was generally accepted during the 1950s, rejected in the 1960s, and resurrected in the mid-1970s.

Richard Ratcliff originally described the process in 1949, but he and most writers immediately after him did not try to distinguish among the various phenomena that accompany, but do not necessarily constitute, filtering. Ira Lowry, in 1960, was the first to recognize and state clearly the central importance of price changes at the lower end of the housing quality distribution spectrum, for understanding the process and for formulating housing policy. He argues that only a decline in quality, not price, for a given unit can occur. The real price for the unit cannot fall because landlords will reduce their expenditures for maintenance until the quality level is again proportional to the rent they can charge, and the return on their investment resumes its initial, market-determined level.

Edgar Olsen, in his 1969 study, came to the same conclusion. Relying on empirical evidence that the supply of new housing is perfectly elastic—as much new housing as the market wants can be provided without driving up its price—Olsen argues that the price per unit will be driven to the minimum long-run average cost of production in a perfectly competitive market. This price will be constant over all quality levels; differences in price between units are therefore proportional to differences in quality in the long run. This theory implies that new private high-quality construction cannot help the poor.

More recently, however, several economists have developed formal housing market models that show that new construction may result in higher-quality and less expensive housing for the poor and an improvement in their overall economic well-being.[7] There are several differences between these models as a group and the earlier work by Lowry and Olsen. The most important concern how difficult it is for a landlord to disinvest in housing. The easier it is, the more realistic are the earlier models. They assume that the landlord is able to reduce maintenance quickly to the point that the quality of the housing declines as much as its market rent. The formal models of the last decade, on the other hand, assume that once a housing unit is built, the owner's expenditure for maintenance is only one of the factors affecting its quality. Therefore, even if the owner does nothing, the quality of the dwelling may not decline as fast as its rent.[8]

Intuitively, there is some truth to both assumptions. Landlords are probably as concerned as other investors with maximizing profits and avoiding losses. Furthermore, it seems implausible that a house or apartment could continue to be a decent place to live if the landlord stopped maintaining it; eventually the unit ought to deteriorate to the point that it is inadequate and finally uninhabitable. But a dwelling is not only "capital" in the abstract but bricks and mortar in the concrete; it continues to stand, and to be livable, even if it is no longer as desirable as when it was new.

A different way of looking at the issue is to ask how long it takes a dwelling to deteriorate to a lower quality level. There is no disagreement that the rising tide will help the poor for some period, until the market fully reacts to the construction. The theoretical argument is whether new construction will help the poor in the long run, after all adjustments have occurred. But there has been little attempt to ascertain the length of the adjustment process. Olsen, following Muth's early empirical work, suggests that about 90 percent of the adjustment will occur within six years.

This adjustment period introduces a policy issue: poor people may benefit from a rising tide for new private construction for only a finite number of years. Is that period long enough to make the promotion of private construction a worthwhile policy to help the poor? Thus the Lowry-Olsen analysis, if valid, does not automatically rule out the rising tide hypothesis; the policy issue depends on how long the adjustment process is. Some models imply that it is much longer than ten years.

Thus it is a somewhat open question whether new private construction can help the poor. The latest theoretical work indicates that it probably can, but the literature does not establish that it does.

Empirical Evidence

There have been very few empirical studies of the rising tide hypothesis and no time-series analysis; the data simply do not exist. The research that has been done is cross-sectional; it usually compares either differences in the incidence of substandard housing across cities or metropolitan areas at a particular date or differential changes among cities over a period.

William Grigsby produced the first and for a long time virtually the only empirical study in 1963. He found that rents and house prices increased least during the 1950s in those metropolitan areas with the most new construction. His study was limited to nine areas, however, and he was unable to adjust for quality changes. In the early 1970s, Frank deLeeuw began to develop a housing market model to simulate various housing policy options, using census data for four metropolitan areas as prototypical markets. This model demonstrates that new private construction results in a reduction in the price and quantity of low-quality housing over a decade.[9] More recently, Thomas G. Thibodeau and I have analyzed the *Annual Housing Survey* data for sixty large metropolitan areas during the early 1970s. We find a very strong negative relationship between private construction during a five-year period and substandard housing at the end of the period and a weaker but still negative effect from units built five to fifteen years earlier. The short-run impact is about one fewer substandard unit at the end of the period for every three to four built during the period.[10] The only contrary evidence is a recent paper by Donald F. Vitaliano, who found no relationship between new private construction and the incidence of low-quality housing five to fifteen years earlier. His analysis is based on a sample of New York State communities of various sizes, rather than large metropolitan areas. There have been no other empirical investigations of the relationship between private new housing construction and the incidence of substandard housing. Two of the most extensive studies of substandard housing—by George W. Hartman and John C. Hook and by Otto A. Davis, Charles M. Eastman, and Chan-I Hua—omit new private construction but include a large number of other independent variables. Werner Hirsch and C. K. Law, who have a narrower focus on the relationship between changes in landlord-tenant law and housing quality, also leave out new construction.[11]

It is surprising that there have been so few studies of the rising tide or filtering hypothesis and of substandard housing in general. Cross-sectional data on housing quality have been available since the *1940 Census of Housing*, and public concern about substandard housing goes back much earlier. But though there is not a great deal of empirical evidence to substantiate the rising tide hypothesis, nearly all the evidence that does exist supports it.

Subsidized Production and Quality Improvement: The "Diverted Flow"

Discussions about housing policy often contrast the filtering hypothesis with subsidized production programs such as public housing. The usual assumption is that subsidized production benefits the poor; the burden of proof thus falls on the advocates of filtering to show that new private construction also benefits the poor. In fact, when the same standards are applied to both policies, it is subsidized production that appears to be clearly inferior.

Conventional public housing, the oldest and simplest subsidized production program, has received the most attention. Analysts agree on one fundamental point—households that move directly into public housing clearly benefit. These families are removed from the private housing market and placed in better housing than they previously occupied.

Analysts have reached diverse conclusions about the effects on low-income households that are not assisted and on the housing market generally. Olsen, for example, concludes that all low-income households not assisted by the program are unaffected; they have the same incomes and face the same price for housing of a given quality as they did before the program was established. Ultimately, as many units drop from the private housing stock as there are households occupying public housing. James Sweeney, however, concludes that public housing benefits all low-income households because demand for private low-quality units declines and the rents of these units therefore fall as well; the number of households occupying the lowest quality of housing also falls. But James C. Ohls gets the opposite result. His simulation model indicates that the quality of housing deteriorates on balance for low-income households that are not assisted. Ohls does not attempt to explain his result. It is possible that public housing construction causes a decrease in private construction at the low-cost end of the housing market, leading in the long run to a reduction in the private stock and a fall in its quality. Thus the various studies allow one to conclude that the total reduction in low-quality housing (the marketwide effect) may be greater, the same as, or less than the number of new public housing units.[12]

According to most of these studies, the effects on households other than those directly assisted occur as a result of relative price changes for different qualities of housing. Thus in this important respect, subsidized production, if effective, works to improve housing by the same filtering process as private construction.

Empirical Evidence

Whereas theoretical studies are ambivalent, empirical studies of the relationship between subsidized housing and quality in the private stock generally support the view that subsidized production has an insignificant or negative impact on the incidence of substandard housing. Studies by Davis, Eastman, and Hua and by Hirsch and Law conclude that subsidized production resulted in an improvement in housing quality only when substandard housing was defined differently at the beginning and end of the study period. When the definition was consistent over time, the subsidized production was unrelated to the incidence of low-quality housing.

My own work with Thomas G. Thibodeau (forthcoming), the most extensive study undertaken to date, found an insignificant relationship most of the time, regardless of the definition of inadequacy and using a variety of data sources on subsidized production. Disaggregating by program type and by year of construction did not improve the results. Moreover, even the most generous estimates of the benefits of subsidized production demonstrate less than a unit-for-unit reduction in substandard housing.

These results are unexpected; they fly in the face of economic theory and conventional wisdom—perhaps even of common sense. If subsidized housing helps poor people directly, it is hard to believe that its side effects can be so perverse as to negate its direct benefits and leave the poor as a whole no better off.

An important partial explanation for this apparent contradiction is that public housing occupancy is not restricted to those who have previously lived in substandard housing. Data on federal government programs show that fewer than half of new residents in assisted housing during the late 1960s and early 1970s moved on from substandard housing.[13] Moreover, the program definition of "substandard" is not the same as criteria used in policy analyses but is an elastic, rather vague notion, based on the perceptions of the tenant and the staff of the local housing authority. Thus public housing in the real world may well have different effects from the abstract concept used in most housing market models.

A more general explanation is that subsidized housing production is in large part a substitute for private production that would probably have occurred without the program. The two most detailed studies, by Michael Murray and Craig Swan, conclude that most public housing has simply replaced private new construction in the long run, although the substitution effect takes a few years.[14] If this is true, then one might describe public housing as a "diverted flow," in contrast to the "rising tide" of private production.

Flotsam and Jetsam: Losses from the Inventory

The rising tide has other consequences besides a reduction in the occupancy of low-quality housing: the reduction occurs through the removal of these units from the housing stock. It is therefore worthwhile to investigate whether the loss of older housing is actually related to private new construction.[15]

One important distinction should be noted: housing *loss* is not the same as housing *abandonment.* A loss occurs when a dwelling unit is no longer available for occupancy; abandonment occurs when the owner surrenders title to the structure and the land under it. Losses therefore may happen for any number of reasons: some are accidental because of fire or natural disaster; some result from government actions as, for example, when highways or urban renewal projects are built in residential areas; some result from property owners deciding that a different use will be more profitable. In general, owners will permit the removal of a dwelling unit if the land has more value if used another way. Owners will abandon a dwelling—and the land under it—if both have no value in the foreseeable future. Date limitations make it difficult to distinguish among losses from whatever cause. The sketchy evidence available suggests that losses and abandonments do correlate positively, but by no means perfectly, across metropolitan areas, so the discussion may be applicable to both.

New private construction does appear to cause housing losses. Loss rates are higher in metropolitan areas with higher construction rates relative to household formation. The magnitude of the effect, however, seems to be surprisingly small: one unit lost for six units built during a five-year period and almost one additional loss in the succeeding decade. This means that 70 percent of new construction leads to changes in the housing market other than loss. Logically, there are only three other possible changes: formation of additional households because more housing is available; a higher vacancy rate; and fewer conversions of existing housing to provide more units or of nonresidential structures to housing. Higher vacancy rates, however, may cause some losses in the long run because losses are responsive to vacancy rates. Thus private construction can result in losses indirectly, over a longer period, by first affecting the vacancy rate.

A related issue is the spatial relationship between new construction and losses. It does not appear that the intrametropolitan location of losses is affected by the location of construction, at least when location is described by a gross city/suburban classification. Lost units are predominantly the worst and smallest, as the rising tide theory would predict. These units drop out of the inventory, wherever they are, as a result of new construction, wherever it is. In most large metropolitan areas, construction typically occurs in the suburbs and the worst housing is in the city, so suburban construction leads to city losses; but in a few southern and western areas, the opposite happens.

For comparative purposes, it is also interesting to consider the effect of public housing and other subsidized production programs on loss rates. There seems to be no relationship between subsidized production and losses, either immediately or with a lag. Nor does the location of public housing or middle-income subsidy programs such as Section 235 and 236 affect the location of losses. Building subsidized housing in the suburbs does not increase the loss rate in either the cities or the suburbs.

This evidence is consistent with the conclusion that subsidized production does not improve the quality of housing for the poor. Apart from those actually occupying the subsidized units, the poor seem to be living in the same quality of housing, and indeed in the same housing, as they would in the absence of the program.

Conclusions and Policy Implications

It appears that there is a rising tide, or filtering process, by which new housing built for the well-to-do ultimately results in better housing for the poor. By academic standards, the theoretical and the empirical evidence is not as conclusive as one might wish. Most recent theoretical analyses support the rising tide theory, but the most elegant ones do not definitely establish the proposition, and there is some disagreement. The preponderance of the empirical evidence, however, supports the theory, although there have not been many studies.

The most fundamental question for policy purposes is whether there are mechanisms that the government can employ to increase the rate of new construction: do we know how to make the tide rise? Three causes of a filtering process were listed earlier: technological progress, reduced regulation of housing construction, and rising incomes for the rich. The first two make new housing cheaper; the last increases the demand for it.

There has been gradual technological progress in the building industry throughout the postwar period, which has probably contributed to general improvement in housing quality. But government has had little to do with this progress and has been unsuccessful in accelerating its rate. Operation Breakthrough, the federal government's most ambitious attempt, is generally regarded as a failure, and rightly so.[16] Technological progress in housing construction seems to come from the cumulative effect of many small changes over a long period. General incentives to innovation, such as research and development tax credits, might be effective, although the evidence is not encouraging.

Reducing government regulation is a favorite proposal of builders, among others. This strategy probably would not accomplish a great deal, however. The anecdotal evidence that regulation raises costs is impressive, but the results of systematic academic research are much less supportive.[17]

The possibility that government policy could increase the income of the rich without at the same time lowering the income of the poor—in other words, without simply redistributing income—seems remote, and few Americans would have much enthusiasm for such a policy, even if it were Pareto optimal. It is worth mentioning only for the sake of completeness.

Although explicit policies to increase the income of the rich find little favor, the federal government from time to time has enacted programs designed to stimulate the production of new housing to be occupied by families in the upper half of the income distribution. The usual rationale is macroeconomic—the programs are an effort to stimulate the economy, or at least the housing industry, during a recession. In this situation, the new housing might use resources that would otherwise be idle, and the subsidy may in fact reduce the cost of housing to the well-to-do without imposing costs on the poor. The government in this way may be able to promote a rising tide, though that is usually not its objective.

The most common policy has been to stimulate the demand for new housing by reducing the cost of mortgage credit. These programs have some cyclical effect but, contrary to the conventional wisdom, are not important in the long run. This apparently applies even to such extensive interventions as the federally sponsored credit agencies.[18] The best that can be said is that they smooth out the filtering process, enabling it to continue during recessions to at least a minor extent. Furthermore, in the wake of the financial market reforms of the 1970s and early 1980s, it is likely to become even harder to divert credit to housing.

The United States has also tried once—and briefly—to stimulate demand for housing by subsidizing the down payment on a house. Evaluations of the 1975 tax credit found that it had little impact even on a countercyclical basis.[19] Canada's long-term down-payment subsidy—the Registered Home Ownership Savings Plan—similarly produced no discernible increase in housing production.[20]

Thus the record of specific government attempts to promote new construction is not encouraging. But this does not invalidate the rising tide argument. Something has been generating an improvement in housing quality for the poor for many years. The high rate of housing construction is no doubt one important contributing factor, whatever the extent to which it has resulted from government policy. Steadily rising real incomes also have been important. Subsidized housing production programs have not been large enough to be very important, and moreover they have not so far been shown to have any measurable beneficial effect. If further research substantiates their conclusion, then subsidized construction is ineffective as well as inefficient.

Notes

1. For the best definition of "a decent home" at the time this goal was established, see U.S. Congress (1949:9).

2. U.S. Bureau of the Census (1967).

3. Kristof (1968:Appendix C).

4. Crowding is reported for nonwhites in the 1940 census (40.0 percent) and for rural residents in 1940 (26.5 percent) and 1950 (20.6 percent). For nonfarm households only, there are 1950 data on crowding by income class: 15.8 percent for the poorest quarter and 17.4 percent for those with incomes below $10,000 in 1980 dollars. These figures supplement the picture of steady improvement shown in Table 3.5.

5. See, for example, Quigley (1979).

6. The earliest full description of this process, in Ratcliff (1949), is not very rigorous but serves as a good model for discussion purposes. This discussion draws on Weicher and Thibodeau (forthcoming).

7. Sweeney's commodity hierarchy model is the first and most important of these (1974a, 1974b); others have been constructed by Ohls (1975), Braid (1981, 1984), and Schall (1981). These models differ in both methodology and detail. But in all, the housing stock consists of a large number of quality classes (or alternatively a continuum of housing quality), with units deteriorating exogenously over time and typically with constant returns to scale in the production of new housing. In most of them, construction clearly results in these improvements under any circumstances. In two instances—the long-run models of Sweeney (1974b) and Braid (1984)—these implications are rigorously deduced only for certain specified new construction subsidy programs, rather than for a general proportional reduction in the cost of construction, such as would occur as a result of technological progress. But Sweeney considers it likely that the same qualitative conclusions would hold (p. 310). Braid does not discuss this situation.

8. Sweeney (1974b:308) argues that the fundamental difference between his model and Olsen's concerns whether capital is malleable after it has been embodied in housing; Olsen assumes that it is, Sweeney that it is not. The importance of this assumption has subsequently been brought out by Fisch (1977), in a model patterned after Sweeney's. Fisch assumes that capital is malleable and then finds that filtering does not occur; he is forced to introduce an additional assumption that new construction is concentrated at the urban fringe to derive

housing consumption patterns similar to those actually observed (for example, new housing being built primarily for higher-income households).

9. DeLeeuw and Struyk (1975).

10. Weicher and Thibodeau (forthcoming); see also Weicher, Yap, and Jones (1982).

11. Vitaliano (1983); Hartman and Hook (1956); Davis, Eastman, and Hua (1974); Hirsch and Law (1979).

12. Sweeney (1974b:312–13); Ohls (1975).

13. This is the latest period for which such data are available. It corresponds to the period covered in many of the empirical studies.

14. Murray (1983); Swan (1973).

15. This section draws on my research on housing losses, as reported in Weicher, Yap, and Jones (1982) and Weicher (1982).

16. For an evaluation of Operation Breakthrough, see Weicher (1980:chap. 8) and the literature cited there.

17. For a review of the anecdotes and the academic literature, see Seidel (1978); for an elaboration of my opinion, see Weicher (1980:chap. 8).

18. For a review of the relevant literature to the mid-1970s, see Grebler (1976). For a recent analysis, see Tuccillo, Van Order, and Villani (1982).

19. See Weicher (1980: 134–38), for a review of the evidence.

20. Clemmer and Weicher (1983).

References

Braid, Ralph M. 1981. "The Short-Run Comparative Statics of a Rental Housing Market." *Journal of Urban Economics* 10:286–310.

———. 1984. "The Effects of Government Housing Policies in a Vintage Filtering Model." *Journal of Urban Economics* 16:272–96.

Clemmer, Richard B., and John C. Simonson. 1983. "Trends in Substandard Housing, 1940–1980." *AREUEA Journal* 10:221–36.

Clemmer, Richard B., and John C. Weicher. 1983. "The Individual Housing Account." *AREUEA Journal* 11:221–36.

Davis, Otto A., Charles M. Eastman, and Chan-I Hua. 1974. "The Shrinkage in the Stock of Low-Quality Housing in the Central City: An Empirical Study of the U.S. Experience over the Last Ten Years." *Urban Studies* 2:13–26.

deLeeuw, Frank, and Raymond J. Struyk. 1975. *The Web of Urban Housing.* Washington, D.C.: Urban Institute Press.

Fisch, Oscar. 1977. "Dynamics of the Housing Market." *Journal of Urban Economics* 4:428–47.

Grebler, Leo. 1976. "An Assessment of the Performance of the Public Sector in the Residential Housing Market: 1955–1974." In Robert M. Buckley, John A. Tuccillo, and Kevin E. Villani, eds., *Capital Markets and the Housing Sector.* Cambridge, Mass.: Ballinger.

Grigsby, William. 1963. *Housing Markets and Public Policy.* Philadelphia: University of Pennsylvania.

Hartman, George W., and John C. Hook. 1956. "Substandard Urban Housing in the United States: A Quantitative Analysis." *Economic Geography* 23:95–114.

Hirsch, Werner, and C. K. Law. 1979. "Habitability Laws and the Shrinkage of the Substandard Rental Stock." *Urban Studies* 16:19–28.

Kristof, Frank S. 1968. *Urban Housing Needs through the 1980's: An Evaluation and Projection.* Research Report No. 10, prepared for the National Commission on Urban Problems, Washington, D.C.

Lansing, John, Charles Clifton, and James C. Morgan. 1969. *New Homes and Poor People.* Ann Arbor: University of Michigan Press.

Leven, Charles, James Little, Hugh O. Nourse, and Richard Read. 1976. *Neighborhood Change.* New York: Praeger.

Lowry, Ira. 1960. "Filtering and Housing Standards: A Conceptual Analysis." *Land Economics* 36:362–70.

Murray, Michael P. 1983. "Subsidized and Unsubsidized Housing Starts: 1961–1977." *Review of Economics and Statistics* 65:590–97.

Muth, Richard F. 1960. "The Demand for Non-Farm Housing." In Arnold C. Harberger, ed., *The Demand for Durable Goods.* Chicago: University of Chicago Press.

———. 1973. "A Vintage Model of the Housing Stock." *Papers of the Regional Science Association* 30:141–56.

Ohls, James C. 1975. "Public Policy towards Low Income Housing and Filtering in Housing Markets." *Journal of Urban Economics* 2:144–75.

Olsen, Edgar O. 1969. "A Competitive Theory of the Housing Market." *American Economic Review* 54:612–21.

President's Commission on Housing. 1982. *Report of the President's Commission on Housing.* Washington, D.C.: U.S. Government Printing Office, pp. 7–8.

Quigley, John M. 1979. "What Have We Learned about Urban Housing Markets?" In P. Mieszkowski and Mahlon Straszheim, eds., *Current Issues in Urban Economics.* Baltimore: Johns Hopkins University Press, chap. 12.

Ratcliff, Richard U. 1949. *Urban Land Economics.* New York: McGraw-Hill.

Schall, Lawrence. 1981. "Commodity Hierarchy Chain Systems and the Housing Market." *Journal of Urban Economics* 10:141–43.

Seidel, Stephen R. 1978. *Housing Costs and Government Regulation.* New Brunswick, N.J.: Rutgers University Press.

Struyk, Raymond J., Sue A. Marshall, and Larry J. Ozanne. 1978. *Housing Policies for the Urban Poor.* Washington, D.C.: Urban Institute Press.

Swan, Craig. 1973. "Housing Subsidies and Housing Starts." *AREUEA Journal* 1:119–40.

Sweeney, James. 1974a. "A Commodity Hierarchy Model of the Rental Housing Market." *Journal of Urban Economics* 1:288–323.

———. 1974b. "Quality, Commodity Hierarchies, and Housing Markets." *Econometrica* 42:147–67.

Tuccillo, John, Robert Van Order, and Kevin Villani. 1982. "Homeownership Policies and Mortgage Markets, 1960 to 1980." *Housing Finance Review* 1:1–21.

U.S. Bureau of the Census. 1967. *Measuring the Quality of Housing.* Working Paper No. 25.

U.S. Congress, Joint Committee on Housing. 1949. *Housing Study and Investigation, Final Majority Report.* Part 1. 80th Cong., 2d sess., 15 March, 1949, p. 9.

Vandell, Kerry E. 1981. "The Effects of Racial Composition on Neighborhood Succession." *Urban Studies* 18:315–33.

Vitaliano, Donald F. 1983. "Public Housing and Slums: Cure or Cause?" *Urban Studies* 20:173–83.

Weicher, John C. 1980. *Housing: Federal Policies and Programs.* Washington, D.C.: American Enterprise Institute.

———. 1982. "The Relationship between Subsidized Housing Production and Loss Rates within Metropolitan Areas." Urban Institute Contract Report No. 1484-01.

Weicher, John C., and Thomas G. Thibodeau. Forthcoming. "Filtering and Housing Markets: An Empirical Analysis." *Journal of Urban Economics.*

Weicher, John C., Lorene Yap, and Mary S. Jones. 1982. *Metropolitan Housing Needs for the 1980s.* Washington, D.C.: Urban Institute Press.

4

The Leaky Boat
A Housing Problem Remains
William C. Apgar, Jr.

Inadequate Housing:
How Much of a Problem Today?

Overall housing conditions have improved for all Americans—rich and poor alike—since World War II, but in recent years this improvement has stalled. There are indications that inadequate housing persists and actually is on the rise in parts of the country. Moreover, in many areas the decline in inadequate units has been offset by a worsening of neighborhood conditions.

America's housing problem is one of affordability as well as inadequacy. Housing costs declined in real terms in the postwar period, but this trend too has been reversed in recent years. Since the mid-1970s, housing costs have increased rapidly for both renters and homeowners. In many cases, incomes have failed to keep pace with rising housing costs.

Low-income renters, who historically have lived in inadequate housing in marginal neighborhoods and have paid an inordinate share of their incomes for housing, have been particularly hard hit by these recent trends. By 1981, 1.6 million renters with incomes below $5,000 lived in inadequate units and another 6.4 million paid more than 35 percent of their incomes for rent. Both figures are up sharply from 1974.

This chapter explores the overall improvement in housing in the postwar period and the causes and extent of current housing problems. It describes measures of housing and neighborhood dynamics, pointing out the limitations of these measures. The chapter identifies the groups of Americans having the most severe housing problems.

Census data show improvements between 1940 and 1980 in broad measures of crowding and housing quality. As Figure 4.1 illustrates, there were long downward trends in the percentages of units that have more than one person per room, that lack some or all plumbing, and that are dilapidated or needing repairs. The downward trends in the two crowding measures logically follow an increase in the average number of rooms per unit and a decline in the average size of households.

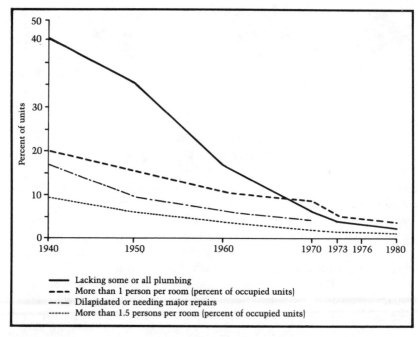

Figure 4.1. *Measures of Housing Inadequacy*

Source: Compiled from data supplied by the U.S. Department of Commerce, Bureau of the Census, and the President's Commission on Housing, *Report of the President's Commission on Housing* (Washington, D.C.: U.S. Government Printing Office, 1982).

Interpreting the two measures of housing quality is more difficult. The presence of plumbing as a measure does not reveal much about the condition of a unit because practically all units today have plumbing. Between 1940 and 1980 many otherwise adequate units were modernized with the addition of plumbing facilities, and with the advent of building codes in most jurisdictions, it has been virtually impossible since 1950 to build a new unit without minimum plumbing such as a flush toilet or hot and cold running water.

Recognizing the limitations of using the presence of plumbing as a measure of housing conditions, the Bureau of the Census produced a broader measure—units that are dilapidated or needing major repairs. Unfortunately, this measure, which the bureau used between 1940 and 1970, has drawbacks, too. Evaluation of census procedures suggested that there was little consistency on how census enumerators judged individual units. This is perhaps understandable, given the heterogeneity of the nation's housing and the dependence on enumerators' subjective judgment. The bureau prepared estimates of this measure until 1970 but decided to drop it from decennial and mid-decade housing data-collection efforts.

Notwithstanding these problems, the data from this measure between 1940 and 1970 are revealing. For example, the sharp decline reported in units without plumbing was not accompanied by an equally sharp decline in units judged to be dilapidated, calling into question the value of the absence of plumbing measure as an indicator of improvement in housing quality. By 1970, 3 million dilapidated units remained on the housing inventory, a figure that was cited widely as a rationale for continued federal efforts to improve the condition of the nation's housing.

In an effort to improve measurement of the adequacy of housing, beginning in 1973 the U.S. Department of Housing and Urban Development joined with the Bureau of the Census to gather the *Annual Housing Survey*. In addition to basic data about the nation's households, the *AHS* collects data on more than twenty-five housing deficiencies. Questions probe not only the presence or absence of a piece of equipment but also whether the item is in good working order. In contrast to the decennial census, which contained a single question on the need for major repairs, the AHS includes several questions on such structural defects as the presence of leaky roofs, cracks or holes in walls or ceiling, or holes in interior floors.

The *AHS* data are based on respondents' assessments of their own units. Therefore, the assessments in part depend on the characteristics of the households making the assessment. For example, studies suggest that a homeowner is less likely to report defects than a renter occupying the same unit. Likewise, low-income and elderly households tend to underreport defects, whereas higher-income households and households headed by younger persons tend to be critical of their dwellings.

The *AHS* data show that from 1974 to 1981 units lacking complete plumbing, complete kitchen facilities, or private bathroom facilities continued to decline (see Table 4.1). The absolute number of occupied units deficient in basic maintenance and upkeep, however, was on the rise. In 1981, 4.9 million dwelling units had leaky roofs, an increase of nearly two hundred thousand units or 4 percent. Furthermore, the absolute number of units with selected defects continued to grow: 4.6 million had cracks or holes in walls or ceilings, 1.9 million experienced a breakdown in the water supply, and 10.5 million showed signs of rats or mice.

In an effort to translate these data on individual defects into com-

Table 4.1.

*Number of Occupied Dwelling Units with Selected Structural
Defects, 1974 and 1981 (in thousands)*

Defect	1974	1981	Percent change 1974 to 1981
Mechanical subsystems			
Shared or not complete kitchen	1,582	1,330	−15.9
Shared or no bathroom	2,633	2,120	−19.5
Lacking some or all plumbing	2,076	1,626	−21.7
No heating equipment	329	447	35.9
Maintenance and upkeep			
Some or all wiring exposed	2,375	2,375	0.0
Lacking working outlets in some rooms	3,078	2,728	−12.8
Breakdown in water supply	1,549	1,850	19.4
Breakdown in sewer/septic/ cesspool	833	923	10.8
Inadequate heat	2,890	2,937	1.6
Cracks or holes in walls or ceilings	4,024	4,647	15.5
Holes in interior floors	1,308	1,561	19.4
Roof leaks	4,737	4,928	4.0
Signs of rats or mice	6,676	10,499	57.3

Source: U.S. Department of Commerce, Bureau of the Census, *Annual Housing
Survey* (Washington, D.C.: U.S. Government Printing Office, 1974 and 1981).

prehensive measures of housing condition, the Congressional Budget
Office (CBO), HUD, and the Office of Management and Budget (OMB)
have used *AHS* variables to develop widely used indexes of housing
quality. These indexes differ in the *AHS* variables they use, yet conclusions based on these measures do not differ significantly.

The measure of housing quality used here is similar to the HUD
index. This measure rates a unit in six areas: plumbing, heating,
electricity, upkeep, hallways, and kitchen (see Table 4.2). Unlike the
HUD index, however, the categories "seriously inadequate" and
"moderately inadequate" are combined into a single category incor-
porating eighteen separate *AHS* questions. The purpose of combining the categories is to create a comprehensive measure of housing
condition that is consistently defined between 1974 and 1981.

Table 4.2.

Definition of Structural Inadequacy: A Unit Is Inadequate If It Has One of the Following Problems

Plumbing	Lacking hot or cold piped water or a flush toilet, or lacking both hand basin and shower, all inside the structure for the exclusive use of the household, or having only one toilet, which broke down three times in the last six months.
Heating	Having three or more breakdowns of the heating equipment last winter, or having unvented gas, oil, or kerosene heaters as the main source of heat.
Electricity	Having all of the following three electric problems: exposed wiring; a room with no working wall outlet; and three blown fuses or tripped circuit breakers in the last ninety days.
Upkeep	Having three of the overall list of five problems: leaky roof; holes in the floors; holes or open cracks in walls or ceilings; more than a square foot of peeling paint or plaster; or signs of rats and mice in the last ninety days.
Hallways	Having two of the following three problems in public areas: no working light fixtures; loose or missing steps; and loose or missing railings.
Kitchen	Lacking a sink, range, stove, or refrigerator, all inside the unit for the exclusive use of the unit.

Using this measure, 11.6 million units or approximately 16.4 percent of all occupied units in 1974 were structurally inadequate (see Table 4.3). The number of structurally inadequate units fell slightly from 1974 to 1981, but this overall decline can be attributed to a decline in structurally inadequate *owner-occupied* units. During the same period, the number of structurally inadequate *renter-occupied* units increased by nearly two hundred thousand.

The number of adequate renter-occupied units, however, grew at a greater rate than the number of inadequate units. New construction added more than 12 million units of good-quality housing to the national inventory, and demolitions removed nearly 4 million units, a quarter of which were inadequate. The total number of structurally inadequate units declined by only 158,000. At the same time, lack of maintenance and repair led to a deterioration of the existing in-

Table 4.3.

Number of Occupied Dwelling Units by Tenure and Structural Adequacy, 1974 and 1981 (in thousands)

Defect	1974	1981	Percent change 1974 to 1981
Owner-occupied units			
Adequate structure	39,679	48,587	22.5
Inadequate structure	6,105	5,755	−5.7
All structures	45,784	54,342	18.7
Renter-occupied units			
Adequate structure	19,523	23,118	18.4
Inadequate structure	5,523	5,715	3.4
All structures	25,046	28,833	15.1
Total occupied units			
Adequate structure	59,202	71,705	21.1
Inadequate structure	11,628	11,470	−1.4
All structures	70,830	83,175	17.4

Source: Joint Center for Housing Studies of the Massachusetts Institute of Technology and Harvard University, "Special Tabulations of *Annual Housing Survey* Data for 1974 and 1981" (Cambridge, Mass., 1984).

ventory. Thus, for every thousand inadequate units removed from the inventory between 1974 and 1981, 842 units of existing housing moved from the adequate to the inadequate category as a result of lack of maintenance and upkeep.

Neighborhood Conditions and Housing Quality

Although neighborhood amenities and local public services are important in influencing a household's satisfaction with a particular dwelling, such features are not included in the HUD, CBO, or OMB indexes of housing condition. Thus studies based on these indexes refer only to the *structural* condition of housing.

This limitation is serious because there is ample evidence that the condition of many neighborhoods has deteriorated since 1974. *AHS* data suggest that America's neighborhoods have deteriorated signifi-

Table 4.4.

Number of Occupied Dwelling Units by Selected Neighborhood Deficiencies, 1974 and 1981 (in thousands)

Condition present in neighborhood	1974	1981	Percent change 1974 to 1981
Crime	12,115	18,371	51.6
Unsatisfactory police protection	6,357	8,460	33.1
Abandoned buildings or structures	4,834	6,396	32.3
Trash, litter, or junk	10,308	12,730	23.5
Streets in need of repair	13,741	14,399	4.8
Odors	7,240	6,640	−8.3

Source: Joint Center for Housing Studies of the Massachusetts Institute of Technology and Harvard University, "Special Tabulations of *Annual Housing Survey* Data for 1974 and 1981" (Cambridge, Mass., 1984).

cantly. The *AHS* asks respondents to rate their neighborhood on a number of neighborhood and public service quality variables by indicating whether or not a negative condition exists in their neighborhood. (As mentioned earlier, answers to *AHS* questions may vary from one respondent to another, even within the same neighborhood, depending on their characteristics and their perceptions of conditions.)

Whether the data collected represent actual or perceived conditions, they indicate that between 1974 and 1981 the number of households that felt that crime was a problem in their neighborhood or that police protection was inadequate increased sharply (see Table 4.4). Since the number of households increased by 17.4 percent during the period, both the number and the incidence of households reporting crime and unsatisfactory police protection increased. In addition, the number and incidence of households reporting the presence of abandoned buildings or of trash, litter, or junk in their neighborhood increased as well. Little change was reported in the other two measures (streets in need of repair and odors).

Combining the information on the six neighborhood measures gives a single index of the number of neighborhood deficiencies present (see Table 4.5). In 1981, 43.8 million households reported no deficiencies, and 22.7 million reported one. The number of house-

Table 4.5.

Number of Occupied Dwelling Units by Number of Neighborhood
Deficiencies, 1974 and 1981 (in thousands)

Number of deficiencies	1974	1981	Percent change 1974 to 1981
No deficiencies	37,072	43,825	18.2
One deficiency	20,101	22,715	13.0
Multiple			
Two	8,683	9,939	14.5
Three	3,449	4,367	26.6
Four	1,055	1,713	62.4
Five or more	467	615	31.6
All units	70,830	83,175	17.4

Source: Joint Center for Housing Studies of the Massachusetts Institute of Technology and Harvard University, "Special Tabulations of *Annual Housing Survey* Data for 1974 and 1981" (Cambridge, Mass., 1984).

Table 4.6.

Number of Occupied Dwelling Units by Tenure and
Neighborhood Adequacy, 1974 and 1981 (in thousands)

Tenure and structural adequacy	1974	1981	Percent change 1974 to 1981
Owner-occupied units			
Adequate neighborhood	37,182	44,622	20.0
Inadequate neighborhood	8,602	9,720	13.0
All neighborhoods	45,784	54,342	18.7
Renter-occupied units			
Adequate neighborhood	19,992	21,929	9.7
Inadequate neighborhood	5,054	6,904	36.6
All neighborhoods	25,046	28,833	15.1
Total occupied units			
Adequate neighborhood	57,174	66,551	16.4
Inadequate neighborhood	13,656	16,624	21.8
All neighborhoods	70,830	83,175	17.4

Source: Joint Center for Housing Studies of the Massachusetts Institute of Technology and Harvard University, "Special Tabulations of *Annual Housing Survey* Data for 1974 and 1981" (Cambridge, Mass., 1984).

Table 4.7.

Number of Occupied Dwelling Units by Tenure, Neighborhood, and Structural Adequacy, 1974 and 1981 (in thousands)

Tenure, neighborhood, and structural adequacy	1974	1981	Percent change 1974 to 1981
Owner-occupied units			
Adequate neighborhood and structure	37,748	40,361	23.2
Inadequate neighborhood and/or structure	13,036	13,981	7.2
Total structures	45,784	54,342	18.7
Renter-occupied units			
Adequate neighborhood and structure	16,089	18,376	14.2
Inadequate neighborhood and/or structure	8,957	10,457	16.7
Total structures	25,046	28,833	15.1
Total occupied units			
Adequate neighborhood and structure	48,837	58,737	20.2
Inadequate neighborhood and/or structure	21,993	24,438	11.1
Total structures	70,830	83,175	17.4

Source: Joint Center for Housing Studies of the Massachusetts Institute of Technology and Harvard University, "Special Tabulations of *Annual Housing Survey* Data for 1974 and 1981" (Cambridge, Mass., 1984).

holds reporting multiple deficiencies increased substantially, with especially sharp increases in those reporting three, four, or more deficiencies.

The data in Table 4.6 suggest that the increases in neighborhood deficiencies are primarily associated with renter households. Table 4.6 defines an adequate neighborhood as one with zero or one of the six neighborhood deficiencies and an inadequate neighborhood as one with two or more. Using this measure, the number of units in inadequate neighborhoods increased from 13.7 million in 1974 to 16.6 million in 1981, with nearly two-thirds of the increase the result of increases in renter-occupied units in inadequate neighborhoods. Indeed, for renters, the incidence of neighborhood inadequacy increased from 20.2 percent in 1974 to 23.9 percent in 1981.

Combining the structural inadequacy and neighborhood inadequacy measures provides further evidence of the slow pace of housing improvement between 1974 and 1981, especially for renter households. As Table 4.7 indicates, the number of occupied dwelling units that were structurally inadequate and/or in inadequate neighborhoods increased by 11.1 percent from 22 million in 1974 to 24.4 million in 1981. The two measures are correlated, but they are not substitutes for each other. Of the 22 million in 1974, 3.3 million were deficient in structure and/or in neighborhood. By 1981, the number had grown to 3.7 million.

The number of rental units that are either structurally inadequate or located in inadequate neighborhoods has increased faster than the number of all rental units. As Table 4.7 shows, the number of units with either deficiency has increased even faster, jumping from 1.6 million in 1974 to 2.2 million in 1981, a 33.4 percent increase.

Regional Trends in Structural and Neighborhood Quality

The true picture regarding housing in our cities is actually bleaker than the aggregate data suggest because the small overall reduction in the number of structurally inadequate units is the result entirely of a substantial decline in the inadequate housing of *nonmetropolitan* (meaning rural and small town) areas (see Table 4.8). As the number of dwelling units in these areas increased, the number of structurally inadequate units fell from 5.4 million to 4.5 million. The greatest improvement was in the owner-occupied sector, in which the number of inadequate units fell by 19.3 percent from 1974 to 1981. In contrast, the number of structurally inadequate units in metropolitan areas increased by more than 10 percent, with equal percentage increases recorded for both owner and renter units. Thus problems of housing inadequacy increasingly were concentrated in the most urbanized parts of the nation.

Although nonmetropolitan areas recorded substantial reductions in the number of inadequate units, this progress was offset, in part, by growing neighborhood problems. The number of dwellings in *inadequate neighborhoods* increased in both metro and nonmetro areas, but the increase was markedly slower for owner-occupied units in nonmetro areas. The number of nonmetro renters reporting two or more neighborhood deficiencies rose fastest of all, suggesting

Table 4.8.
Number of Structurally Inadequate Dwelling Units or Dwelling Units in Inadequate Neighborhoods by Tenure and Metropolitan Status (in thousands)

Tenure and Location	Inadequate structure 1974	1981	Percent change	Inadequate neighborhood 1974	1981	Percent change
Metropolitan						
Own	2,810	3,097	10.2	5,511	6,435	16.7
Rent	3,471	3,838	10.6	4,150	5,551	33.8
Total	6,281	6,935	10.4	9,661	11,986	24.1
Nonmetropolitan						
Own	3,295	2,658	−19.3	3,091	3,285	6.3
Rent	2,052	1,877	−8.5	904	1,353	49.7
Total	5,347	4,535	−15.2	3,995	4,638	16.1

Source: Joint Center for Housing Studies of the Massachusetts Institute of Technology and Harvard University, "Special Tabulations of *Annual Housing Survey* Data for 1974 and 1981" (Cambridge, Mass., 1984).

that the growth of rental housing in the more densely populated nonmetro areas was bringing with it neighborhood problems more traditionally associated with the greater urbanization of metro areas.

There are further differences in housing in metro and nonmetro areas, broken down by region. Historically much of the nation's worst housing has been located in nonmetro areas, particularly the low-income, marginal farm areas of the North Central and southern states. The recent surge of development in those regions has added new standard units but has also swept away much inadequate housing. As Table 4.9 indicates, the combination of a growing inventory and absolute decline in structurally inadequate units has had a pronounced effect on the incidence of structural inadequacy in nonmetro areas. By 1981, only 13.6 percent of all owner-occupied units in nonmetro areas were structurally inadequate, down sharply from 20.5 percent in 1974. Similarly, reductions in the incidence of structural inadequacy were recorded for the nonmetro renter stock. This decline in incidence of inadequacy was widespread. Only the owner-occupied stock in the nonmetro Northeast failed to exhibit a decline.

Table 4.9.

Structurally Inadequate Dwelling Units as a Percentage of Total
Occupied Units by Tenure, Region, and Metropolitan Status

Region and location	Owner		Renter	
	1974	1981	1974	1981
Metropolitan				
Northeast	7.1	8.0	20.4	19.1
North Central	7.7	7.7	14.8	16.2
South	14.7	13.2	24.1	21.1
West	7.9	5.8	12.3	13.1
Total	9.5	8.9	18.3	17.5
Nonmetropolitan				
Northeast	11.3	11.7	22.3	16.1
North Central	15.2	10.3	23.1	17.2
South	29.0	17.2	48.7	38.7
West	13.5	10.2	21.0	20.7
Total	20.5	13.6	33.8	27.0

Source: Joint Center for Housing Studies of the Massachusetts Institute of Technology and Harvard University, "Special Tabulations of *Annual Housing Survey* Data for 1974 and 1981" (Cambridge, Mass., 1984).

Although the absolute number of inadequate owner and renter units in metro areas increased from 1974 to 1981, the incidence of inadequacy fell slightly. Thus for metro areas in 1981, 17.5 percent of all rental units and 8.9 percent of all owner units were inadequate, down slightly from 1974. The incidence of structural inadequacy of renter units showed most improvement in the South but nonetheless remained high. The renter stock of northwestern metro areas also improved somewhat. The metro areas in North Central and western states, however, ended the period with increased shares of their renter stock in structurally inadequate condition.

Data on the share of units located in inadequate neighborhoods reveal striking differences by tenure, metro status, and region. Metro area renters have the greatest likelihood of living in inadequate neighborhoods. But neighborhood inadequacy is increasing for nonmetro renters as well (see Table 4.10). In contrast, the incidence of neighborhood inadequacy has declined sharply for nonmetro area owners. At the beginning of the period, nonmetro areas had a higher share of their owner-occupied units located in inadequate neighbor-

Table 4.10.

Dwelling Units in Inadequate Neighborhoods as a Percentage of Total Occupied Units by Tenure, Region, and Metropolitan Status

Region and location	Owner		Renter	
	1974	1981	1974	1981
Metropolitan				
Northeast	16.5	19.9	23.9	30.4
North Central	18.6	17.5	23.5	27.4
South	21.0	21.3	20.6	23.5
West	17.7	14.6	19.0	20.2
Total	18.7	18.5	21.9	25.4
Nonmetropolitan				
Northeast	17.6	10.6	19.3	19.6
North Central	15.0	15.4	11.7	15.6
South	22.2	19.3	14.4	21.5
West	21.4	18.4	18.7	24.6
Total	19.2	16.8	14.9	19.5

Source: Joint Center for Housing Studies of the Massachusetts Institute of Technology and Harvard University, "Special Tabulations of *Annual Housing Survey* Data for 1974 and 1981" (Cambridge, Mass., 1984).

hoods than did metro areas. By 1981 the incidence of neighborhood inadequacy was lower in nonmetro areas. Indeed, with the exception of the western region, nonmetro owners reported the fewest complaints with their neighborhoods.

Who Lives in Inadequate Housing?

Despite more than three decades of federal, state, and local government efforts, a large share of households remain poorly housed. As Table 4.11 indicates, inadequate housing is far more common among renters than owners, in part because homeowners have more control over the maintenance and upkeep of their units. Even for middle- and upper-income households (those with income greater than $15,000), the incidence of living in inadequate housing among renters is anywhere from 50 to 100 percent higher than for owners.

The group most likely to live in inadequate housing is renters who are poor. In 1981, 28 percent of all renters with incomes of $5,000 or

Table 4.11.

Percent of Households Living in Inadequate Structure or Inadequate Neighborhood by Tenure and Income, 1981

Income class (in thousands)	Percent living in inadequate structure		Percent living in inadequate neighborhood	
	Own	Rent	Own	Rent
$ 0 to 5	21.3	28.0	19.5	28.2
5 to 10	15.4	22.5	22.0	22.8
10 to 15	12.9	18.0	18.9	23.9
15 to 20	10.9	15.1	21.7	23.6
20 to 25	10.4	14.8	17.3	25.5
25 to 30	7.9	15.8	16.1	20.7
30 to 40	6.3	14.7	15.5	20.1
40 or more	6.1	9.9	13.9	15.2
Total	10.5	19.7	17.8	23.9

Source: Joint Center for Housing Studies of the Massachusetts Institute of Technology and Harvard University, "Special Tabulations of *Annual Housing Survey* Data for 1981" (Cambridge, Mass., 1984).

less lived in structurally inadequate units. Another 28.2 percent lived in inadequate neighborhoods. For owners with incomes less than $5,000, nearly one in five live in structurally inadequate housing. For both owners and renters, the incidence of structural inadequacy decreases slightly as income increases.

Although owners overall live in better housing than renters, they do not have any advantage over renters with respect to neighborhood condition. Neither owners nor renters have direct control over the level of neighborhood amenities. Although most owners will fix a leaky roof or repair a broken fixture in their own housing, it appears that fewer are willing or able to solve neighborhood problems.

In addition to having low income and being renters, occupants of poor-quality housing are more likely to be black and/or families with children (see Table 4.12). The differences by race are particularly striking. In 1981, 32.2 percent of all black renter households lived in structurally inadequate housing, compared to 17 percent for white households. Similar differences are found between blacks and whites for the incidence of neighborhood inadequacy. Even among owners, blacks are more than twice as likely as whites to live in inadequate housing and in inadequate neighborhoods.

Table 4.12.

Percentage of Households Living in Inadequate Structure or Inadequate Neighborhood by Family Type and Race, 1981

Family and race	Living in inadequate structure		Living in inadequate neighborhood	
	Own	Rent	Own	Rent
Head 65 or younger,				
no children				
Married couple	8.9	17.6	16.9	21.6
Other household	12.7	17.8	18.9	24.2
Head 65 or older,				
no children				
Married couple	8.0	16.1	13.3	19.4
Other household	16.0	18.3	17.5	16.0
Household with children				
Married couple	9.5	23.0	18.7	24.7
Other household	15.8	24.9	25.4	32.7
Race of head				
White	9.6	17.0	16.8	20.9
Black	23.4	32.2	30.2	37.2
Total	10.5	19.7	17.8	23.9

Source: Joint Center for Housing Studies of the Massachusetts Institute of Technology and Harvard University, "Special Tabulations of *Annual Housing Survey* Data for 1974 and 1981" (Cambridge, Mass., 1984).

The high incidence of inadequate housing among renters is in part the result of a decline in their real incomes. Measured in 1981 dollars, the share of renter households with incomes less than $5,000 increased from 15.3 percent in 1974 to 20.2 percent in 1981. The number of renter households with real incomes less than $5,000 increased from 1.3 million in 1974 to 1.6 million in 1981. In absolute terms, low-income owners fared little better, with the absolute number of households living in structurally inadequate housing increasing from 827,000 in 1974 to 920,000 in 1981. Thus between 1974 and 1981, the problems of structural inadequacy were increasingly associated with very low-income households.

The continued growth in absolute numbers of poor households

Table 4.13.

Number of Subsidized Rental Housing Units by Structural and Neighborhood Adequacy, 1974 and 1981 (in thousands)

	1974	1981	Percent change 1974 to 1981
Total number of subsidized units	2,178	3,067	40.8
Adequate structure	1,897	2,610	37.6
Inadequate structure	281	457	62.6
Adequate neighborhood	1,623	2,147	32.3
Inadequate neighborhood	555	920	65.8

Source: Joint Center for Housing Studies of the Massachusetts Institute of Technology and Harvard University, "Special Tabulations of *Annual Housing Survey* Data for 1974 and 1981" (Cambridge, Mass., 1984).

living in inadequate units is somewhat surprising in light of the fairly substantial increase in the number of subsidized units available and the increased efforts to target these units to low-income renters. In 1981, 3.1 million households reported in the *AHS* that they lived in either public housing or other subsidized rental housing, up from 2.2 million in 1974. In the six-year period, the stock of subsidized units increased by more than 40 percent.

At least part of the failure of the subsidized units to have more effect on the number of poorly housed low-income renters is because much of the subsidized inventory is inadequate (see Table 4.13). In 1981, 457,000 subsidized renter units (or 14.8 percent) were in inadequate structures, up by more than 62.6 percent from 1974. Of all subsidized rental units, 30 percent were located in inadequate neighborhoods.

Trends in Housing Affordability

For all households, renters and owners alike, adequate housing has become more affordable in the postwar period. Recent data suggest, however, that in the 1970s the real cost of housing for owners and renters began to rise, reversing the long-term trends. Since 1979, the real costs of homeownership have increased dramatically. Real rents,

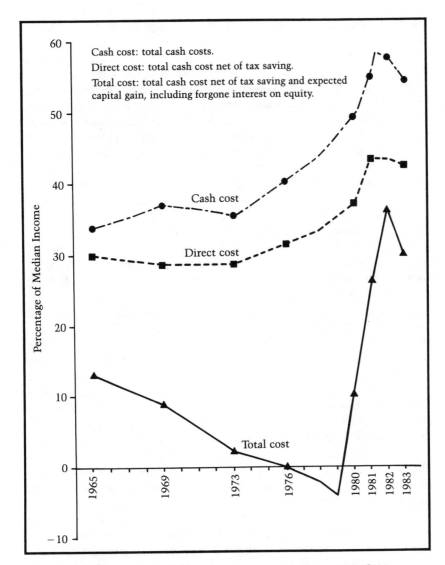

Figure 4.2. *Homeownership Costs as Percentage of Median Family Income, 1965–1983*

Source: H. James Brown, Karl Case, and Kermit Baker, *Homeownership and Housing Affordability in the United States, 1963–1983* (Cambridge, Mass.: Joint Center for Housing Studies of the Massachusetts Institute of Technology and Harvard University, 1983).

adjusted for changes in housing quality, have increased steadily since at least 1975.

The increase in homeownership costs since 1970 was documented by James Brown, Karl Case, and Kermit Baker of the Joint Center for Housing Studies of the Massachusetts Institute of Technology and Harvard University in a study examining changes in homeownership costs relative to income since 1965. As Figure 4.2 indicates, the Joint Center study traced the cash cost, the direct cost, and the total cost of owning a home. The latter two measures adjust out-of-pocket costs for the effects of tax savings and of expected capital gains, including foregone interest on equity. Adjusted for expected capital gains, the total cost of owning a home declined steadily for much of the period and even may have turned negative from 1977 to 1979. Since 1979, however, the total homeownership costs rose sharply. By 1982, higher home prices, interest rates, and utility costs—combined with a reduction in the expected gains from appreciation—resulted in a rise in the total cost of owning a home to nearly 40 percent of the median family income.

The recent increase in real homeownership costs has been matched by increases in real rents (see Table 4.14). From 1974 to 1981, the number of renter households paying more than 35 percent of their income for rent increased from 5.8 million to 9.1 million, or from 23.1 percent to 32 percent. As would be expected, the nation's poorest households faced particularly severe cost burdens. In 1981, 6.4 million renter households with incomes less than $5,000 paid more than 35 percent of their income for rent. Further, the incidence of overpayment increased for a wide range of family types, with particularly sharp increases occurring among married couples with children. The failure of the income of large numbers of renter households to keep pace with inflation exacerbated an already severe housing affordability problem.

Increases in the rent-to-income ratio can, of course, be a misleading indicator of changes in the affordability of rental housing. A ratio can change as a result of changes in the denominator (in this instance income) as well as changes in the numerator (in this instance rent). Over the postwar period, the growth of the real income of renters did, in fact, lag behind that of owners. Moreover, during this period, many upper-income renters became owners, reducing the average income of those who remain as renters. Finally, lower-income people have always had difficulty paying for rent as evidenced by the high rent-to-income ratios for that group in all time periods. Thus, those arguing that the rising rent-to-income ratio is not to be interpreted as a sign of worsening housing condition maintain that the

Table 4.14.
Percentage of Renter Households Paying 35 Percent or More of Income for Rent

	1974	1981
Households with no children, head aged 65 or less		
Married couples	8.1	16.7
Other households	28.2	34.9
Households with no children, head aged 65 or older		
Married couples	24.6	32.2
Other households	42.0	36.7
Households with children		
Married couples	9.5	21.1
Other households	41.6	49.6
Total	23.1	32.0

Source: Joint Center for Housing Studies of the Massachusetts Institute of Technology and Harvard University, "Special Tabulations of *Annual Housing Survey* Data for 1974 and 1981" (Cambridge, Mass., 1984).

movement of upper-income renters into homeownership explains the sharp increases in apparent rent burden that have occurred in recent years.

Although these explanations are plausible, the data for the period 1974 to 1981 fail to support the central features of the argument. The rate of homeownership did increase from 1974 to 1981 for households with real incomes in excess of $15,000 (in constant 1981 dollars). At the same time, for households with real income of less than $15,000, the rate of homeownership fell. Yet this shift in the relationship between the rate of homeownership and real income is not sufficient to explain the decline in real incomes of renter households. By way of illustration, Table 4.15 presents information on the distribution of renter households by income in 1974 and 1981. As in the previous discussion, incomes are measured in constant 1981 dollars. In addition to the actual data for 1974 and 1981, the table also presents a predicted distribution based on the assumption that the ownership rate for each real income category remained at 1974 levels.

As these calculations reveal, even without changes in the income/tenure relationship, the share of renters in the lower income catego-

Table 4.15.

*Percent Distribution of Renter Households by Real 1981 Incomes:
1974 and 1981 Actual, and 1981 Predicted*

Households (in thousands)	1974	1981 predicted	1981 actual
Less than 5	15.3	17.8	19.7
5 to 10	20.7	22.2	23.1
10 to 15	17.1	19.2	21.2
15 to 20	14.3	13.3	13.4
20 to 25	10.6	9.4	8.8
25 to 30	9.0	6.8	5.5
30 to 40	7.2	6.3	5.6
40 or more	5.8	5.0	2.7
Total	100.0	100.0	100.0

Source: Joint Center for Housing Studies of the Massachusetts Institute of Technology and Harvard University, "Special Tabulations of *Annual Housing Survey*
Data for 1974 and 1981" (Cambridge, Mass., 1984).
Predicted distribution for 1981 assumes that rates of owner occupancy for each
real income class equal 1974 actual owner occupancy rates.

ries would have increased over the period. That declining rates of
homeownership among lower-income households added to the share
of low-income renters explains but a portion of the trend. Another
way to illustrate the same point is to note that over the period,
the median income of renter households declined from $14,100 to
$11,400 in constant 1981 dollars. Of this decline only $1,200, or approximately 44 percent, is the result of changing patterns of homeownership for households in a given real income category.

Just as changing patterns of homeownership are an insufficient explanation for the declines in the real incomes of renters, so is the fact
of declining real incomes for renter households an insufficient explanation for the increases in households with high rent-to-income
ratios. As noted earlier, the number of renter households paying
more than 35 percent of their income for housing increased from
5.8 million in 1974 to 9.1 million in 1981. The growth of the total
number of renter-occupied households accounts for 874,000 of the
increase, and the decline in the real incomes of renters accounts for
an increase of another 1.5 million. Thus more than 960,000 renters
were added to the list of households paying more than 35 percent of
their income for housing as a result of factors other than the growth
of total renter households or the declining real incomes of renters.

Table 4.16.

Selected Measure of Change in Prices, Rents, and Incomes

	Percent change		
Item	1970 to 1975	1975 to 1980	1970 to 1980
CPI All items, old series	39	54	113
CPI residential rents	25	39	73
CPI All items, new series	36	47	99
Lowry residential rents	34	51	103
Median income of owners	40	46	104
Median income of renters	25	33	67
Median gross rents	44	55	123

Source: Annual Housing Survey and periodic reports of the Bureau of Labor Statistics on consumer prices. For a discussion of the effect of alternative measures of homeownership affordability on the Consumer Price Index, see U.S. Department of Labor, Bureau of Labor Statistics, *CPI Issues, No. 593* (Washington, D.C.: U.S. Government Printing Office, 1980). For definition of the Lowry rent index see Ira S. Lowry, *Inflation Indexes for Rental Housing* (Santa Monica, Calif.: Rand Corporation, 1981).

Some note that rising rent-to-income ratios could result from pure increases associated with the general improvement in the condition of the housing stock. The evidence of an absolute increase in units with structural and neighborhood deficiencies makes this explanation hardly plausible. Table 4.16 presents information for the period 1970 to 1980 and breaks the data into two time periods. As measured by the official Consumer Price Index (CPI), all consumer prices increased by 39 percent in the first half of the decade and at a somewhat sharper rate in the second half. In both periods, the residential rents as measured by the CPI lagged behind. These declines in real residential rents as measured by the CPI continued a pattern that had been in effect since the 1950s and appear to support the "quality" explanation for higher rent-to-income ratios.

Nevertheless, this notion may be flawed. The CPI rent component is derived from rents on a set of dwellings, which are resurveyed from year to year, with adjustments being made only for major changes in the quality of the dwelling units. As a result, minor changes attributable to depreciation are not picked up, nor are the cost increases of utilities paid directly by the tenant. Recognizing these difficulties, Ira Lowry prepared a constant-quality rent index that incorporates adjustments for both factors. As noted in Table 4.16, the Lowry rent index increases more rapidly than the CPI residential rent index, suggesting that the deficiencies in the CPI index substantially overstated the extent to which real (meaning quality-adjusted) rents declined during the period.

For the entire period 1970 to 1980, the adjusted all items CPI increased by only 99 percent. Yet the Lowry residential rent index increased by 103 percent, suggesting that real rents actually *increased.* Moreover, the data also suggest that constant quality rents may have increased more slowly than all other prices at the beginning of the decade, but this was more than offset by relatively faster increases in constant quality real rents at the end of the period. The supposed decline in real rents is an important element in many attempts to explain what happened to housing consumption in the 1970s. If real rents did not decline yet the rent-to-income ratio rose, we must conclude that at the end of the recent decade, the poor were worse off than they were at the beginning.

Summary and Conclusion

Low-income households and particularly low-income renter households have historically been consigned to live in inadequate housing in marginal neighborhoods. The housing conditions of all Americans—rich and poor alike—have improved in the postwar period, but since 1974 this progress has stalled. This chapter presents evidence that since 1974, the rapid inflation in housing costs, combined with the inability of renter income to keep pace with inflation and the seeming decline of many basic urban services, has exacerbated the problems of affordability and inadequate housing for many low-income renters. By 1981, 1.6 million renters with incomes less than $5,000 lived in structurally inadequate housing and 6.4 million paid more than 35 percent of their income for rent. Both figures were up sharply from those for 1974 for households with equal real incomes.

Just as the income distribution of the housing problems changed, so has their spatial distribution. The recent rapid growth of nonmetropolitan areas has swept away much of the most severely inadequate housing but at the same time added substantially to the stock of new adequate housing. Unfortunately, the improvement in the structural adequacy of nonmetropolitan housing was largely offset by increases in the number of structurally inadequate metropolitan area housing units. The plight of the low-income residents of metropolitan areas still must be viewed as largely a problem of inadequate income. Inadequate income alone cannot explain the recent increases in rent burden or the growing concentration of inadequate housing in deteriorated city neighborhoods. A universal housing allowance program as some propose that would provide cash assistance to the more than 6.4 million low-income households now paying excessive amounts for housing undoubtedly would help, but such a program by itself might prove insufficient because of the surprising persistence of housing quality as a problem.

Adequately to address the housing problems of low-income households will require a careful balancing of demand- and supply-oriented programs. This is hardly a new idea. Yet such a program will not be developed unless policy analysts are more fully aware of the extent of current housing problems and understand better the dynamics of the housing market in the recent period that produced them. In attempting to put a good face on the presumed improvements in the housing situation, the recent studies and reports that celebrate the long-term improvements in housing not only fail to state the true magnitude of current housing problems but also help to foster numerous misconceptions concerning housing market dynamics. The nation's housing problems deserve more careful attention.

References

Abt Associates. 1981. *Participation and Benefits in the Urban Section 8 Program: New Construction and Existing Housing.* Cambridge, Mass.: Abt Associates.

Brown, H. James, Karl Case, and Kermit Baker. 1983. *Homeownership and Housing Affordability in the United States, 1963–1983.* Cambridge, Mass.: Joint Center for Housing Studies of the Massachusetts Institute of Technology and Harvard University.

Joint Center for Urban Studies of the Massachusetts Institute of Technology and Harvard University. 1984. "Special Tabulations of Annual Housing Survey Data for 1974 and 1981." Cambridge, Mass.: Joint Center for Housing Studies of the Massachusetts Institute of Technology and Harvard University.

Lowry, Ira S. 1981. *Inflation Indexes for Rental Housing.* Santa Monica, Calif.: Rand Corporation.

President's Commission on Housing. 1982. *Report of the President's Commission on Housing.* Washington, D.C.: U.S. Government Printing Office.

U.S. Department of Commerce, Bureau of the Census. 1974. *Annual Housing Survey.* Washington, D.C.: U.S. Government Printing Office.

———. 1981. *Annual Housing Survey.* Washington, D.C.: U.S. Government Printing Office.

U.S. Department of Labor, Bureau of Labor Statistics. 1980. *CPI Issues, No. 593.* Washington, D.C.: U.S. Government Printing Office.

5 Where Should the Poor Live?

Ira S. Lowry

Where should the poor live? This question seems urgent to those concerned with low-income housing for several reasons.

One reason is that the poor have chosen to live primarily in the central cities of major metropolitan areas, where they contribute little to the municipal fisc but draw heavily on the city's resources. Those who used to pay central-city taxes all too often have voted with their feet, moving to suburban jurisdictions that are not required to share the fiscal burden of support programs for the poor. The managers of central-city governments can readily see the virtue of spreading the poor around so that suburban jurisdictions bear more of the responsibility of caring for their needs.

A second reason is that those who are not poor are rarely enthusiastic about having poor people as neighbors. Their objections partly reflect concern about the financial ability of poor neighbors to maintain their homes and children up to the neighborhood standard; but the objection is often less to poverty per se than to differences in social values and lifestyles that are perceived as threats to neighborhood safety, morals, and congenial social life. This is especially true when the poor are also different from their prospective neighbors in race or ethnicity. In our time, at least, the issue of residential location for the poor is bound tightly to the issue of racial segregation.

A third reason is that the homes of the poor often stand in the way of progress. As cities grow and their economic bases and transportation technologies change, the configuration of land uses becomes increasingly irrational unless modified by redevelopment. The targets of opportunity are usually urban slums, strategically located by accidents of urban history and cheaper to acquire and redevelop than better-off neighborhoods. Less dramatically, low-income neighborhoods may be "gentrified" by venturesome private purchase and rehabilitation that displaces poorer residents in favor of more prosperous ones.

Intervention by a public agency to improve the housing conditions of the poor usually sharpens these issues by explicitly raising the question of residential location. Nearly every siting proposal for low-income housing encounters objections from prospective neighbors and often from the local government. Nearly every program of slum clearance, urban development, or even neighborhood improvement displaces residents who must be helped to relocate. What otherwise might be a gradual process of residential rearrangement mediated by the private market becomes a controversial public decision.

Where should the poor live? A meaningful answer must specify the public purposes to be served by the proposed residential rearrangement; a helpful answer must specify a process that reliably leads to the desired outcome. In this chapter I first address public purposes, concluding that our highest priority should be to create neighborhood environments that support the social needs and aspirations of their residents. Then I review a half century of federal programs aimed at improving housing and neighborhood conditions, concluding that we do not know how to create safe, healthy neighborhoods for poor people. Consequently, our best hope is to facilitate private choice, enabling people to congregate residentially in neighborhoods that offer the physical facilities and social milieus to which they aspire.

The Aims of Public Policy

Public intervention to improve the housing conditions of the poor goes back at least a century in cities such as New York and Chicago but was not firmly adopted as national policy until the Housing Act of 1949 (63 Stat. 413), which called for "the realization as soon as feasible of the goal of a decent home and suitable living environment for every American family." On many occasions since 1949, the Congress has reaffirmed its commitment not only to "decent housing" but to a "suitable living environment."[1]

The attributes of a decent home have been specified for practical purposes by the American Public Health Association. They reflect fairly primitive notions of human requirements for health, comfort, and social development: privacy for the nuclear family (a separate dwelling for each family and separate sleeping rooms for adults and children); protection from the elements (a weatherproof structure that can be heated in cold weather and illuminated at night); plumbing equipment that facilitates personal cleanliness and inhibits the transmission of disease; equipment for the sanitary storage of food and the preparation of hot meals; and a minimum of well-ventilated airspace for each household member.[2]

Recent census data indicate that about 95 percent of all occupied dwellings now meet these requirements, and more would do so if the occupants reasonably exerted themselves as housekeepers and handymen. That is not to say that one cannot find dilapidated, un-heated, or rat-infested buildings, only that it is hard to find them without a corollary of contributory negligence by the building's oc-cupants. The more salient issue today is the "suitable living en-vironment," by which Congress obviously means the neighborhood.

From the perspective of public policy, what neighborhood condi-tions are important, and why? Three clusters of neighborhood at-tributes have been matters of concern in urban reform over the years:

- Factors affecting the health and safety of a neighborhood's resi-dents. These include protection from those age-old urban hazards, fire, burglary, theft, and criminal assault, but also pro-visions for public sanitation, controlling street traffic, safe out-door playspace, and access to emergency services.
- Factors affecting the social performance of a neighborhood's residents, particularly the young. These include the social atti-tudes and beliefs that are passed from one generation to the next, or from prior residents to new arrivals; the quality of formal institutions of socialization and training such as schools and churches; and the array of opportunities for ap-prenticeship in the world of gainful employment.
- Factors affecting the larger community. These include the en-vironmental impact of each neighborhood on adjacent neigh-borhoods; the fiscal contributions and demands for public ser-vice that each neighborhood makes on local governments; and, often, the obstacles to rationalization of the urban economy that arise from the existing configuration of land uses.

In these respects, not all neighborhoods are equal, and none are perfect. But there is a broad consensus among both the public and the policy-making elite as to what constitutes better and worse neighborhood environments. The paradigm of a good environment is a suburban neighborhood whose tree-lined streets carry local traffic only and whose roomy houses are set well apart. It is a neighborhood with good schools, a library, and supervised recreation for children; with efficient and responsive public services; and with a sense of community such that every resident has a respected social role and there is a high degree of trust in casual encounters between individu-als. In contrast, the paradigm of a bad environment is a central-city slum of decrepit tenements, trashy streets, and scrawled walls; where children and old people dodge traffic in the streets, drug pushers on the corners, muggers in the alleys, and winos sleeping on the sidewalks; where the schools are bad jokes, knifings are common on the playgrounds, unemployed men and women lounge on doorsteps, and pregnant fourteen-year-olds lean out windows.

Despite the consensus on desirable and undesirable neighborhood characteristics residents of most neighborhoods are satisfied with the conditions they perceive around them, and many prefer their present environments to alternatives both better or worse. In 1978, a national survey found that three-fourths of those who lived in large central cities were "delighted," "pleased," or "mostly satisfied" with their neighborhoods; blacks, whites, and Latins expressed roughly the same levels of satisfaction, and satisfaction increased only slightly with income.[3] This statistical consensus reflects the fact that although most people who live in slums are poor, most of the poor do not live in slums. The poor are spread over a wide range of neighborhood environments, although they naturally are concentrated where housing is cheap.

Where should the poor live? To ask this question is to invite a bad answer because it emphasizes the wrong common denominator for residential grouping: poverty, rather than personal and family circumstances, lifestyles, and aspirations. By the Orshansky standard of poverty, about a sixth of all U.S. households are poor; by the rule of thumb among housing professionals, about a fifth are poor.[4] Within either group, there are not only degrees of financial poverty but enormous differences in personal and family circumstances, lifestyles, and aspirations.

Whether poor or not, the appropriate place for students to live is near their universities. The appropriate place for elderly widows is a sheltered community that provides services to compensate for their infirmities. The appropriate place for parents with children, especially single parents, is one that specializes in education and supervised recreation. The appropriate place for an intact family whose breadwinner has been disabled or is temporarily unemployed is the place they chose before their financial reversal. The appropriate place for an extended family of new immigrants is close to a concentration of low-skilled jobs and fellow-countrymen.

The real question is whether the poor can sort themselves out, with or without the aid of government, into neighborhoods whose physical facilities and social milieus support their needs and aspirations. The evidence of the 1978 survey, cited earlier, is that most urban residents have managed to do this.

Despite general satisfaction with their neighborhoods, however, urban residents are deeply concerned about personal safety, the use of drugs, and the quality of schools. According to the survey, four-fifths of the residents of large cities considered crime a serious problem in their communities, two-thirds mentioned drug addiction, and over half were dissatisfied with the schools.[5]

What We Have Tried

An implicit assumption of the question, Where should the poor live? is that government has the power to affect the outcome. Over the years since housing assistance for the poor found a place on the national agenda, we have tried a number of ways of helping the poor arrive at "a decent home and a suitable living environment." Before addressing the future it is worthwhile to review those attempts.

Slum Clearance and Public Housing. The first major venture in rehousing the poor was the federal public housing program. The United States Housing Act of 1937 authorized federal contributions to local authorities that were empowered to acquire sites, build dwellings, and manage them as low-rent housing for poor people. Public housing construction was tied to slum clearance; for each new unit built, an "unsafe or unsanitary dwelling unit" was to be demolished and the displaced inhabitants were to be relocated in low-rent housing either on the site or elsewhere within the jurisdiction of the local housing authority. On paper, it was a neat arrangement.

A perceived virtue of the public housing program was that multi-unit projects under public management could provide not only better dwellings for the poor but a supportive neighborhood environment. Until well into the 1960s, this concept worked rather well because the local public housing authority was able to choose its tenants.

During the early years of public housing, tenant selection was a prerogative of local housing authorities, constrained only by federal dwelling-unit occupancy standards and federal approval of local income limits for participation. Rent schedules were also set by local authorities, constrained by the need to cover operating costs out of rental revenues.[6]

Most local authorities set rents that varied with the size of the dwelling but not with its occupant's income. In effect, all tenants got a discount on market rent that was roughly equal to the ratio of capital costs to total costs. Public housing was a substantial bargain to all eligible applicants, and most authorities had long waiting lists.

The local authorities devised a variety of formal and informal procedures for excluding "problem families" and those unable to afford project rents, choosing tenants who were predominantly the "working poor" and the elderly. Though they might chafe under paternalistic project management, the tenants by and large accepted the underlying value system, paid their rents, and maintained their homes. Those who did not were evicted.

So populated and so managed, a public housing project might show signs of its occupants' poverty, but it was a place where decent people could live decently. For many of the working poor (including one recent president of the United States), it was a way station to a better life.

This description still applies to many projects in small towns. But in the larger cities, public housing projects today usually are distinguishable from neighboring slums mainly by the vintage of their buildings. The clear reasons for the decline of public housing are the shift to a policy of income-based rent determination and a series of court decisions and federal regulations that altered the rules for tenant selection and eviction.

The Brooke Amendment of 1969 limited public housing rents to no more than 25 percent of the tenant's income. Under this provision, public housing became virtually free to the destitute, while those with incomes near the eligibility ceiling paid market rents. Naturally, project populations became increasingly composed of the very poor: "During the period from 1960 to 1972, the median income of all U.S. families rose by 90 percent, while the median income of families moving into public housing rose only 21 percent. Of the families moving into public housing in 1960, 35 percent were receiving welfare assistance and/or [unemployment or social security] benefits, compared to 71 percent in 1972."[7]

Along with increasing poverty and dependency on welfare have come increasing social problems in big-city projects. Vandalism, theft, drug abuse, juvenile delinquency, and parental irresponsibility make life in projects dangerous and miserable for those with more constructive values and overwhelm project management with expenses for security and repairs. Only projects designed for and limited to the elderly have escaped degradation by their own occupants.

Not all these problems originate with project residents, and probably no more than 5 percent of project tenants are serious threats to their neighbors. But the end of "arbitrary" selection rules and the elaboration of due process in evictions remove project managers' surest methods of social control.[8] In some cities (St. Louis, Jersey City, Chicago, and Washington, D.C.), the "good" tenants have left in such numbers that whole projects have been abandoned.

These events, no doubt magnified by rumor and racial prejudice, have made middle-class neighborhoods fiercely unwilling to play host to public housing projects—even to the small "scattered site" projects undertaken in the late 1960s as an alternative to the high-rise "barracks for the poor" so scorned by liberal critics of the program.

Though public housing has and could again improve the lives of many poor people whose values are consistent with program purposes, its future in large cities, except for projects limited to the elderly, is bleak. HUD increasingly has turned to various arrangements for subsidizing low-income tenants in privately owned rental housing, at least partly in the hope that private managers can exercise controls no longer available to public authorities.

Slum Clearance and Urban Redevelopment. The second major effort by the federal government to help cities cope with slums and urban blight was the urban redevelopment program, authorized by Title I of the Housing Act of 1949. Title I offered local authorities financial aid to acquire blighted urban land, clear it, and resell it to private developers.

The law loosely linked urban redevelopment to both housing improvement and city planning. It stipulated that project sites be "predominantly residential" either before acquisition or after redevelopment, that displaced residents be relocated in housing within their means, and that local authority prepare a project redevelopment plan that conformed to the city's general plan.

Whatever Congress had in mind, city mayors knew what they wanted from urban redevelopment: to replace eyesores in the environs of the central business district—dilapidated housing, crumbling warehouses and lofts, shabby small businesses—with hotels, high-rise apartments, office buildings, shopping malls, and convention centers. They wanted to strengthen the downtown in its losing struggle with the suburbs for jobs and retail trade, to add to the city's tax base, and perchance to dislodge some of their poorer constituents who consumed a distressing share of public services.

As the program developed along these lines, it generated a counter-lobby of those who favored clearing strictly residential slums and using the sites for low-rent public or nonprofit housing for the poor. Others discovered functioning social systems in run-down neighborhoods slated for the bulldozer and objected to their destruction, stressing the emotional as well as the financial hardships of forced relocation. There was also general discomfort with the subsidy through land "write-downs" to already prosperous investors in large enterprises.[9]

Under pressure from both sides, Congress waffled. In a series of amendments between 1949 and 1968, it both loosened the constraints on nonresidential reuse of cleared land and encouraged re-development in the form of low-rent housing. It provided relocation grants for those who were displaced and encouraged housing re-habilitation and code enforcement as alternatives to demolition. Successive administrators in HUD were able to choose among con-flicting signals those that were congenial to their own or their presi-dent's appraisal of urban priorities.

The urban redevelopment program was extraordinarily successful in meeting the objectives of its local sponsors. By the end of 1974, nearly eighty thousand acres of urban land had been acquired and nearly forty thousand had been redeveloped. In completed projects, about a fourth of the land was shifted from private to public uses as parks, playgrounds, public housing, schools, or public buildings. Yet the assessed valuation of all taxable land and structures within project areas roughly tripled.

No one seems to know exactly how much housing was demolished in the process. HUD's estimate through mid-1971 was 600,000 dwell-ings.[10] As of the end of 1974, HUD reported plans for 411,000 new dwellings on these sites, 302,000 of which had been completed. These plans included 59,000 units of low-rent public housing of which 47,000 had been completed. The remainder ranged from middle-income housing assisted by federal interest subsidies to luxury apart-ments that were unsubsidized except for the land write-down.[11]

Thus there was a substantial net reduction in residential use within redevelopment sites and an overwhelming shift from housing for the poor to housing for the prosperous. At the same time, the later empha-sis on rehabilitating adjoining neighborhoods with urban renewal and neighborhood development funds resulted in some improvement to about 240,000 dwellings, with an equal number targeted for future action.

Although the housing demolition raised many hackles at the time and unavoidably created individual hardships, it is hard to fault in retrospect. Had the housing remained, most of it would now be vacant and vandalized. A stronger argument could be made for the construc-tion of more low-rent public housing to replace what was demol-ished—but preferably not in the same places. In fact, public housing authorities were generally able to find cheaper sites for smaller projects; and the private market throughout the 1950s and 1960s was releasing housing to the poor about as fast as they could absorb it.

Housing Rehabilitation and Neighborhood Preservation. In 1954, Congress amended Title I of the Housing Act of 1949, changing "ur-ban redevelopment" to "urban renewal." The act's sponsors thereby recognized that neighborhood decay was a continuing social process rather than an inherited physical condition. They hoped that means could be found to prevent decay or remedy it in its early stages, thus avoiding the trauma and expense of the ultimate remedy—evacuation, clearance, and redevelopment.

Congress was uncertain what those means might be, so it opted for planning and demonstration grants. Thereafter, to qualify for assistance with specific projects, a city had to prepare a communitywide "workable program" for urban renewal and general development. The projects themselves no longer were limited to land acquisition and clearance but could include restoration of deteriorating areas. Demonstration grants were offered for developing, testing, and reporting on new methods of renewal and preservation.

By 1959, a "workable program" had become a "Community Renewal Program," and in 1968 it became a "Neighborhood Development Program." The new planning requirements were significant in two respects. First, although the emphasis was still on physical changes, explicit recognition was given to economic and social conditions bearing on the feasibility and benefits of the proposed renewal measures. Second, the planners were asked to explain how and when they proposed to achieve their specific objectives and how plans for different areas interrelated.

From this beginning, specific instruments for neighborhood rehabilitation and preservation emerged gradually over the next two decades. Federal grants were used for improving public facilities in deteriorating neighborhoods, for spot clearance of dilapidated structures, and for acquiring, rehabilitating, and reselling dwellings. Additional grants were made to support "concentrated code enforcement" in designated areas. Low-interest loans and outright grants were offered to homeowners in renewal and code enforcement areas for rehabilitation and home improvements. Low-interest loans were offered to finance new or rehabilitated rental properties. Mortgage insurance was made available on special terms to cover the risks of private lenders who financed new construction or rehabilitation in designated neighborhoods. Finally, and most ominously, Congress authorized HUD to provide crime and fire insurance to property owners unable to obtain it from normal sources. By 1973, federal assistance for housing rehabilitation and neighborhood preservation was available under some two dozen legislatively distinct programs.[12]

Two issues dominated in planning urban renewal as opposed to redevelopment. One was the search for means to create a neighborhood consensus on the actions to be taken and then to secure the cooperation of individual property owners. The second concerned the technical feasibility and economic efficiency of rehabilitating older dwellings without permanently displacing their occupants. The problems of community participation will be discussed in the next section of this essay. The following account captures the flavor of the problems of housing rehabilitation.

In the early 1960s, the Federal Housing Administration (FHA) undertook a series of rehabilitation experiments in New York City, Chicago, Pittsburgh, Boston, and Detroit, collaborating with city governments, nonprofit foundations, building materials manufacturers, and private rehabilitation contractors. Financed by 3 percent FHA loans, the sponsors bought deteriorated and dilapidated dwellings that ranged from row houses in Pittsburgh to four-story tenements in Manhattan, and from scattered buildings to entire blocks. Acquisition costs generally ranged between $2,000 and $5,000 per dwelling. Rehabilitation costs varied with initial condition and final standards, ranging from $8,000 to $18,000 (and much higher for the famous forty-eight-hour rehabilitation of two New York tenements).

Upon completion, each experiment was heralded as a promising prototype if not itself the perfected model. But Carter McFarland, who directed most of these experiments for FHA, revisited the sites a decade later and found that most of the mortgages had been foreclosed and most of the buildings had been vandalized. None of the projects were financially or functionally successful.

Although McFarland argues that neighborhood rehabilitation can succeed if applied to essentially sound structures in a neighborhood where morale is high, owner occupancy is common, support for the enterprise is strong, occupants' incomes are stable, and adequate subsidies are available, these requirements virtually define away the targets. He concludes reluctantly that "improving housing is not enough to reverse the downward spiral in neighborhoods afflicted with deep social pathologies. We do not know exactly how to deal with these more fundamental causes of the slum condition. It follows that money and energy spent on housing improvement in neighborhoods significantly affected by these pathologies are likely to be wasted and to produce no permanent neighborhood improvement."[13]

Mobilizing the Poor. Slum clearance, public housing, and urban redevelopment mainly were directed at improving the housing and physical environments of city dwellers. Poverty was seen primarily as an impediment to participation in these improvements, an impediment that could be overcome by subsidies. Over the years, the limitations of this view had become increasingly clear. In 1964, the Johnson administration sought to remedy poverty itself.

The "War on Poverty" had many fronts. The campaigns of concern here are the Office of Economic Opportunity's (OEO) Community Action Program (CAP) and HUD's Model Cities Program. Those who designed and implemented the new policies generally shared two salient perceptions. One was that poverty resulted from a complex of reinforcing causes—poor health, lack of education and marketable skills, family instability, lack of visible opportunity for betterment, inability to deal with impersonal social institutions, susceptibility to fraudulent practice—together leading to loss of confidence and motivation. Poverty as social pathology could thus be best remedied by mutually supporting therapies.

The second perception was that a critical element of the therapy was giving the poor a new sense of control over their personal and communal destinies. To this end, the poor were encouraged to organize politically, assert their claims on society, and formulate and administer their own programs of self-help, aided by federal grants of cash and technical assistance.

In its short history, OEO managed to fund an amazing variety of loosely articulated programs for housing betterment, medical care, legal services, education and training, child care, and indigenous business ventures. The Community Action Program, approved by Congress in 1964, organized many of these activities under local leadership with vaguely territorial constituencies. OEO was willing to do business with nearly anyone who, by virtue of race, place of residence, or organizational connections, could plausibly claim to represent the poor. It even sponsored formal elections for CAP boards, the voters presumably being poor and entirely self-selected.

The actual delivery of benefits and services by CAP organizations to their constituents was fragmented, haphazard, and often incompetent. But the effort to plan, organize, and administer social programs at the local level provided leadership training for hundreds of blacks and Latins whose talents had theretofore languished for lack of a forum. Moreover, OEO-funded lawyers challenged local, state, and federal bureaucrats on behalf of the poor, winning precedents for due process and equal entitlement that have since sharply limited (for both better and worse) the discretion of public officials.

Within two years of its founding, the Community Action Program was under fire: "The strain caused by [its] emphasis on maximum feasible citizen participation and control, as well as the direct funding of the cities' poor (rather than of city agencies), caused increasing attacks by the mayors, who now initiated a counter-revolution against what had turned out, as they saw it, to be a guerilla warfare in their own territory under the sponsorship of the federal government."[14]

Congress gradually withdrew its support from CAP, and the Nixon administration, entering office in 1969, easily dismantled OEO. Few would claim that CAP's legacy was enduring either in the physical appearances or the social and economic statistics of urban slums. The principal reminders are the faded names of defunct community organizations occasionally visible on boarded-up storefronts. But the whole adventure did educate many people still in public life to the rhetoric and ambitions of indigenous leaders of the poor.

A more cautious Congress authorized the Model Cities Program in 1966. The program's sponsors proposed a series of local projects to demonstrate that a comprehensive attack on the physical, social, and economic problems of specific urban neighborhoods could produce marked improvements in a short time. Observing the antagonisms and administrative chaos engendered by OEO-style direct democracy, they opted rather for planning, coordination, and working through city hall. At the same time, they stressed local initiative and "widespread citizen participation" in program formulation and administration.

Applications for planning grants were solicited from city governments, which were to designate a needy neighborhood encompassing no more than 10 percent of the city's population or fifteen thousand people, whichever was larger; to diagnose its ills and describe the proposed remedies; and to outline the proposed structure of the Community Development Agency that would administer the program.

Those cities that won planning grants then were required to prepare an extremely detailed plan of action comprehending neighborhood public facilities, housing, transportation, education (from preschool to adult), manpower training, economic development, recreation and cultural enrichment, crime reduction, health care, and social services. They were also responsible for securing the cooperation of the multitude of local, state, and federal agencies that controlled resources bearing on each of these elements of community betterment and for showing that the residents of the neighborhood had a "meaningful role" in policy making and, subsequently, in its implementation.

The scheme was long on planning and short on authority over resources. Most of the money came not from HUD's Model Cities Administration but from categorical grants administered by other federal departments that had their own priorities. And the Nixon administration, in office by the time selected model cities had completed their obligatory plans, placed local control firmly in the mayor's office. Neighborhood residents and community organizations retained little more than advisory powers.

By early 1973, Model Cities Programs were active in 148 cities but had spent only about $1 billion of the $2.3 billion Congress had appropriated. The original purpose of comprehensive attention to the physical, social, and economic needs of a limited area was increasingly shifted by executive interpretation to general attention to city-wide needs and to strengthening the local government's capacity to plan and implement programs. From 1971 on, the administration shaped Model Cities as a bellwether for Community Development Block Grants.

Although cooperation from other federal agencies administering categorical grants never materialized, about two-thirds of HUD's urban renewal funds were allocated to Model Cities neighborhoods between 1968 and 1971. The Model Cities Administration directly funded a variety of activities in these neighborhoods, most of its budget going to education (20 percent), environmental improvement (17 percent), housing improvement (16 percent), and health services (11 percent).[15]

After all this activity, the hypothesis that motivated the Model Cities Program remains unproven if not disproven. The experiment showed instead that federal resources could not be mobilized by interdepartmental negotiation and that the idea of rational planning in applying diverse resources to solve complex social problems was hopelessly out of touch with both the state of sociological knowledge and the technical capacities of local governments. Charles Haar, who as an assistant secretary of HUD designed the Model Cities Program, describes it in retrospect as "a Waterloo for 'urban planning' . . . and a Pearl Harbor for 'local capacity.'"[16]

Turning the Job over to City Hall. In 1969, the Nixon administration inherited from its predecessor a bewildering variety of overlapping programs aimed (if that is the word) at improving the conditions of urban life, most explicitly for the poor and for racial minorities. The new administration promptly dismantled the more controversial of these and by 1970 had articulated its ideas for a sweeping change in the strategy of federal assistance.

The New Federalism conceded that the limited fiscal resources of local governments prevented them from doing much that was desirable or even necessary for the welfare of their own communities. Although it recognized Washington's proficiency as a tax collector, it doubted the competence of federal government to set local priorities or to design solutions to local problems. It proposed instead to send a check to city hall and let the mayor and council decide how to spend the money.

This plan for "general revenue sharing" was embodied in the State and Local Fiscal Assistance Act of 1972, which authorized nearly $30 billion in unrestricted grants to state, county, and city governments over a five-year period. Subsequent legislation consolidated existing categorical grant programs by general function, again leaving the grantee free to decide on specific ways and means with minimal federal supervision. By 1976, about a fourth of all federal transfers to state and local governments were either general or specific revenue-sharing grants.

The funds were allocated among units of government according to formulas that balanced population against various indicators of need: local incomes and tax effort in the case of general revenue sharing; unemployment rates for the Comprehensive Employment and Training Act (CETA); and indexes of poverty and overcrowded housing for Community Development Block Grants. Within each jurisdiction, however, neither the geographic nor the programmatic allocation was specified.

Scholars are still comparing the redistributive effects of these formulas to federal transfers under categorical grant programs; in general, the formulas favored the older central cities. Perhaps more important than the allocation among units of government is how they used the funds. The question cannot easily be answered because both general revenue-sharing funds and block grants are more or less fungible with locally raised tax revenues.

Section 8 and Housing Allowances. Having turned neighborhood preservation and redevelopment over to the cities, the administration and Congress moved next to turn residential choice over to the recipients of federal housing assistance. This move was reflected in two new programs, one experimental and the other operational.

In the Housing Act of 1970, Congress instructed HUD to test the concept of direct cash payments to low-income households that would enable them to afford decent housing in the private market. By 1972, HUD had launched the Experimental Housing Allowance Program (EHAP) to learn whether cash allowances could be successfully earmarked for housing improvements and whether a full-scale program would disturb local housing markets in ways that negated program purposes, to test variations in assistance formulas and associated behavioral responses, to explore the advantages of alternative administrative forms, and to estimate the cost of a national program. HUD used three research contractors and twelve sites. On most of the sites, it conducted two-year limited-enrollment programs, but in two sites it conducted ten-year open-enrollment programs. The experiment was not completed until 1981, at which time HUD estimated its cost at $153 million.

Congress, however, made its next major commitment of federal resources without waiting for the results of these experiments. In the Housing and Community Development Act of 1974, it authorized the Section 8 rent assistance program. Section 8 had two parts, only one of which, the Existing Housing Program, was innovative. A household enrolled in this program could nominate the dwelling it wished to occupy, often its current residence. If the landlord was willing to participate, the administering agency (a local housing authority) would inspect the dwelling and negotiate repairs (if needed) and a "fair market rent" pursuant to HUD standards. The enrolled tenant agreed to pay a fourth of his income toward the negotiated rent, and the agency agreed to pay the balance. If the tenant subsequently moved, his Section 8 certificate moved with him, although his former landlord was partially sheltered from vacancy losses by the terms of his contract with the administering agency.

Although the second part of Section 8, the New Construction Program, had the same payment formula, HUD chose the dwellings. The agency negotiated long-term contracts with developers of rental property, guaranteeing housing assistance payments on behalf of low-income tenants enrolled in the program. If the tenant subsequently moved, the subsidy stayed with the dwelling. From the tenant's viewpoint, the main differences between Section 8 New Construction and public housing were that the property was privately managed and often housed unassisted as well as assisted tenants.

Section 8 was generously funded, and within a few years it rivaled the public housing program in size and cost. By the end of fiscal 1981, HUD had signed assistance contracts covering 791,000 new or rehabilitated dwellings and 973,000 existing dwellings, entailing cumulative subsidy obligations then estimated at $136 billion.[17]

The Existing Housing Program was popular with both landlords and assisted households. The landlords were happy because they were able to negotiate substantial rent increases when they brought dwellings into the program and because they were partially protected against vacancy losses thereafter.[18] The assisted households were happy because they were often able to stay in familiar surroundings or to move to places they particularly preferred; since their contributions to rent were strictly income-determined, they were unaffected by the rent increases that benefited their landlords.[19]

The New Construction Program was also attractive to developers and assisted households, but the subsidy costs were high. In fiscal 1981, the average annual subsidy payment for dwellings under contract was estimated to be $5,100, about twice the cost per dwelling in the Existing Housing Program. Because of escalating development and financing costs, the most recent contracts carried even higher subsidies to bring rents down to a fourth of the incomes of eligible tenants.

The President's Commission on Housing, appointed early in the Reagan administration to review existing programs and propose new policies, consulted the findings of HUD's Experimental Housing Allowance Program.[20] The commission recommended in 1982 that housing allowances (also known as "housing vouchers" and "housing assistance payments") should become the federal government's principal mode of low-income housing assistance. This recommendation was accepted by HUD Secretary Samuel R. Pierce, Jr., who in each subsequent session of Congress sought authorization for such a program.

In 1982, for example, the administration proposed ending construction subsidies for both public housing authorities and private developers (except for a small program of construction for elderly persons), raising tenants' contributions in assisted housing programs, and consolidating rent assistance in a "Modified Section 8 Housing Certificate Program" as current Section 8 contracts expired. The modified Section 8 program would include two key features of the housing allowance concept: the subsidy would attach to the enrolled household rather than to the dwelling it occupied, and the amount of the assistance payment would be based on the household's income and a local housing-cost standard rather than on income and actual rent.

For two years, Congress and the administration could not agree on the basic direction of federal housing policy, and no authorization bill even reached the floor. They finally reached a compromise in November 1983. The Housing and Urban-Rural Recovery Act of 1983 repealed the Section 8 New Construction Program, substituting a two-year program of cash grants to private parties for building or rehabilitating rental housing and promising to include low-income tenants. The law also provided $242 million for a housing voucher "demonstration."

Most of the estimated fifteen thousand vouchers were used to supplement the cash grants made to owners of rental property for rehabilitation, although HUD used a third of the vouchers in a "free-standing" demonstration of the voucher concept. At least in this demonstration, the vouchers were portable, moving with participating households as they changed residences. Since 1984, the administration has regularly requested additional voucher authority and Congress has appropriated funding to support vouchers for about 140,000 households. By 1986, housing allowances were firmly established in the federal program portfolio, though not yet—as the President's Commission recommended—the principal mode of low-income housing assistance.

What We Have Learned

In the early days of housing reform in the United States, the government gave highest priority to improving the dwellings of the poor in ways that would benefit their health and safety. For practical purposes, that agenda has been accomplished—partly by enforcement of housing codes, partly by housing subsidies, but mostly by the general rise in real incomes and living standards. The problem that remains unsolved is the persistence of neighborhood social environments that endanger the residents' lives and property, handicap their children, and cause socially valuable citizens to move elsewhere if they have the means.

Government has demonstrated its capabilities and limitations in addressing this problem. A public housing authority can create a well-regulated community by carefully selecting its tenants, excluding those among the poor who lack the competence or values needed to participate constructively in community life. A city government can uproot a slum neighborhood with a bulldozer, but its social system usually reassembles elsewhere or seeds its destructive elements into hitherto "sound" neighborhoods. Urban renewal can improve a neighborhood's dwellings, add playgrounds, and redirect street traffic; but unless the social system is reformed, neighborhood problems persist and the physical setting soon deteriorates. And, as evidenced by the Community Action and Model Cities programs, we lack the institutional tools and probably the sociological knowledge needed to reform a neighborhood social structure that is already in place.

What makes a neighborhood a safe, comfortable, and congenial place to live is a sense of community among its residents. If they share social values and interests, they can and do join to supervise the use of public space and support neighborhood churches, schools, and social clubs that make their lives richer and keep them in touch with each other. In such a community, social roles and standards of behavior in daily life are well-defined. To be sure, not everyone consistently abides by the prevailing social norms, but there is a consensus as to what constitutes deviant behavior and an informal but effective system of sanctions to bring deviants back into line. Because people know each other, they can recognize possible predatory intruders and can deal with them by summoning the police or by vigilante action. In a variety of small but ultimately important ways, people look out for their neighbors.

Today, such a sense of community exists in some small towns and in smaller metropolitan suburbs. Apparently, strong neighborhoods were formerly common in large cities, generally organized around a shared ethnic heritage. Because of the diverse sources of immigration to our cities and the density of urban settlement, adjacent neighborhoods often differed in ethnic composition, and interneighborhood animosities were sometimes intense. But within each neighborhood there seemed to be a social system that worked.

Urban life is substantially less wholesome than it was because of a loss of social control at the neighborhood level. The poor are not the only but are certainly the greatest losers thereby. Those poor who want to live safely and decently need help to protect their neighborhoods from predators and bad examples, but our society seems unable to provide such help.

There are contemporary instances in which the residents of low-income neighborhoods have organized to protect their mutual interests. Most often, such voluntary associations have formed to oppose a specific threat (demolition of homes by a private or public developer) or to secure a specific benefit (a park or a new elementary school). Once formed, they may persist as watchdogs and lobbyists for community interests. There are other examples of residents of low-income neighborhoods organizing as vigilantes to expel drug dealers or to patrol unsafe streets. Some cities have sought to institutionalize neighborhood government by granting the residents a collective voice in the allocation of public resources within their neighborhood.[21]

A prerequisite to effective social control is the existence of a value-consensus among residents of a neighborhood. A great deal of sorting out occurs naturally in the marketplace. Like-minded people congregate residentially in neighborhoods that seem to offer the physical facilities and social milieu to which they aspire. Even though public intervention to create or maintain such a milieu has not been very successful, we can still help the poor find, among the alternatives available, places that suit their particular needs and circumstances.

That seems to be the strategy to which the federal government is turning. The Section 8 Existing Housing Program, especially in its looming metamorphosis into housing allowances, enables assisted households to choose where they will live, broadening their options by subsidizing the rents of the dwellings they choose—so long as those dwellings meet minimum standards for health, safety, and decency.

So it seems that, for the present at least, the best answer we can give to the question, Where should the poor live? is, Where they individually choose, with the aid of whatever financial assistance the nation is willing to provide them.

Notes

1. For example, the preamble to Title I of the Housing and Community Development Act of 1974 (88 Stat. 633) says, "The primary objective of this title is the development of viable urban communities, by providing decent housing and a suitable living environment and expanding economic opportunities, principally for persons of low and moderate income."

2. American Public Health Association (1941).

3. U.S. Department of Housing and Urban Development (1978).

4. The Orshansky standard, which has been adopted by federal statistical agencies, is based on the current cost of a nutritionally adequate diet (Orshansky, 1965). Housing professionals have traditionally applied a standard based on the current cost of adequate housing (Lane, 1977).

5. U.S. Department of Housing and Urban Development (1978).

6. The federal subsidy then covered only capital costs, paying interest and amortization on bonds issued by local authorities.

7. U.S. Department of Housing and Urban Development (1974: 154).

8. Starr (1971); Scobie and Starr (1973).

9. Anderson (1964); Gans (1965); Rossi and Dentler (1961); Seeley (1959).

10. Congressional Research Service (1973).

11. U.S. Department of Housing and Urban Development (1977).

12. Sternlieb and Hughes (1976).

13. McFarland (1977).

14. Haar (1975: 25).

15. Congressional Research Service (1973: 184–91).

16. Haar (1975: 204–5).

17. President's Commission on Housing (1982: 15).

18. Rydell, Mulford, and Helbers (1980).

19. For a while, program rules offered a "bargaining incentive" to encourage tenants to choose low-rent dwellings, but no one understood how it worked and it was seldom invoked.

20. The findings of the Housing Allowance Demand Experiment are summarized in Kennedy (1980); those of the Housing Assistance Supply Experiment in Lowry (1983); and those of the Administrative Agency Experiment in Hamilton (1979). The Urban Institute's integrated analysis, written before the Supply Ex-

periment was completed, is presented in Struyk and Bendick (1981). HUD's own summary also precedes completion of the Supply Experiment (HUD, 1980).

21. Hallman (1974); Yin and Yates (1975).

References

American Public Health Association. 1941. "Basic Principles of Healthful Housing." 2d ed. (1939). In *Housing for Health*. Lancaster, Pa.: Science Press Printing Company.

Anderson, Martin. 1964. *The Federal Bulldozer*. Cambridge, Mass.: M.I.T. Press.

Congressional Research Service, Library of Congress. 1973. *The Central City Problem and Urban Renewal Policy*. A study prepared for the Subcommittee on Housing and Urban Affairs, U.S. Senate. Washington, D.C.: U.S. Government Printing Office.

Gans, Herbert J. 1965. "The Failure of Urban Renewal: A Critique and Some Proposals." *Commentary*, April.

Haar, Charles M. 1975. *Between the Idea and the Reality: A Study in the Origin, Fate, and Legacy of the Model Cities Program*. Boston: Little, Brown.

Hallman, Howard W. 1974. *Neighborhood Government in a Metropolitan Setting*. Beverly Hills: Sage.

Hamilton, W. L. 1979. *A Social Experiment in Program Administration: The Housing Allowance Administrative Agency Experiment*. Cambridge, Mass.: Abt Books.

Kennedy, Stephen D. 1980. *Final Report of the Housing Allowance Demand Experiment*. Cambridge, Mass.: Abt Associates.

Lane, Terry S. 1977. *What Families Spend for Housing: The Origins and Uses of the Rules of Thumb*. Cambridge, Mass.: Abt Associates.

Lowry, Ira S., ed. 1983. *Experiment with Housing Allowances. The Final Report of the Housing Assistance Supply Experiment*. Cambridge, Mass.: Delgeschlager, Gunn & Hair.

McFarland, M. Carter. 1977. "The Rehabilitation and Revival of Decayed or Decaying Residential Neighborhoods." In *Subsidized Housing: Where Do We Go from Here?* A study prepared by the Congressional Research Service, Library of Congress, for the Subcommittee on HUD-Independent Agencies, Committee on Appropriations, U.S. House of Representatives. Washington, D.C.: U.S. Government Printing Office, pp. 228–33.

Orshansky, Molly. 1965. "Counting the Poor: Another Look at the Poverty Profile." *Social Security Bulletin*, January, pp. 3–29.

President's Commission on Housing. 1982. *The Report of the President's Commission on Housing*. Washington, D.C.: President's Commission on Housing.

Rossi, Peter H., and Robert A. Dentler. 1961. *The Politics of Urban Renewal: The Chicago Findings*. New York: Free Press.

Rydell, C. Peter, John E. Mulford, and Lawrence Helbers. 1980. *Price Increases Caused by Housing Assistance Programs*. R-2677-HUD. Santa Monica, Calif.: Rand Corporation.

Scobie, Richard S. 1973. "'Problem Families' and Public Housing." Roger Starr. "A Reply." *Public Interest*, No. 31, Spring, pp. 126–34.

Seeley, John. 1959. "The Slum: Its Nature, Use, and Users." *Journal of the American Institute of Planners.*

Starr, Roger. 1971. "Which of the Poor Shall Live in Public Housing?" *Public Interest*, No. 23, Spring, pp. 116–24.

Sternlieb, George, and James W. Hughes. 1976. "Analysis of Neighborhood Decline in Urban Areas." In National Housing Policy Review, *Housing in the Seventies, Working Papers*, vol. 2. Washington, D.C.: U.S. Department of Housing and Urban Development, pp. 1117–78.

Struyk, Raymond J., and Marc Bendick, Jr., eds. 1981. *Housing Vouchers for the Poor*. Washington, D.C.: Urban Institute Press.

U.S. Department of Housing and Urban Development. 1974. *Housing in the Seventies: A Report of the National Housing Policy Review.* Washington, D.C.

——. 1978. Office of Policy Development and Research. *The 1978 HUD Survey on the Quality of Community Life: A Data Book.*

——. *Experimental Housing Allowance Program: Conclusions, the 1980 Report.* Washington, D.C.

——. Various years. *Statistical Yearbook.* Washington, D.C.: U.S. Government Printing Office.

Yin, Robert K., and Douglas Yates. 1975. *Street Level Governments.* Lexington, Mass.: D.C. Heath.

6

Creative Reuse of the Existing Stock

Howard J. Sumka

As federal deficits swell and budgets for social programs shrink, subsidizing the construction of new housing for the poor has become increasingly unpopular. At the same time, there has been growing interest in housing the poor in existing stock.

Many local and federal programs make use of existing stock. Their objectives range from assuring adequate maintenance and preservation of occupied standard housing, to rehabilitating substandard but essentially sound units, to reclaiming abandoned structures. The proclaimed merits of these programs over massive land clearance and new construction include cost-effectiveness, the conservation of residential neighborhoods and social networks, and the ability to tailor programs effectively to local needs and conditions. Numerous questions about rehabilitation remain unresolved, however, such as where it works well and where it does not and its effectiveness in increasing the supply of housing.[1]

This chapter provides new insights into these issues. After briefly discussing the major reasons for the rising interest in using existing stock, the chapter develops a broad framework for such strategies. Five programs are described, analyzed, and compared, considering their effectiveness, the environments in which they best operate, and the clients they best serve. Of the five programs, four are active and scheduled for indefinite continuation (three were expanded in the Housing Act of 1983[2]); the last was only recently discontinued. The final section considers the potential and limitations of relying on existing stock to serve the needs of the poor.

Moving from New Construction to Reliance on Existing Stock

Use of existing stock looms as the major approach to serving low-income housing needs in the coming years for a number of reasons.

The predominant reason is cost. Housing production programs have become very expensive. From 1975 to 1983, the per unit costs of the flagship federal housing production program, Section 8, increased dramatically. The government was entering twenty- to forty-year contracts with private housing developers as direct annual subsidy costs of as much as $5,000 per unit, not counting financing subsidies through Government National Mortgage Association (GNMA) tandem and generous tax advantages.[3]

From 1977 to 1980, the government maintained emphasis on new construction in the Section 8 program in the face of these rising costs. The volume of Section 8 activity fell from 388,000 units in FY 1977 to 325,000 in FY 1979, but the proportion of new construction (as opposed to certificates for existing housing) increased from 52 percent to 61 percent. In FY 1980, total activity was cut nearly in half to 187,000, but new construction accounted for 63 percent of the units. From FY 1981 until the termination of the program with the Housing Act of 1983, activity fell precipitously to 52,000 and 62,000 units in FY 1982 and 1983, respectively, with new construction at only 12 percent and 8 percent of new budget authority.[4]

Another reason for the turn away from new construction is the perception that the nation's problem of housing quality, as distinct from affordability of housing, has been virtually solved. Since 1940, substandard housing has declined from nearly 50 percent of the inventory to about 6 percent.[5] Subsidized new construction, therefore, is not generally required to replace substandard housing—and could even weaken the market demand for the existing stock.

Rehabilitation strategies also offer advantages in neighborhood preservation and revitalization. To prevent neighborhood decline in the form of physical deterioration, population loss, diminution of the tax base, decay of infrastructure, and loss of economic activity, local officials will look to programs that visibly and dramatically pump new dollars into neighborhoods. Housing rehabilitation is far more visible than an allowance program, at least in the short run.

Strategies for Using Existing Stock

It is important to understand how housing deteriorates because strategies to use existing stock, in effect, are attempts to overcome the forces that led to deterioration. Once a dwelling unit is built, it begins to deteriorate.[6] This deterioration usually occurs at a very slow rate during the early life of the dwelling and then accelerates as major systems require replacement or as structural elements need repair. The rate of deterioration in the early years also depends on the amount of maintenance the dwelling receives, relative to the wear and tear to which it is subjected.

At critical points in the dwelling's life, however, substantial resources will be required for major repairs or replacements. These efforts, theoretically, can bring the dwelling back to, or at least very near, its original quality level—from which it again will begin the process of decline. There is no theoretical reason a dwelling cannot last indefinitely. With some exceptions, dwellings are capable of providing adequate housing indefinitely if maintenance and repair are more cost-effective than replacement of the units through new construction. Why, then, is there such extensive housing deterioration and abandonment?

Answering this question requires an understanding of some fundamental economic and sociological principles. Three forces, under certain circumstances, inevitably lead housing to deteriorate: low income, lack of social control, and market externalities. Any program that fails to counter these forces will face an exceptionally high risk of failure.[7]

The contribution of low income to housing deterioration is fairly straightforward. If a household is unable or unwilling to spend enough to keep ahead of the natural decay process (or pay a rent that will support such expenditures), deterioration begins. At some point, the housing will fall below accepted community standards.

Increased maintenance could be enforced through housing codes or subsidized in a variety of ways if a household cannot afford the needed expenditures. If the major concern were with individual units, this would be a simple matter of working out the details of providing the necessary enforcement or assistance. But housing deterioration in an urban setting is not an isolated process. Deterioration proceeds in an infectious manner through a neighborhood, causing the expectations of residents, investors, and other institutions to fall.[8]

For example, after World War II, middle-income families moved in droves from inner cities to the suburbs, leaving behind old but generally sound housing for lower-income families. In many cases, the process resulted in complete racial change in the neighborhood, which contributed to institutional disinvestment and decay well in excess of what the lowered economic demand alone would have produced.

As disinvestment continued, many neighborhoods attracted residents least able to control their futures and with the least stake in the environment. Increasing crime and family dissolution, combined with low incomes, often created environments seriously deficient in social control. Ultimately, many of these areas were abandoned. The resulting urban environment is a mosaic of neighborhoods at various stages of health and decline.[9]

Strategies that rely on using the existing stock must operate to reverse these processes and, therefore, must proceed from three basic principles. First, they must overcome the gap between housing cost and income, which low-income families confront. Doing so involves a number of considerations, including the form subsidies should take, alternative financing arrangements, and appropriate levels of rehabilitation.[10] Second, the problem of housing deterioration in the context of neighborhood environments must be addressed. Strategies must be coordinated with broader community development efforts and, for maximum effectiveness, target well-defined areas. Further, because local situations vary substantially from city to city and even within cities, this principle requires that the strategies be implemented by local governments. Third, strategies must be cognizant of the social environments in which they will operate. This suggests that local community organizations should be involved when possible and that ownership by low-income people rather than tenant status be encouraged.

Underlying these principles is a concern for efficiency. To the extent possible, programs must rely on direct cash assistance to reduce excessive rent burdens and assure optimal maintenance of the stock. Supply-side subsidies should favor moderate over substantial rehabilitation whenever possible to keep costs and debt service requirements low. A strategy of this form should be very efficient in using resources. It also has an aura of political plausibility. The real question, though, is whether the theoretical benefits of this policy approach would be realized in practice.

It is with this question in mind that I will review a variety of recent efforts to use existing housing stock. The focus primarily is on how successfully these approaches have addressed the problem of income, externality, and social control and in what environments they have been or could be most effective. It is essential to discuss approaches to multifamily housing and single-family housing separately because they present qualitatively different sets of problems and, therefore, require fundamentally different interventions.

Single-Family Housing

Cities tend to focus on owner-occupied single-family homes and to provide relatively little support for rental housing. The General Accounting Office (GAO) estimates that only 8 percent of the cities with populations over fifty thousand have assisted more than one hundred rental units since 1980.[11] This bias is not based on relative need and in fact runs counter to the cities' own stated perceptions of the needs of their rental and homeowner populations. Rather, it likely reflects the attempt by cities to implement relatively simple programs that will produce a maximum return on the public dollar.

Homeowners are stable, generally reliable, and often enthusiastic participants in revitalization programs. They control their housing environments and need not worry whether problem tenants will render their rehabilitation short-lived and unprofitable. As relatively long-term residents who probably expect to remain indefinitely, they clearly perceive the consumption and investment benefits of improving their homes and participating in neighborhood improvement.

From the city's perspective, the attractiveness of programs for homeowners is further enhanced by the simplicity of the physical plant, the lack of complicated ownership or management problems, modest capital requirements, and uncomplicated financing arrangements. Underlying these concerns is the general perception that homeownership contributes to social stability and personal well-being and should therefore be encouraged wherever possible.

There are a variety of programs that focus on single-family stock. The following discussion focuses on two types: the partnership approach to neighborhood preservation and urban homesteading. The discussion shows how they address key problems, the environments in which they operate most effectively, and their potential for the future.

Neighborhood Preservation Partnerships. One of the urban development code words of the 1980s is "partnership." The popularity of the term reflects the recognition that most urban problems can be alleviated only through the coordinated efforts of a variety of interested and influential parties. The partnership approach to neighborhood preservation recognizes that neighborhood decline, generally the result not only of low income but also of deteriorating public facilities and reduced expectations among financial and insurance institutions, can be reversed only by including all of the institutional actors in a comprehensive neighborhood revitalization plan. In its most common form, a partnership brings together the local government, lenders, and neighborhood residents. The programs such partnerships implement normally include code inspections, technical assistance regarding home repair, and assisted loan programs for high-risk or lower-income homeowners. Many of these programs received funding through the locality's CDBG allocation.[12]

The best-known and most extensive partnership is the Neighborhood Housing Services program (NHS), developed and supported by the federally chartered and funded Neighborhood Reinvestment Corporation (NRC). For more than a decade the NRC, serving as theorist, catalyst, technical assistance provider, program designer, and nurturer, has replicated the NHS program, originally developed locally in Pittsburgh, in nearly two hundred cities. In addition, NHS has served as a model for many locally developed programs.

The NHS structure and approach are well known.[13] A partnership of lenders, residents, and the city creates a local NHS organization to encourage home improvements in a well-defined target neighborhood. Lenders are expected to provide operating funds for the organization and to look favorably on mortgage applications from neighborhood residents. The city, which usually plays a minor role in the organization itself, commits resources for improving public facilities in the neighborhood and for providing subsidized rehabilitation loans. The NHS implements a systematic program of code inspections to encourage home repair and rehabilitation. It provides technical assistance regarding executing repairs and finding contractors and financial assistance in the form of low-interest, high-risk loans.

By design, the NHS program is a preservation approach that is generally applicable to predominantly homeowner neighborhoods that have suffered only modest decline (although they very well may be on the road to serious decay in the absence of any coordinated intervention). Only homeowners are directly assisted, although a number of renter-oriented pilot programs have been used to support NHS activities in neighborhoods with special problems. NHS is effective in neighborhoods of modest income where basic social control mechanisms are present. Through a variety of actions, it bolsters confidence in the neighborhood's future and counteracts the externality problem. The technical assistance helps alleviate problems related to inertia and lack of information.

In a recent self-assessment, NRC concluded that NHS serves as a means to reasonably quick rehabilitation.[14] The assessment also uncovered some problems.[15] Lenders worried about having made an open-ended commitment to the programs, a concern exacerbated by the financial problems plaguing the savings and loan (S&L) industry in the early 1980s. The local S&L retrenchment created budget problems for NHS at a time when other resources were diminishing.[16]

The longer-term problem is that as lending institutions' contributions decline, there is more reliance on local CDGB funds, creating an undesirable (to the NRC) increase in the cities' control over the programs. In nominal terms, operating costs of local programs increased about 75 percent from 1975 to 1980, when they averaged $74,000 per year. Over the same period, contributions by lenders declined from 80 to 45 percent of operating costs, and those of local governments increased from 4 to 39 percent.[17]

In an independent evaluation, HUD came to the same broad conclusions that the NHS programs have been highly successful as builders of local organizations and catalysts for neighborhood reinvestment and housing improvement.[18] The HUD evaluation, however, raised some difficult questions regarding the costliness and limited focus and applicability of the programs. NHS programs have worked with a relatively small portion of the residents in their target neighborhoods. Only about 35 percent of the residents in a typical neighborhood were even aware of the program, and only 7 percent actually received direct assistance.

Nearly all clients (97 percent) were homeowners with incomes ($18,000 in 1980) about 25 percent above the average for their neighborhoods. Clients who received low-interest loans from the revolving fund had incomes at about the neighborhood average ($13,700). Clients tended to be long-term residents of the area, nearly 58 percent having been there for ten years or more, compared to 29 percent for all residents. Clearly, NHS, as promulgated by the corporation, is a decline-prevention strategy that focuses on the most stable, higher-income families in neighborhoods that are not suffering from serious decay.

The HUD evaluation went on to ask whether the neighborhoods were improving in measurable ways that could be attributed to the NHS program. Using the ratio of neighborhood conditions, HUD found that NHS neighborhoods showed marked improvement during the 1970s but no greater improvement than similar inner-city neighborhoods without NHS programs. This overall improvement can be attributed to general changes in the economy that made older neighborhoods more attractive to households that otherwise might have moved elsewhere. Investments in repair and renovation exceeded the national average. Thus, although NHS and non-NHS areas have experienced similar improvements, NHS program activity is clearly associated with home improvement. The recipients of high-risk loans would not otherwise have been able to finance repairs.

A final question in evaluating NHS regards cost, an especially difficult issue when assessing programs that provide technical assistance and services rather than direct subsidies. In 1980, the development of a local NHS, which can take as long as two to three years, averaged $203,000, including $35,000 to $50,000 from local governments. Locally raised annual operating costs averaged $74,000 and the annual value of technical and administrative services this corporation provided about $39,000. Averaging development costs over a five-year period, and making certain technical adjustments, produces an average total annual NHS program cost of $135,000. Measured against output, these figures indicate that on average, it costs NHS programs about $980 for every family that received technical assistance regarding rehabilitation, $650 for every family that received a private loan through NHS referral, and $2,980 to process and close a revolving loan. The last figure amounts to $410 per $1,000 borrowed, or a 41 percent service cost.[19] Program costs are substantial but not out of line for a labor-intensive, hands-on assistance effort.

Although the NHS success demonstrates the potential usefulness of partnership approaches to housing rehabilitation and neighborhood preservation, it is not clear whether NHS per se or the general economy has made the larger contribution to the improvement of NHS neighborhoods. To the extent that partnership interventions such as NHS can create neighborhood confidence, counteract neighborhood externalities, and help maintain social control by using minimal direct subsidies, they are an efficient approach to the preservation of homeowner housing stock and can serve as a key component of an existing stock strategy.

Urban Homesteading. At about the same time that NHS was being developed as a response to incipient neighborhood decay, local governments began experimenting with single-family urban homesteading to deal with property abandonment, one of the most frustrating aspects of decline. The concept of urban homesteading is fairly simple: publicly owned, abandoned property is transferred to households in exchange for their commitment to repair, occupy, and maintain the property. In essence, the family receives in-kind subsidy as an incentive to move into a neighborhood it would not likely choose otherwise. This approach to conserving the existing housing stock addresses all three aspects of decline: low- or moderate-income families receive assistance to lower their housing costs; a serious blighting influence is removed from the neighborhood; and the stabilizing influence of homeownership is increased.

Despite its promise and the exceptionally good press it received a decade ago, homesteading has not been widespread. Most has occurred under Section 810 of the Housing and Community Development Act enacted in 1974, which allows federally owned residential properties to be given to local governments for homesteading. Although some cities operate their own local programs, most participate in the federal program because they then become eligible for additional federal subsidies to finance rehabilitation. Through FY

1982, 107 cities had participated in the homesteading program, and 91 were active. In aggregate, 7,115 properties—including 690 local properties—had been homesteaded between 1974 and 1982.[20]

Although homesteading programs vary according to local circumstances, all entail four essential functions: neighborhood designation, property selection, homesteader selection, and management and financing of rehabilitation. How those functions are implemented determines the focus and potential success of a homesteading program. To measure the success of homesteading in the first twenty-three cities participating in the HUD demonstration, an in-depth evaluation was undertaken. It examined programs according to each of the four basic functions and the programs' overall effectiveness. The primary objective was to assess homesteading's potential as a mechanism for reclaiming abandoned housing stock and providing opportunities for homeownership.[21]

Neighborhood selection was based on the expectation that homesteading could best serve as a device for stabilizing and preserving marginal neighborhoods rather than for reviving seriously blighted areas. The neighborhoods tended to house minority families of modest incomes. From 1970 to 1977, they had changed on average from 45 to nearly 70 percent minority, and incomes had increased to $11,200 at a rate well below the national average. Housing in the neighborhoods was predominantly owner-occupied; house values averaged about $21,400. The average rent was below $200. Compared to NHS areas, homesteading neighborhoods were somewhat further along the path of decline: families had lower incomes and property values were nearly 30 percent lower.

Property selection created a dilemma for many programs. A dwelling to be homesteaded should have little or no market value to avoid the appearance of a government giveaway and to be consistent with the theory of homesteading. Cities found, however, that their most common problem was the selection of properties for which they could generate no interest. Therefore, many cities adjusted their property selection criteria during the course of their programs, raising the minimum value, placing greater emphasis on the condition of the surrounding neighborhood, or involving only larger or attractive properties. Some cities have received considerable publicity for homesteading programs that market seriously deteriorated properties, but these are not typical. Generally, these programs have been concentrated in neighborhoods with some historical significance or locational advantage. They usually have catered to reasonably well-to-do young people who have considerable resources for rehabilitation and who view homesteading as an adventure.

The selection of homesteader families presented a similar tension.

Cities attempted to restrict participation to families with a demonstrated housing need, while at the same time assuring that homesteaders had the capacity to complete the rehabilitation. The characteristics of the original homesteader families clearly reflect the need and capacity criteria. Families were typically minority (70 percent), male-headed (64 percent), and young (average age thirty-six). Most were small families, and two-thirds included at least one child under age eighteen. The vast majority of the household heads were employed, but nearly 20 percent of the households received some form of government assistance, and they reported average liquid assets of only $900. Their average incomes approximately equaled the national median and were above average for the homesteading neighborhoods. (Over the first three years of the demonstration, average incomes of homesteaders increased from just under $12,000 to almost $17,000, reflecting not only inflation but also a tightening of the income criteria by many of the cities.) Virtually all families were renters before entering the program, and almost all reported an improvement in their housing conditions even before the rehabilitation of the homestead was completed. In many respects, the homesteaders are very similar to other homeowners in the neighborhoods although they are younger, suggesting that urban homesteading appears to facilitate and accelerate the process leading to homeownership for families less endowed than but otherwise not unlike other neighborhood residents.

Substantial proportions of the actual rehabilitation of deteriorated and abandoned housing were completed through self-help, which generally took longer to complete but produced work that was equal in quality to that performed by professional contractors. Homesteading relied on moderate rehabilitation; the average total value was about $12,400, of which 27 percent was contributed by self-help. Homesteaders spent nearly three hundred hours working on their properties, mostly performing lower-skill tasks related to demolition, site improvement, and interior finishing. In addition to saving about $3,000 on labor, homesteaders saved an additional $350 through the direct purchase of materials.

There is some evidence that homesteading was able to counteract neighborhood externalities and produce spillover benefits. The original programs were implemented in areas receiving CDBG support from local government, however, making it difficult to disentangle the causes of improvement. Over the course of the HUD evaluation (1977–79) the relative decline in the income of neighborhood residents was arrested, and racial change slowed considerably. Investment activity by owner-occupants increased significantly. The proportion of nonhomesteader homeowners who invested in their homes increased from 58 to 65 percent, and the average amount per investment increased from $1,130 to $1,635. Property values, which had been declining relative to those in the rest of the SMSAs, were maintained. From 1970 to 1976, property values increased 65 percent in the homesteading neighborhoods, compared to 77 percent in similar areas and 86 percent in the metropolitan areas. Between 1976 (when homesteading began) and 1978, property values in homesteading neighborhoods increased 36 percent, the same as for comparison areas and only slightly below the 39 percent rate for metropolitan areas.

Despite these achievements, there are reasons why homesteading may never be used extensively. First, the attention the program requires may discourage local administrators operating under tight budgets. Second, it is not clear that an adequate supply of appropriate housing exists, despite data that suggest housing abandonment has not substantially abated in recent years.[22] In older, northeastern cities, abandonment rates may reach 5 percent or more of the stock, yet relatively little if any homesteading is occurring. One clue may be the process of acquiring properties and the legal restrictions on their disposition. Most state legislation prescribes long, tedious procedures for foreclosing on tax-delinquent property. Requirements for *in persona* proceedings, along with long redemption periods during which clear title cannot be obtained, prevent cities from conducting aggressive acquisition programs. Thus for many cities, the potential resource of homesteading properties is essentially unreachable.

Cities in states that do allow fast-take foreclosures, however, often find themselves the owners of occupied or partially occupied properties that create serious management problems and are not easily disposed of. Another problem is that foreclosure procedures may not allow the city to discriminate between homeowners who have fallen behind in tax payments and absentee investors who have no intention of paying the taxes or who use the delays in the collection system as a form of public loan. Thus, though the reform of legislation regarding acquisition and disposition of state property would improve the ability of cities to conduct homesteading programs and to cope more effectively with neighborhood decline, such reform must leave the cities sufficient discretion in dealing with the properties they acquire.[23]

Even if cities could readily acquire and homestead abandoned properties, they face yet another problem. Abandonment, which older cities are experiencing, often reflects either the "falling out of the bottom" of the worst housing in the stock as new units are built or weak demand for entire neighborhoods as the cities lose population. In either case, homesteading may not be an appropriate and effective strategy. Although many city neighborhoods would benefit greatly from, and perhaps even be revived by, the infusion of new blood that homesteading could bring, many others are far beyond the stage at which homesteading holds any promise. Certainly, in the absence of support for housing rehabilitation and other general neighborhood improvements, it would be fruitless to introduce homesteading into many of these neighborhoods.

Single-family homesteading, as implemented to date, is a moderate-income homeownership program that achieves modest levels of rehabilitation and operates in the larger context of local neighborhood preservation efforts. The trends have been to increase the income requirement of families selected, as well as the value of abandoned houses used. Homesteading has operated successfully in more difficult neighborhoods than has NHS but has directly served essentially the same income group. The major differences between the two client groups are that homesteaders were more likely to be minorities and virtually all were renters. Although nearly 60 percent of the homesteaders exceeded local Section 8 income guidelines, fewer than one-fourth had sufficient assets to make a down payment on a house with the postrehabilitation value of their homesteading properties.

Multifamily Housing

The maintenance and rehabilitation of the multifamily housing stock presents an exceptional challenge to local housing officials. The predominance of local programs that focus on owner-occupants reflects the reluctance of cities to tread into the complexities of multifamily rental housing. Yet such housing is an exceedingly important sector of the inventory serving low- and moderate-income households. Multifamily buildings also have an enormous neighborhood impact. By virtue of their size, they are very visible in the neighborhood and, if in deteriorating condition, can have a deleterious impact on the surrounding area.

Conversely, the rehabilitation of large structures can have a strong positive influence, sending signals to nearby property owners and to financial institutions that the neighborhood has a promising investment climate. In addition, such structures may allow scale economies. Compared to working with single-family homes on an individual basis, one would expect certain administrative efficiencies and

expensive

slow
complex

construction cost advantages on a per unit basis. Rarely, however, is that the case. Efforts at rehabilitating multifamily housing are notoriously expensive, slow to process administratively, and slow to bring to completion. The difficulties are the result of the technical complexity of the construction process, substantial capital requirements, complicated financing arrangements, and community resistance resulting from displacement and relocation issues.[24]

A variety of multifamily housing strategies have been attempted in recent years in continuing efforts to conserve this portion of the nation's housing resources, especially that portion most accessible to lower-income households, and to stabilize deteriorating inner-city neighborhoods. Most local efforts rely to some degree on federal resources.[25] At one extreme are strategies designed for buildings that are on the verge of decline but essentially sound and capable of being stabilized under effective management and careful refinancing. Such an approach is the Apartment Improvement Program developed in Yonkers, New York, and propagated as a counterpart for multifamily buildings to the NHS programs for single-family homes.[26] Other attempts at halting decline through improved or innovative management include the less than successful "work-out" approaches for federally assisted projects by Advisory Services for Better Housing and the more promising tenant management programs for public housing.[27]

By and large, however, solving the problem of multifamily housing calls for more dramatic efforts, which include large infusions of money for rehabilitation. To keep the newly rehabilitated dwellings affordable to lower-income families, cities have employed various financing and subsidy mechanisms as well as different requirements for the amount of rehabilitation needed. Most efforts have recognized the problem of neighborhood externality, although attempts to coordinate housing and community development activities often have been unsuccessful. Even when cities coordinate their CDBG activities with privately sponsored, subsidized rehabilitation, they still often ignore the problems of community alienation. In response to this problem, and often to recover housing so seriously deteriorated or in such unattractive neighborhoods that private action is extremely unlikely, a variety of multifamily homesteading efforts have sprung up around the country.

This section examines three strategies for rehabilitation of multifamily dwellings that illustrate a variety of ways to address the problems of income gap, externality, and control. The first is HUD's Neighborhood Strategy Areas (NSA) Substantial Rehabilitation Demonstration, an effort to coordinate community development activities and rehabilitation of multifamily housing in declining areas. Under the general category of multifamily homesteading, there are a number of community and tenant-controlled efforts at rehabilitation, management, and low-income cooperative ownership. Finally, HUD's new Rental Rehabilitation Program (RRP), a moderate rehabilitation approach, leverages private funds and uses a split-subsidy mechanism.

Neighborhood Strategy Areas. The Section 8 program included provisions for new construction and substantial rehabilitation of existing housing under the same general process. Cities received allotments of funds, but local developers submitted proposals to HUD; cities essentially could only approve or veto the submission. This process left the cities without meaningful participation in the design and execution of Section 8 projects; nor did it allow them to coordinate housing and community development activities in a comprehensive neighborhood revitalization strategy.

The NSA Demonstration was designed to overcome both of these shortcomings by giving cities the authority to select neighborhoods and designate sites for rehabilitation. Cities were required to use their Section 8 substantial rehabilitation allocations in areas slated for comprehensive improvement using CDBG funds and other resources. In addition, cities were required to minimize the displacement of families and to provide relocation assistance when necessary. It was expected that giving cities control over the entire process would encourage more extensive use of substantial rehabilitation and would focus rehabilitation on relatively small, multifamily buildings, which make up the bulk of rental stock.

The demonstration began in 1979 in 150 neighborhoods. Largely because of serious credit problems, only about 10 percent of a planned 36,700 dwellings were in construction two years later, and 43 percent of the NSAs had not started. Apart from production and financing problems, which were specific to the Section 8 model and the state of the economy, the NSA experience illustrates a number of important aspects of multifamily housing rehabilitation. The Section 8 subsidy mechanism required that the program address tenants' income gap. Of more interest are its approach to and impact on externality problems, relocation problems, and the roles of the various actors in the demonstration. These issues were addressed in a HUD evaluation of the demonstration during 1979 to 1981.[28]

The NSAs tended to be large inner-city areas with primarily rental housing and declining and unstable populations. In the largest NSAs, the cities usually focused their limited resources on small subareas.

Section 8 allocations covered only 16 percent of the rehabilitation needs documented by the cities, and all other resources had to be provided by the city from its CDBG allocations or other sources. Despite population losses (averaging 13 percent during the 1960s and as high as 30 to 50 percent in a few cases) and increasing minority populations, the neighborhoods were generally at the point at which decline could be arrested. In 1981, only 2 percent of the housing stock was judged to be deteriorated, and only 3 percent was obviously vacant and abandoned. Based on windshield surveys, 51 percent of the structures were rated well-maintained, and half the NSAs received eighty out of one hundred points on an assessment scale that measured street and sidewalk conditions. Environmental quality—as indicated by litter, yard maintenance, and street landscaping—was more variable; one-third of the NSAs were rated as seventy or above and one-third at thirty or below.

HUD's evaluation revealed a relationship between completed rehabilitation and environmental improvement. In NSAs in which 50 percent or more of the Section 8 units were being constructed, the condition ratings of residential blocks improved by nearly 20 percent from 1979 to 1981. In less productive NSAs, the ratings improved less than 10 percent. There was also a clear correlation between the amount of CDBG funds spent in the NSA and Section 8 completion rates. In a sample of cities, those with 50 percent or better start rates had spent more than three times the amount of CDBG funds than the others.

There are several possible explanations for the relationship between rehabilitation and neighborhood improvement. One is that a local staff capable of successfully managing the rehabilitation was also likely to be able to coordinate and implement its CDGB activities. The relationship also may demonstrate the local commitments to neighborhood targeting. In fact, local officials responded that linking housing and CDBG activities was an important component of success and should be encouraged. Participating developers and state housing finance agencies also favored targeting, presumably because they felt more secure about their investments. The strong relationship between rehabilitation and neighborhood improvement at the least suggests that a measurable and mutually reinforcing impact can be achieved; it also may have created a more optimistic feeling about the neighborhood that led to other private investments not directly measured.

Cities were required to develop plans that minimized displacement but accommodated relocation needs that arose. In efforts to avoid displacement, cities attempted to identify vacant properties for rehabilitation but often found themselves in a trap: the vacant structures were generally in such bad condition that rehabilitation was infeasible or less efficient than rehabilitation of occupied units, even accounting for relocation costs. As a result, 75 percent of the cities with projects in construction used occupied structures, but they were able to find partly occupied buildings so the number of relocations was only 11 percent of the units rehabilitated.

Relocation costs—about $500 for temporary and $7,000 for permanent relocation—were fully or partially paid by CDBG funds in 60 percent of the cities. In the remainder, the developer, usually using syndication proceeds, had to bear the full burden. For cost and equity reasons, it was hoped that all relocation would be temporary. In actuality, less than 60 percent was temporary; an unexpectedly large portion of the relocated tenants were ineligible for Section 8 or would have been overcrowded had they returned to their original units. The NSA relocation experience indicates not only the trade-offs that must be made but also the great potential for abuse of the current residents if there is not strong oversight of the process.

The major innovation of the NSA Demonstration was the process of developing and managing the rehabilitation through unusual partnerships of local officials and developers (including nonprofit development entities). An important objective was to focus on the smaller rental structures that predominate in most neighborhoods and to attract smaller-scale developers with links to the neighborhood. To grasp the implications of this approach, it is important to understand the principal forces that powered Section 8 production. Both new construction and substantial rehabilitation were made attractive to developers through the tax laws. Equity syndication, the sale of ownership shares to limited partners in high tax brackets who take advantage of large depreciation tax shelters, was extremely profitable. The fixed administrative and legal costs of syndication, however, effectively restricted Section 8 activity to relatively large projects, typically containing about 90 dwellings.

The demonstration succeeded in achieving rehabilitation of small buildings; the 540 projects in construction in 1981 averaged 31 dwellings each, with 45 percent involving fewer than 25 dwellings. In selecting buildings of this size, cities often found themselves working with inexperienced local developers. These developers generally had strong ties to the NSA neighborhood, either as residents or property owners, and were especially committed to the broad community goals of the demonstration. But the developers were undercapitalized and did not have extensive financing networks on which to rely. They had enormous difficulty coping with the normal delays in Section 8 processing and production, which led to average production periods of more than two years per project. In the sample, developers whose projects averaged forty units had 36 percent of their units at construction in 1981; among experienced developers used to working on a large scale, 63 percent of the projects, which averaged 133 units, were under construction.

Two other problems occurred with small projects. First, spreading the rehabilitation costs over a smaller number of units led to debt service requirements that made it difficult for the rents to fall under the Section 8 fair market rent for the area. Second, HUD field staff viewed small projects as an excessive drain on their time as they strove to meet production goals. As a result, the developers who needed the most help often found themselves at the end of the processing queue.

The lessons of the NSA demonstration are clear. Cities can take control of the multifamily rehabilitation process, coordinate it with local community development efforts, and produce decent housing and living environments for low-income households, albeit with the deep subsidies provided by Section 8. Clearly, the process requires a committed and capable staff. The rehabilitation of small buildings by local developers is also possible and, by and large, desirable. Such developers, however, need extensive technical assistance (for estimating project costs, obtaining financing, coping with processing delays, and finding capable contractors). Cities can provide this help or, as the demonstration found, local limited-profit development entities with strong ties to the area can assist developers and attract outside financial resources, while keeping project administration close to neighborhood residents. The final lesson is that subsidy mechanisms must be appropriate. If the tax system provides a primary incentive for housing rehabilitation it will dictate the kinds of buildings that will be attractive to developers. Small-scale development by local, less-experienced developers requires other support to assure adequate capitalization and the ability to bring the project to successful completion.

Multifamily Urban Homesteading. Multifamily urban homesteading can be broadly defined as the cooperative renovation, ownership, and management of a multifamily building by its residents. Numerous variations on the multifamily urban homesteading concept are possible. Some efforts have used city-owned abandoned property and relied almost exclusively on self-help rehabilitation; in other cases, properties have been purchased from private owners and much of the repair work has involved professional laborers supervising unskilled

trainees from the neighborhood. Projects may be owned by a resident cooperative or by a community-based, nonprofit organization
and managed by a tenant cooperative. The common overall objectives are to reclaim deteriorating housing resources while keeping
the production costs low and ensuring tenant control.

Most multifamily homesteading has taken place in New York
City. By virtue of its predominantly high-density, multifamily housing stock, its very active and sophisticated community-based organizations, and its long tradition of cooperative housing, the city has
served as a fertile testing ground. The first project, begun by an East
Harlem neighborhood group in 1969, used sweat equity to rehabilitate a number of abandoned buildings. In 1973, the Urban Homesteading Assistance Board (UHAB) was created to provide technical
assistance in community organizing, real estate, law, and finance to
groups attempting homesteading.[29]

The earliest projects were sweat equity homesteading efforts.
A minimal amount of mortgage financing was used to cover property
acquisition, construction materials, professional services, and some
interim costs; virtually all the labor was in the form of sweat equity.
Projects completed under this model in New York City in the early
1970s produced dwelling units, after gut rehabilitation, at $5,000
each, but the work took as long as four years. The excessive time required to complete these projects and the need for skills that are
often beyond the capability of the cooperative households led to
modified approaches, including varying amounts of purchased labor.
Three such projects in New York City were completed in eighteen
months at an average cost of about $15,000 per unit, illustrating the
clear trade-off between time and cost in the sweat equity process.

By the late 1970s multifamily homesteading was still rare. In its
1977 annual report, UHAB listed fifty-four buildings containing
slightly over a thousand dwellings as being inclusive of "all known
urban homesteading/sweat equity projects in New York City." Con-
firmation of that number was provided by a 1981 HUD study, which
identified fewer than fifty low-income cooperatives in the entire city.[30]

The rate of homesteading activity in New York has increased dramatically in recent years, a direct but unintended result of the enact-
ment in 1977 of fast-take foreclosure proceedings. The process was
designed to discourage abandonment by investors by shortening the
time between tax delinquency and public acquisition of the property.
What occurred, however, was a massive taking of residential property by the city, which found itself in the uncomfortable and in-
appropriate role of landlord to a vast number of its lower-income
households living in substandard housing. The city created a Divi-

sion of Alternative Management Programs (DAMP) in the hopes of finding innovative ways to improve the management and stabilization of these properties and hasten their return to private ownership.[31] Two of the six programs embody basic homesteading concepts and objectives.

Under DAMP's Community Management Program (CMP), established community groups enter into contracts with the city to manage buildings.[32] Although this process differs from homesteading in that the tenants neither own nor operate the building, CMP does create substantial community control over lower-income housing. In 1982, CMP included 116 buildings containing more than 2,250 dwellings and had a $10 million budget. The large budget reflects the rehabilitation needs of the CMP buildings. More than half the buildings were old law tenements, and the average repair cost was over $9,400 per dwelling unit. A recent evaluation of the DAMP programs found CMP to be especially successful in bringing buildings up to standard quality, largely because of the relatively high rehabilitation budget.[33] In getting the buildings to the point at which rents, including Section 8 certificate receipts from eligible tenants, covered operating and maintenance costs, CMP performed about average for all DAMP programs, with three-quarters of the CMP buildings judged to be fiscally sound. CMP also was assessed as average in overall management, performing worse than one private sector management program but better than two others. The evaluation concluded that despite the community roots and established reputation of the CMP managers, there was no guarantee that management would be efficient or responsive or that the usual tenant-landlord conflicts would disappear.

The homesteading concept was taken a step further in the Tenant Interim Lease (TIL) program, under which the city turns management over to the tenants with the objective of ultimately selling the property to a tenant cooperative. In 1982, TIL had a $5 million budget and 227 buildings containing more than 5,400 dwellings. Under TIL, the city provides training and technical assistance, most often through UHAB, and funds for major repairs; the tenants are responsible for all other aspects of management. Because of its limited budget, TIL is intended only for a building that is in good condition and has a viable tenant organization. The building must be at least 60 percent occupied, on a block that is at least 60 percent occupied, and need no more than the equivalent of one major system replacement. In addition, the application to join TIL must be made by 60 percent of the tenants.

In fact, TIL buildings were found to be in relatively poor condition, requiring more than $9,200 per dwelling in repairs. Because TIL has only limited rehabilitation resources, the program was rated lowest of the five DAMP programs in achieving standard physical condition. Largely because of tenant self-management, however, the TIL buildings were the most fiscally sound of all those in DAMP; very high rent collection rates and stable, high occupancy were the primary reasons. Overall management capability for TIL was judged to be average, reflecting continuing needs for training the tenant organizations. TIL groups share a dual goal of controlling their housing and maintaining ties in the neighborhood. Even when experiencing management difficulties, the groups were confident about tenant management and the possibility of buying the building in the future.[34]

Despite these positive views, however, the TIL program can be judged only moderately successful. The continuing inability or unwillingness to rehabilitate the buildings to standard condition will continue to impede the sale of the buildings to tenant groups, which is the consummation of the homesteading process. During the first two years of operation, only six sales occurred. In 1982, there were forty-five sales, below the goals for the program.

In its effort to stimulate multifamily homesteading activity nationwide, HUD developed two demonstrations, which, if nothing else, attest to the difficulty and complexity of the process. In 1978, UHAB received funding to transfer its basic model to six cities, adapting it to meet the specific needs of each situation. Six years later, only two of the ten projects had succeeded in completing the rehabilitation and forming the cooperative, and one of these is a middle-income project.[35] A second demonstration, authorized under Section 510 of the 1978 Housing Act, attempted to develop low-income cooperatives through local partnerships without reliance on sweat equity. The 510 demonstration began as a pilot in three New York City neighborhoods in 1979 and expanded to six other cities in 1981. By early 1984 only one of the New York projects had finished the rehabilitation and formed a cooperative. Of the six other projects, only two were close to completion, two had failed to form low-income cooperatives, and two were still in progress, with the eventual outcome still uncertain. Despite its spotty record, the 510 demonstration holds a number of lessons regarding the problems and the promise of multifamily homesteading.[36]

The 510 model was implemented by a special-purpose organization (SPO)—a nonprofit partnership of a community-based organization and a local developer. The goal was to rehabilitate a deteriorating multifamily building and form a cooperative among existing tenants or new households moving in after the rehabilitation was complete. The rehabilitation (usually of fifty units per neighborhood) was coordinated with an equal number of Section 8 substantial rehabilitation units in an effort to concentrate the effect. (In addition, a portion of the syndication proceeds from the Section 8 buildings was earmarked as a private sector contribution to the cooperative.) Federal subsidies included a demonstration grant for SPO operation and technical assistance, and cities contributed the properties, CDBG funds, and other resources. Sweat equity rehabilitation was eschewed because of the time it requires and the management difficulties it creates; it was expected that affordability would be assured through the various subsidies. The demonstration can best be assessed by considering the three New York City pilot projects.

Although the three New York neighborhoods had somewhat different population and housing characteristics, they were all declining areas of predominantly low- and moderate-income families. The buildings selected were all city-owned, four-to-six-story structures built between 1890 and 1925. Except for one fifty-six-unit building, the buildings had eight to sixteen units. Two were abandoned and completely vacant; two were fully occupied and two half-occupied. A careful prerehabilitation physical inspection uncovered numerous physical deficiencies. On a per room basis, 25 percent had an electrical deficiency, 34 percent had sagging floors, and 26 percent needed replacement windows. Virtually all of the dwellings in one neighborhood were old law tenements with incomplete bathroom facilities. Among the other structures, one-third of the bathrooms had evident water damage, and half had corroded or leaking pipes.[37]

The residents in these buildings typically were young, minority households; half received some form of public assistance, more than half were female-headed, and half had children under the age of eighteen. The average income was about $8,400 in 1980. The tenantry was, however, fairly stable. About 40 percent had lived in the building for five or more years and another 25 percent for three to four years. They were paying rents of $150 to $215 per month, largely because substantial subsidies were provided to the buildings through the city's building management programs.[38]

Efforts were made to perform only moderate rehabilitation averaging $10,000 per unit. Through its CDBG grant and other programs, the city provided about $2.4 million for one rehabilitation. Because of anticipated costs for deficiencies not revealed during the early building inspections, another $1.1 million in private financing had to be negotiated. This additional need had serious repercussions for final carrying costs and required the issuing of Section 8 existing certificates for many in-place residents whose postrehabilitation monthly costs increased 18 percent, 40 percent, and 165 percent in the three projects, respectively.

Despite these unanticipated costs, the 510 projects compare favorably with typical Section 8 substantial rehabilitation projects. On a per unit basis, the average total direct subsidy for a 510 unit was $4,900 per year, compared to $5,360 for a comparable Section 8 project. In addition, Section 8 projects provide indirect tax subsidies, which typically average nearly $800 per unit annually. Thus the public subsidy cost for a Section 510 unit was about $1,200 less per year. The primary source of the savings was the reduction in financing costs made possible by the use of CDBG subsidies.[39]

One rehabilitation project in New York has been completed and the cooperative is functioning. At a second site, the rehabilitation is complete, but the building is still being run on a rental basis. At the third site, continued squabbles between the community group and the developer have delayed occupancy of the rehabilitated units and the completion of the remaining units; formation of the cooperative appears to be far in the future. The lessons of 510 are numerous, but two issues of most interest are the effectiveness of the SPO model as a mechanism for community control over the rehabilitation process and the viability of the cooperative approach for low-income, multi-family ownership.

Contrasting the most successful of the New York projects with the other two reveals the problems of establishing community control through special entities such as the SPO.[40] The successful SPO consisted of two nonprofit members with extensive experience in low-income cooperatives and housing development and a developer experienced with federal housing programs. The other two SPOs were considerably less experienced in these areas and relied very heavily on volunteer staff. This suggests that although the organizational model is basically sound, the process is too complex to be implemented by novices or part-time unpaid staff without considerable technical assistance.

It is useful to consider the experience of the other six cities in which the demonstration was implemented.[41] In all but one case, the SPO has proven to be ineffective in managing the cooperative projects. The one success appears to be the result of the SPO being a partnership of mature, experienced groups able to resolve differences, effectively divide the labor, and focus on completing the project. In two cities, the developers demanded a fee for their SPO-related activities, and the community organizations decided they could manage the project themselves; in only one case were they correct. In three cities, the developers took control of the SPO as a result of either disinterest by the nonprofit partner or serious conflicts between their interests. In sum, the SPO concept, intended to weld development experience to community commitment and control, has been ineffective in seven out of nine projects. Very special circumstances are required for the SPO to succeed.

The second issue is whether 510 really created, or can create, viable low-income ownership. Some insights can be drawn by comparing the most and least successful of the New York projects. The successful project had a base of older, working-class tenants who were committed to the project. The other project's tenants were a predominantly welfare-dependent group of larger, mostly female-headed households who expressed dissatisfaction with their housing and neighborhood. Not surprisingly, then, success was related to the basic ability of the tenants to assume leadership and take control of their housing through the cooperative. Families who, disregarding income and assets, would not be successful homeowners are not likely to be good multifamily cooperators.[42]

Equally important may be the potential benefits of the cooperative to the tenants, an issue that relates to neighborhood selection. In the successful site, the 510 project served as an antidisplacement strategy in a neighborhood that was in the path of advancing reinvestment. The cooperative not only provided protection but also held the promise of some future financial gain. The other neighborhood promised no such gain, nor were the tenants threatened with displacement. Thus two basic incentives were missing.[43]

In sum, the 510 demonstration has shown that low-income cooperatives can serve as a relatively cost-effective means to rehabilitate and stabilize deteriorating buildings in declining neighborhoods. It also has shown, however, that considerable technical assistance is required and that the risk of failure is fairly high. The better the condition of the building and neighborhood, the more likely the effort will be to succeed. But better condition implies higher acquisition costs and reduced affordability.

Bringing community groups into partnership with developers proved to be extremely tenuous. Success in this aspect of homesteading would be far more likely if the developer served a clearly circumscribed fee-for-service role in support of the community group. This would preserve the community interest, and the developer would in effect be serving a client. Although this system might add to costs, developers with other interests in the neighborhood may be enticed to discount their services with the prospect for an improved neighborhood environment. Finding community-based organizations capable of managing the process is not difficult. They were successful in NSA sites and have served as rehabilitation developers in many cities.

Market-Oriented Approach to Rehabilitation

Since 1981, HUD has been testing an alternative, market-oriented approach to the rehabilitation of rental housing. This demonstration served as a prototype for the recently enacted Rental Rehabilitation Program (RRP) included in the 1983 Housing Act.[44] In concept, RRP is a substantial departure from previous rehabilitation programs in two principal ways. First, it minimizes the need to regulate the program, relying on market discipline to moderate rent increases after rehabilitation and to optimize postrehabilitation maintenance and investment. Second, it uses a split-subsidy mechanism, which makes a clear distinction between production assistance to the investor and rental assistance to the household.[45]

The split-subsidy concept has been around for many years, especially in western Europe, where programs often make distinctions between object (building) and subject (household) subsidies.[46] In this country, the basic concept has often been employed in a variety of ways (welfare assistance for public housing tenants, for example), but it has never been explicitly designed into a federal program.[47] Theoretically, the approach is an especially appropriate strategy for existing stock. Demand-side subsidies to low-income families allow them to rent privately owned standard housing, and production subsidies for moderate rehabilitation assure an adequate supply of standard housing in the market. The two subsidies are only loosely linked. Households that receive vouchers are not required to live in the subsidized rehabilitation dwellings, nor are all of the dwellings occupied by voucher holders. As in the NSA program, emphasis is placed on the program's flexibility and adaptability to local circumstances. Unlike NSA and homesteading, general neighborhood improvement is not an objective directly supported or required by the program. Although RRP has been touted as a neighborhood preservation tool, it relies on market-control mechanisms rather than public action to erase the effects of negative externalities. It uses the split-subsidy scheme to address the cost-income gap but essentially ignores the issues of externality and control.

The basic elements of the program are straightforward. Owners of rental housing receive a rehabilitation subsidy to bring their dwellings up to local program standards. The form of the subsidy can vary depending on local needs and preferences, but the most common are grants or deferred payment loans for principal reduction. The maximum allowable subsidy is the lesser of $5,000 per dwelling or 50 percent of the rehabilitation cost. This is therefore a moderate rehabilitation program, explicitly designed to correct substandard conditions. After rehabilitation, the units must meet the Section 8 existing housing quality standards.[48] Rehabilitation beyond this level is clearly discouraged, consistent with a conclusion by the GAO, that in eighteen communities that were surveyed, as much as one-third of rental rehabilitation costs could have been saved if repairs were restricted to items violating local housing codes.[49]

In the pure model, the owner, having completed the rehabilitation, is virtually free of government regulation. The benefits to lower-income households are derived from a linked voucher, which they may use to remain in occupancy after rehabilitation or to relocate to standard housing before the rehabilitation is done. Alternatively, a household not previously occupying the building may use the voucher to move in after rehabilitation. Thus the program accomplishes the moderate rehabilitation of one dwelling and the subsidization of one household at the same theoretical cost as using a Section 8 subsidy, but without requiring the household to live in that specific unit to receive a benefit from the program. (In actuality, one voucher is provided for every five rehabilitated units because some lower-income households can afford the market rent for standard dwellings.) The theoretical benefits of the nonregulatory approach come in two forms: reduced administrative costs because of less need for oversight and control and lower subsidies because of reduced investor uncertainty.

Robert Dodge has argued that less bureaucratic control is needed because postrehabilitation rents are allowed to move with the market and, therefore, need not be monitored.[50] Moreover, the lack of rent control eliminates disinvestment incentives so that housing quality standards do not require bureaucratic enforcement; nor are site and neighborhood standards required because there is no incentive, as in rent-limiting subsidy programs, to locate the rehabilitation in the worst neighborhoods.

It is doubtful, however, that an unregulated program would be set up. The General Accounting Office has expressed concern that local governments conducting rental rehabilitation programs of various types had virtually no idea of the income groups that benefited.[51] GAO recommended that tenants in any rental rehabilitation program be legislatively required to report their income and that local evaluations be conducted to assess cost-effectiveness, benefits to tenants, and displacement problems. These recommendations appear to reflect a mistrust of market discipline as an appropriate control for publicly subsidized rehabilitation. GAO also recommended that rents be limited for "some period of time" to assure occupancy of low-income households while still accounting for increases in owner debt or equity. In effect, the GAO stance was that publicly funded rehabilitation requires guarantees of low-income occupancy and protection against abuses by investors, effectively rejecting a basic tenet of the Rental Rehabilitation Program.

Congress apparently agreed with GAO. The legislation creating RRP required that all dwellings be rehabilitated for the benefit of very low-income families (those with incomes less than half the area median).[52] HUD has interpreted this legislation as requiring all initial occupants to meet the very low income standard, although HUD has the discretion to lower the percentage of units to 70 percent to minimize displacement or to meet the housing needs of special groups. No such controls will be applied after initial occupancy, nor is there any minimum initial occupancy period. The proportion of benefits directly accruing to very low-income families over the longer run is, therefore, uncertain.

In addition to the initial occupancy criteria, four other principal regulatory items will require enforcement: postrehabilitation housing standards, presumably including periodic reviews, at least of units occupied by rent voucher recipients; provisions against overcrowding in rehabilitated dwellings; strict provisions regarding displacement and relocation; and the usual nondiscrimination requirements, including prohibitions against discriminating against holders of rent certificates. There also will be continuous monitoring of grantee performance in three substantive areas, adding yet another layer of control, although failure to meet these performance objectives will not trigger enforcement actions but will reduce the grantee's award the following program year. The major criterion is the proportion of rents that are below established fair market rents for the area. The program goal is that 80 percent of all rehabilitated dwellings rent for less than the fair market rent to assure affordability by low-income families. Cities failing to meet that goal will be severely penalized, and those exceeding it will receive a bonus. A second objective is to serve large families, and cities in which at least 70 percent of the rehabilitated dwellings contain three or more bedrooms will receive a bonus. Finally, cities will receive a bonus to the extent that substandard units occupied by very low-income families are rehabilitated. None of these requirements is unreasonable, nor do they together amount to excessive government imposition on the program's participants. They do, however, appear to be only marginally less imposing than those of other programs.

It has been further argued that investors, in the absence of program-imposed rent limitations, will be better able to optimize their returns as market rent levels change and will, therefore, require lower subsidies to participate in RRP as compared to other rehabilitation programs.[53] Because the dwellings must be located in neighborhoods with median incomes no higher than 80 percent of that for the area, and because rehabilitation is restricted to essential repairs, the program's designers are confident that excessive rent increases will be highly unlikely. As market rents increase, however, subsidized investors may raise rents without prior government approval. This provision removes an element of investor risk common to other programs in which rent increases may not be approved or may be delayed. Market-conditioned rent increases will allow investors' revenues to keep pace with operating costs and to capture market appreciation. They do not, however, assure that the rehabilitated dwellings will remain affordable to low-income families or that private investors will not enjoy windfall returns should their building be in a local market that heats up. Unlike the NSA program, RRP has no public objective to use rehabilitation subsidies to help low-income families benefit from neighborhood revitalization. Should RRP, along with other public sector actions or private market forces, lead to rent increases beyond the increase in rental assistance payment levels, lower-income program beneficiaries will face displacement.

The RRP demonstration began in 1981 with the selection of 23 localities that proposed to rehabilitate 1,200 units. Another 162 localities and 14 states, which planned the rehabilitation of 10,000 units, were selected in a second round in 1982. Although available performance data are not extensive, they do provide some insights into the prospects for the program. Activity under the demonstration got off to a slow start with fewer than 1,000 dwellings selected by local governments by January 1983.[54] Only about one-third of these were actually in construction, and only one-quarter of the first round communities had completed more than 20 percent of program goals by that date. (Preliminary data suggest that the rate of activity accelerated dramatically during 1983.)

Like the NSA program, RRP had the objective of targeting small buildings. In RRP, however, the subsidy mechanism is far more appropriate to the purpose and has been more successful. Among the first round cities, more than half the projects (and one-fifth of the dwellings) are in buildings with one to four units; 85 percent of the projects (and 46 percent of the dwellings) are in buildings with ten or fewer units.[55] The demonstration also met its cost objectives in the first group of rehabilitation projects. The average total rehabilitation cost was just under $11,000 per dwelling, including about $4,300 subsidy (but not including the rent certificates for those tenants receiving them). These costs compare favorably with the Section 312 multifamily loan program, for which the average loan was about $10,500 per unit. Under the Section 8 Moderate Rehabilitation Program, total costs were in the same range, at nearly $7,700 per dwelling. Preliminary data suggest that average total costs and subsidy amounts fell during 1983. Among the first group of completed dwellings, 88 percent of the tenants were low income (less than 80 percent of the area median), and the same percentage of dwellings rented at or below the Section 8 existing fair market rent.

An assessment of the progress of the first round cities which solicited the views of local program administrators revealed a few serious implementation problems but general satisfaction with the program.[56] The most frequently cited major problem (fourteen of twenty-three cases) was in getting investors and lenders interested in the program because of general economic problems and high interest rates and also because of reluctance to invest in small properties in poor neighborhoods. Developing acceptable antidisplacement and relocation plans and subsidy mechanisms was of lesser concern but still a major problem noted by about one-fourth to one-fifth of the participants.

When compared to the Section 312 and Section 8 Moderate Rehabilitation programs, RRP fared well in local administrators' views. Between 56 and 65 percent rated RRP as more effective in increasing local control and flexibility and reducing the public role in the rehabilitation process. About half thought RRP had administrative and processing advantages. Less than one-third, however, rated RRP as a more effective mechanism for maximizing production, and 70 percent saw it as no different from Section 312 and Section 8 in assuring high-quality work. Thus the smaller subsidy and increased private sector involvement led to a slower rehabilitation process; flexibility and streamlining reduced administrative burdens but afforded less public control over quality.[57]

Conclusion: The Viability of Strategies for Existing Stock

The 1983 Housing Act contained new budget authorizations estimated to produce 51,500 dwellings through a variety of new construction programs; of these, only 27,500 are for low-income families.[58] In contrast, new budget authority for existing stock programs including the Section 8 Existing Housing Program, a new rental voucher program, and the Rental Rehabilitation Program will assist 107,500 dwellings. In addition, the act authorized two small changes to the urban homesteading program: the use of HUD-owned multifamily projects and the reimbursement of cities for the cost of acquiring and homesteading local single-family properties. Altogether, about two-thirds of new budget authority is focused on the use of existing housing. Besides reflecting the general retrenchment on the domestic side of the federal budget, the law continues the trend away from approaching the housing problem through new construction in an effort to achieve greater efficiency. How successful this orientation will be remains to be seen, but some inferences can be drawn from past experiences.

By far the most telling factor will be the degree to which the demand-side approaches stimulate minor repairs and adequate maintenance and keep dwellings from falling into disrepair and substandard condition. This is true not because of the current size of these programs, which will account for 47,500 units in 1982, but because they contain whatever potential for growth there is in federal housing budgets in the immediate future. The Rental Rehabilitation Program, with 30,000 units over the next two years, and the small increments to urban homesteading will remain as subsidiary supports to boost the available stock of standard housing. Nonetheless, they will be vital components of overall housing and community development strategies for many communities.

Rehabilitation is inherently a slow process that must be carefully tailored to the local situation. Tenants may have to be relocated, and community groups may have to be involved. Small investors have to be coaxed to participate, as do lenders who shy away from small rehabilitation efforts in shaky neighborhoods. Invariably, unexpected structural problems arise during the course of the work, increasing both the cost and time of construction. These and other problems create the need for careful local control. Attempts to short-circuit the process will invariably produce shoddy workmanship, unsatisfied tenants, and public disappointment. Successful strategies will rely on local control, recognize the diversity of actors who must be brought into the process, and use appropriate subsidy mechanisms. They will also view these approaches as parts of broader community-building efforts and tolerate the time required to complete the rehabilitation.

Urban homesteading, either of single-family or multifamily housing, will never be a large-volume program, but it could be a cornerstone of efforts in communities to stabilize local markets while at the same time giving residents control over housing. To assess homesteading in terms of the number of units produced would be to create

Homestead
Success-
small scale

unreasonable expectations for it. Past experiences have shown it to be a successful strategy in the appropriate environments and with committed participants who have the necessary resources. In contrast, the NSA Demonstration showed the difficulties of trying to use the wrong incentive mechanisms to encourage rehabilitation. Although it had the best intentions and achieved some success, it applied the wrong tool and collapsed of its own weight. In theory, the Rental Rehabilitation Program contains the right mix of incentives, although its expectations for minimal regulation, though superimposing market discipline on a subsidy program, may be somewhat high.

Regardless of the specific strategy, past efforts have demonstrated the necessity of housing and neighborhood interaction. The most successful programs have been implemented within a broader revitalization effort; in many cases, they have generated perceptible spillovers. The success of rehabilitation must be measured by its conformance with larger community goals, its contribution to neighborhood improvement, and the degree to which residents are involved in the process and served by it. Rehabilitation will probably never produce large numbers of dwellings, but then there is no reason to hold it to that performance standard.

Notes

1. McFarland and Vivrett (1966:3–40) discusses the advantages of rehabilitation as well as lessons learned from early experiences. Arthur D. Little, Inc. (1971) notes the specific problems of HUD's Project Rehab. See also Center for Community Change (1978) and Listokin (1972).

2. The Housing and Urban-Rural Recovery Act of 1983 (PL 98-181) is summarized in *NAHRO Monitor* (1983).

3. Congressional Budget Office (1982:15–20).

4. Ibid., p. 26; Struyck, Mayer, and Tuccillo (1983:11–17).

5. Clemmer and Simonson (1983:462); Weicher (1980:chap. 2).

6. Grigsby (1963) discusses the housing deterioration process in conceptual terms.

7. One simplification relates to the role of institutional behavior, which may cause rather than result from decline. For a summary of alternative views see Solomon and Vandell (1982).

8. Goetze (1976) and (1979) discusses the role of expectations and perceptions in neighborhood change.

9. Downs (1981).

10. National Association of Housing and Redevelopment Officials (1979).

11. U.S. General Accounting Office (1983).

12. Robison and Ferguson (1981:159–70). A recent survey, intended to be illustrative rather than exhaustive, uncovered a dozen partnership programs implemented by local governments as well as three states that support locally implemented partnership efforts.

13. For detailed descriptions, see Ahlbrandt and Brophy (1976), Clay (1981), or Robison and Ferguson (1981).

14. Clay (1981:169).

15. Ibid., pp. 171–73. A related point, not raised in the corporation's evaluation, is whether savings and loan institutions will sustain enthusiasm for NHS if they perceive that federal regulatory agencies are less vigorously enforcing the Community Reinvestment Act (CRA); NHS contributions served as a measure of local institutions' adherence to CRA provisions.

16. Cohen and Kohler (1983) analyze the problems of nonprofit neighborhood-based organizations during this period.

17. Robison and Ferguson (1981:chap. 6, esp. tables on pp. 99, 116).

18. Except where noted, all the data in the remainder of this section are from Robison and Ferguson (1981).

19. Although any comparison can be misleading, CDGB entitlement communities spent 14 percent of their grants for administrative purposes (U.S. Department of Housing and Urban Development, 1983b:17).

20. Ibid., pp. 126–35.

21. Unless otherwise noted, the information on the HUD homesteading demonstration and its evaluation are from Urban Systems Research and Engineering (1981a).

22. Burchell and Listokin (1981:chap. 1).

23. See, for example, Lake (1979) and Olson and Lachman (1976).

24. Kolodny (1981) discusses problems peculiar to multifamily housing.

25. These are described in ibid.

26. Clay (1981:229–38) and Kolodny (1981:27–36) describe and assess this program.

27. These are described by Kolodny (1981:chap. 4 and 11).

28. The information on NSA is taken from Bleakly et al. (1982).

29. See Urban Homesteading Assistance Board (1977a; 1977b; 1983) regarding homesteading in New York.

30. Cohen (1981).

31. Citizens Housing and Planning Council of New York (1981); Sullivan (1982:tables 1 and 2).

32. Sullivan (1982:table 5).

33. Ibid., table 10.

34. Ibid., table 10, p. 42.

35. See Sumka and Blackburn (1982).

36. The New York City pilot projects are described and assessed in Urban Systems Research and Engineering (1981b) and Holin and Heintz (1982); the activity in the six expansion cities is described in Holin et. al (1983). Schorr (1981) also describes the New York project.

37. Urban Systems Research and Engineering (1981b:chap. 2).

38. Ibid., chap. 1.

39. Holin and Heintz (1982:4–12ff.).
40. Ibid., pp. 4–7ff.
41. Holin et. al. (1983).
42. Holin and Heintz (1982:chap. 4).
43. Ibid.
44. PL 98-181; see *NAHRO Monitor* (1983).
45. The advantages of this approach are discussed in Dodge (1983).
46. See Dumouchel (1978) and Welfeld (1972).
47. The Baltimore NHS developed a Neighborhood Rental Services program in the late 1970s. It combined Section 312 low-interest rehabilitation loans with Section 8 certificates to make housing available to lower-income families in areas undergoing or likely to experience revitalization.
48. These are summarized in U.S. Department of Housing and Urban Development (1978).
49. U.S. General Accounting Office (1983).
50. Dodge (1983).
51. U.S. General Accounting Office (1983).
52. The legislation and the preliminary HUD program design are described in *NAHRO Monitor* (1983; 1984).
53. Dodge (1983).
54. U.S. Department of Housing and Urban Development (1983b:120).
55. The data on project cost and size are from ibid., p. 120.
56. U.S. Department of Housing and Urban Development (1983a).
57. Ibid., pp. 25ff.
58. New construction under PL 98-181 includes a new development grant program (30,000 units), Section 202 housing for the elderly (14,000), and conventional and Indian Public Housing (7,500). See *NAHRO Monitor* (1983).

References

Ahlbrandt, Roger S., and Paul Brophy. 1976. *Neighborhood Revitalization.* Lexington, Mass.: D. C. Heath.
Arthur D. Little, Inc. 1971. *Project Rehab Monitoring Report.* Washington, D.C.: U.S. Department of Housing and Urban Development.
Bleakly, Kenneth D., et al. 1982. *The NSA Demonstration: A Case Study of Local Control over Housing Development.* Washington, D.C.: U.S. Department of Housing and Urban Development.
Burchell, Robert W., and Listokin, David. 1981. *The Adaptive Reuse Handbook.* New Brunswick: Center for Urban Policy Research.
Center for Community Change. 1978. *Annotated Bibliography on Housing Rehabilitation.* Harrisburg: Pennsylvania Department of Community Affairs.
Citizens Housing and Planning Council of New York. 1981. "In Rem: Recommendations for Reforms." New York: Citizens Housing and Planning Council of New York.

Clay, Phillip L. 1981. *Neighborhood Partnerships in Action.* Washington, D.C.: Neighborhood Reinvestment Corporation.

Clemmer, Richard B., and Simonson, John C. 1983. "Trends in Substandard Housing, 1940–1980." *Journal of the American Real Estate and Urban Economics Association* 10:442–64.

Cohen, Barbara. 1981. "Service Needs of Lower Income Housing Cooperatives." Washington, D.C.: U.S. Department of Housing and Urban Development.

Cohen, Rich, and Miriam Kohler. 1983. "Neighborhood Development Organizations after the Federal Funding Cutbacks: Current Conditions and Future Directions." Washington, D.C.: U.S. Department of Housing and Urban Development.

Congressional Budget Office. 1982. *Federal Housing Assistance: Alternative Approaches.* Washington, D.C.: U.S. Government Printing Office.

Dodge, Robert I. 1983. "The Real Cost of Rent Limitations in Rehabilitation Programs." In David D. Listokin, ed., *Housing Rehabilitation: Economic, Social, and Policy Perspectives.* New Brunswick: Center for Urban Policy Research, pp. 275–83.

Downs, Anthony. 1981. *Neighborhoods and Urban Development.* Washington, D.C.: Brookings Institution.

Dumouchel, Robert J. 1978. *European Housing Rehabilitation Experience: A Summary and Analysis.* Washington, D.C.: National Association of Housing and Redevelopment Officials.

Goetze, Rolf. 1976. *Building Neighborhood Confidence.* Cambridge, Mass.: Ballinger.

———. 1979. *Understanding Neighborhood Change.* Cambridge, Mass.: Ballinger.

Grigsby, William. 1963. *Housing Markets and Public Policy.* Philadelphia: University of Pennsylvania Press.

Holin, Mary Joel, and Kathleen Heintz. 1982. *Coops for Neighborhoods: A Report on the New York City 510 Demonstration.* Springfield, Va.: National Technical Information Service.

Holin, Mary Joel, et al. 1983. *Baseline Report on the Section 510 Homeownership Opportunities Demonstration.* Washington, D.C.: U.S. Department of Housing and Urban Development.

Irby, Iredia. 1983. "Housing Problems in 1980 (A Synopsis)." Washington, D.C.: U.S. Department of Housing and Urban Development.

Kolodny, Robert. 1981. *Multi-Family Housing: Treating the Existing Stock.* Washington, D.C.: National Association of Housing and Redevelopment Officials.

Lake, Robert W. 1979. *Real Estate Tax Delinquency.* New Brunswick: Center for Urban Policy Research.

Listokin, David. 1972. *The Dynamic of Housing Rehabilitation.* New Brunswick: Rutgers University.

———, ed. 1983. *Housing Rehabilitation: Economic, Social, and Policy Perspectives.* New Brunswick: Center for Urban Policy Research.

Lowry, Ira S. 1982. *Experimenting with Housing Allowances: Executive Sum-*

mary. Washington, D.C.: U.S. Department of Housing and Urban Development.

McFarland, M. Carter, and Walter K. Vivrett. 1966. *Residential Rehabilitation.* Minneapolis: University of Minnesota.

NAHRO Monitor. 1983. "The 1983 Housing Act." December 15, vol. 5, no. 23.

———. 1984. "HUD Describes Design of New Rental Rehabilitation Program." January 31, vol. 6, no. 2, pp. 4–7.

National Association of Housing and Redevelopment Officials. 1979. *Designing Local Rehab Programs.* Washington, D.C.: U.S. Department of Housing and Urban Development.

Olson, Susan, and M. Leanne Lachman. 1976. *Tax Delinquency in the Inner-City.* Lexington, Mass.: Lexington Books.

Robison, Maynard T., and Gary D. Ferguson. 1981. *Neighborhood Housing Services and the Neighborhood Reinvestment Corporation.* Washington, D.C.: U.S. Department of Housing and Urban Development.

Schorr, Philip. 1981. "The Homeownership Tool: A 510 Demonstration Program Report." *New York Affairs* 6, no. 4:29–32.

Solomon, Arthur, and Kerry Vandell. 1982. "Alternative Perspective on Neighborhood Decline." *Journal of the American Planning Association* 48 (Winter):81–98.

Struyk, Raymond J., Neill Mayer, and John C. Tuccillo. 1983. *Federal Housing Policy at President Reagan's Midterm.* Washington, D.C.: Urban Institute.

Sullivan, Brian T. 1982. *Analysis and Assessment of the Alternative Management Programs for New York City's in Rem Properties.* Washington, D.C.: U.S. Department of Housing and Urban Development.

Sumka, Howard J., and Anthony J. Blackburn. 1982. "Multifamily Urban Homesteading: A Key Approach to Low-Income Housing." *Journal of Housing* 39(4):104–7.

U.S. Department of Housing and Urban Development. 1978. *Revitalizing North American Neighborhoods.* Washington, D.C.: Office of Policy Development and Research.

———. 1983a. "The Rental Rehabilitation Program Demonstration: Experiences of First Round Participating Communities." Washington, D.C.: Office of Community Planning and Development.

———. 1983b. *1983 Consolidated Annual Report to Congress on Community Development Programs.* Washington, D.C.: Office of Community Planning and Development.

U.S. General Accounting Office. 1983. *Rental Rehabilitation with Limited Federal Involvement: Who Is Doing It? At What Cost? Who Benefits?* RCED-83-148. Washington, D.C.: U.S. Government Printing Office.

Urban Homesteading Assistance Board. 1977a. *Sweat Equity Homesteading of Multifamily Housing in New York City.* Washington, D.C.: U.S. Department of Housing and Urban Development.

———. 1977b. *Third Annual Progress Report.* New York: Cathedral House.

———. 1983. "Current Programs and Projects." New York: Cathedral House.

Urban Systems Research and Engineering. 1981a. *Evaluation of the Urban*

Homesteading Demonstration: Final Report. Vol. 1, *Summary Assessment.*
Washington, D.C.: U.S. Department of Housing and Urban Development.
————. 1981b. *The New York City 510 Demonstration: The Neighborhood
Coop Experiment.* Washington, D.C.: U.S. Department of Housing and Urban
Development.
Weicher, John C. 1980. *Housing: Federal Policies and Programs.* Washington,
D.C.: American Enterprise Institute.
Welfeld, Irving. 1972. "That Housing Problem—the American vs. European Ex-
perience." *Public Interest* 27 (Spring):78–95.

7

Finding the Money to Finance Low-Cost Housing

Kevin Villani

Housing investment in the period from 1945 to 1979 enjoyed a privileged niche in the nation's credit markets and was also subject to generous treatment in the income tax code. The ability of the nation's savings and loan system to secure a large volume of deposits at stable, often below market, interest rates, coupled with the mortgage insurance and guarantee programs of the Veterans' Administration (VA) underwrote several generations of long-term, fixed, low-interest Federal Housing Administration mortgages. At the same time, the deductibility of mortgage interest and local property taxes lowered the cost of homeownership. Housing economists have long argued the question as to whether, on balance, these preferences actually lowered the net cost of housing to its consumers or were merely capitalized to the benefit of incumbent property owners, investors, and speculators. Theory aside, however, the period in which these preferences were operative was marked by a consistently high rate of private housing production, much of it marketed at prices within the reach of a large proportion of the nation's households. As Weicher points out in Chapter 3, the "rising tide" of housing production has undoubtedly improved housing conditions for all income sectors, including the poor.

Without necessarily defending, in regard to allocation of national resources, a system of credit and tax preferences biased toward housing, this chapter will examine the ways in which these preferences have changed since 1979 and how the new credit and tax environment continues to nurture the production and ownership of low-cost housing. The major facts regarding credit and tax preferences in the 1980s are as follows. The deregulation of financial markets has forced housing to compete with other credit users on more equal (and volatile) terms. The potential negative effects of this more competitive credit environment have been offset somewhat by below-market, state-sponsored financing, by the expansion of national secondary mortgage markets, and by new "creative" mortgage finance instruments. The federal tax subsidies embodied in tax-free state credit were supplemented by extensive new housing tax preferences built into the Economic Recovery Tax Act of 1981 (ERTA), although these were curtailed by the 1984 deficit reduction act and altered in favor of low-income housing in 1986 tax reform legislation.

The net effects of these changes, both positive and negative, and of the increasing instability of the credit and tax environment require increasing doses of "creative" private and public entrepreneurship to take maximum advantage of available credit and tax preferences. Everyone involved in housing investment and finance is, in the words of Alice, having to run faster and faster to stay in the same place. This entrepreneurial frenzy appears more urgent to all concerned because of the drying up of direct budget appropriations to subsidized housing. Indirect subsidies represent the only game in town, a game requiring ever greater skill and ingenuity to play.

Policy Context for Financing Housing

Traditionally, the federal government has insulated the system of financing housing from other capital markets, hoping to maintain a steady supply of mortgage funds at reasonable cost. In contrast, the system that has emerged since 1979 is not protected from other credit markets by federal regulations and does not attempt to control the price or quantity of mortgage funds. The system allows capital to flow freely between markets to the sector using the funds most efficiently and therefore providing the greatest return. This strategy opens the mortgage market to new actors and requires the development of new instruments to enable investors to participate in financing housing.

This unprotected system of financing housing places new demands on all housing investors and developers, private as well as public, building for the market rate as well as the subsidized sectors. Linking the system of financing housing with other capital markets also requires strong secondary markets and new financial instruments to bring mortgage funds from a new class of investors to mortgage originators. This function is particularly important because housing must compete for credit with the growing claims of government and business. Private savings in the near term are unlikely to provide enough funds to meet all mortgage demands because government borrowing is expected to consume 80 percent of domestic private savings for the next five years.

Under a deregulated finance system, mortgage funds will continue to be available, but the costs of those funds will be more sensitive to returns on other investments. Therefore, mortgage rates will reflect the demand for credit from all borrowing sectors. Finally, the development of federally subsidized credit will be increasingly driven "underground" primarily through the mechanism of federal income tax subsidies.

Taxation of Housing

Housing has always been well-treated by the federal income tax system. Homeowners have been able to deduct their mortgage interest and property taxes without having to declare their imputed rental income, preferences that have grown in importance with tax bracket creep and rising interest and property tax expenses. Investors in rental housing, and presumably their tenants, have benefited from these provisions as well as from liberal depreciation allowances and generous capital gains treatment.

The long-standing tax preferences available to rental housing were given a significant boost by the tax law changes enacted in 1981. This is the case even though underlying the Economic Recovery Tax Act of 1981 was a desire to revise the tax code provisions affecting capital allocation to redirect capital away from housing, primarily by reducing the tax burden of other sources of income. But although the benefits of ERTA flowed primarily to the corporate sector, residential rental housing also ended up faring very well.

ERTA has had major implications for the residential housing market, particularly low-income housing, because of significant changes in the tax treatment of depreciation, capital recovery periods, and amortization of interest and property taxes during the construction period. ERTA allowed new low-income rental housing to use a 200 percent accelerated declining balance depreciation method. The minimum depreciation period for all rental housing was reduced by ERTA from an average of thirty years previously to fifteen. The 1984 deficit reduction act raised the depreciation period to nineteen years generally but retained the fifteen-year depreciation for low-income housing. As with other new rental housing property, recapture is limited to excess (over straight line) depreciation only. (Before 1981, the principal tax benefit available for low-income rental housing was a phase-out of the recapture liability, which favored low-income rental housing by allowing the developer to write off interest and property taxes accrued during the construction period.)

The combination of these tax provisions resulted in a significant incentive for the rehabilitation of low-income housing. It permitted an investor in low-income housing to elect 200 percent declining balance depreciation and a fifteen-year tax-useful life for the shell and other areas of a building not to be rehabilitated, together with the use of Section 167(k) sixty-month amortization for the areas to be rehabilitated.

The 1981 tax law changes certainly had the potential for reducing rents for low-income tenants in renewal projects. Analysts have found that the difference in tax treatment between low-income and conventional rental housing could create potential rent differences of 10 to 30 percent, depending on a variety of factors. Overall, the required rental income in the post-ERTA environment on a representative low-income housing development was between 11 and 23 percent less than on a comparable project that did not qualify as low-income. The actual difference depended on the prevailing mortgage rates, the cost of construction, and the structure of the development syndication—that is, the tax benefits were divided among investors and tenants.

The tax revenue forgone by the federal government represented the real cost of providing lower rents for low-income housing. Such tax expenditures should be compared to the on-budget costs of providing direct rental housing subsidies for new production to determine whether they are indeed more efficient. My own estimates, on the basis of admittedly slender empirical studies, suggest that a cost comparison between tax incentives and production subsidies would favor tax incentives, although like all tax preferences, they are much more costly than most of their advocates realize or are willing to acknowledge.

The main thrust of tax reform in the mid 1980s was to reduce the role of the tax code in capital allocation. This reversed a long historical trend, as highlighted in Table 7.1. Treatment for low-income housing is actually more favorable under the new Tax Reform Act of 1986. Accelerated depreciation and the long-term capital gain *deductions* have been replaced with significant *credits*. For low-income housing these can represent as much as 9 percent each year for ten years.

The Real Estate Syndication System for Assisted Housing

There has to be a mechanism for channeling the tax advantages of real estate investments for upper- and middle-income individuals to low-income tenants. That mechanism is a real estate syndication. The major participants in real estate syndications are builder-developer teams, syndicators, and investors.

Table 7.1.

Major Tax Changes Affecting Residential Real Estate Investment

Affected tax area	Pre-1964 tax rules	Tax Reform Act of 1964	Tax Reform Act of 1969
Capital gains deduction	50 percent deduction 50 percent taxed as ordinary income	No change	No change
Construction period interest and taxes	1-year write-off	No change	No change
Depreciable life	30–40 years	No change	No change
Depreciation method (maximum)	200 percent declining balance, sum of years digits	No change	Same as pre-1964 for new property, 125 percent declining balance for existing property
Depreciation recapture on "net excess depreciation"	None	Recapture for properties held less than 10 years (120 months)[b]	Recapture for properties held less than 16.7 years (200 months)[c]
Regular minimum tax	None	None	10 percent additional tax on tax preferences (excess depreciation, capital gains deduction) above statutory limits
Low-income housing credit			

[a]Phase in schedule to reach a full ten years by 1982.
[b]Recapture phased out for properties held less than ten years.
[c]Ten-year phase-out maintained for low-income property.

Tax Reform Act of 1976	Revenue Act of 1978	Economic Recovery Act of 1981	Tax Reform Act of 1986
No change	60 percent deduction 40 percent taxed as ordinary income	No change	Deduction repealed
10-year amortization[a]	No change	1-year write-off for low-income units	No change
No change	No change	15 years	27.5 years
No change	No change	175 percent declining balance for new and existing property, 200 percent for low-income property	Straight line
Recapture for properties held less than depreciable life	No change	No change	No change
Rate changed to 15 percent and statutory limits reduced	Capital gains deduction no longer taxed by regular minimum tax	No change	20 percent rate applied to a base of regular taxable income plus preferences: one-half of financial over taxable income, certain otherwise tax-exempt interest
			9 percent credit each year for 10 years for new construction or rehabilitations of low-income housing; 4 percent credit for 10 years if financed by tax-exempt bonds or for purchase of existing housing

A builder-developer team consists of a group of specialists, including a sponsor, architect, builder, manager, and lawyer. The sponsor usually operates as project initiator and developer, selecting project sites, dealing with government agencies and local officials, and preparing and submitting development proposals. Local housing agencies can serve as sponsors directly or indirectly through some nonprofit subsidiaries. In the low-cost housing field the nonprofit sponsor (a church group, for example) is the most common prototype. The builder takes responsibility for construction of the project from a set of plans at an agreed-upon cost. There is often a profit- and risk-sharing arrangement between the builder and sponsor under which the builder contributes to the preconstruction development costs for a share in the project. Other members of the team usually receive fixed fees for services.

A syndicator is a project wholesaler or marketer, who buys the project from the builder-developer, structures a legal ownership package, most often a limited partnership, and sells the partnership shares to passive investors. The passive investors are limited partners, generally individuals seeking a tax shelter to offset income from other sources. Under the Internal Revenue Code, a limited partner deducts a pro rata share of partnership losses and includes a pro rata share of partnership gains in his taxable income. Typically, the partnership experiences a substantial negative cash flow during the construction period and tax losses during the early years of operation even though its actual cash flow may be positive. This occurs when the depreciation allowances exceed the debt service payments.

Activity in apartment syndication during the early 1980s suggested renewed interest in rental housing investment generally. Consolidated Capital Corporation, one of the largest apartment syndicators, brought to the market forty-seven buildings with a total price of approximately $400 million. The buyers were small private placement limited partnerships. Under market conditions of the time, transactions for such properties take place with investors contributing up to 30 percent of the project cost, payable over two to three years. The remainder of the project was financed by variable rate mortgages. These mortgages were negotiated with below-market interest rates applying for five to ten years, at which time they must be refinanced at market rates.

The Tax Reform Act of 1986 may eliminate real estate syndications as a source of equity financing for income-producing housing. The ability of investors to deduct losses from a syndication will generally be limited to offsetting gains from other passive investments. Remaining losses cannot be offset against taxable income until later years, when the investor has excess passive income over losses or when the property is sold. Thus the real estate syndication tax deferral is eliminated, and with it the implicit government housing support.

State Housing Finance Agencies and Mortgage Revenue Bonds

One way or another, virtually all indirect housing subsidies are federal income tax subsidies. The major alternative, or supplement, to the tax subsidy offered directly to investors is the federal tax subsidy channeled through the states' ability to raise funds by issuing tax-free bonds. The typical vehicle for their activity is the state or local housing finance agency (HFA). State and local housing finance agencies participate in housing finance to provide mortgage funds to developers or home buyers at below the prevailing market rate. To do so, HFAs acquire funds at less than the market rate by issuing tax-exempt mortgage revenue bonds (MRBs). This practice began in the 1960s primarily to finance multifamily housing. In 1975 state HFAs issued $900 million in multifamily MRBs, which represented approximately 3 percent of the total municipal bonds issued that year. In the same year, state HFAs began issuing tax-exempt MRBs for single-family as well as multifamily housing. By 1980, single-family tax-exempt MRB issues out-weighed multifamily issues by a factor of 3.6, generating $5 billion. Many of these bonds were issued at the county or city level.

The tremendous increase in state and local HFAs' use of tax-exempt MRBs to finance low-rate single-family mortgages has prompted charges that the program was not achieving its original objectives of targeting benefits to low-income households. Many analysts claimed that most of the projects financed would have been built without the subsidized funds, that the subsidy (because of the bond's tax-exempt status) was not cost-effective, and that the tax revenue losses were growing unacceptably large. In response to the unfavorable review of the MRB device, Congress passed the Mortgage Bond Tax Act of 1980 (the Ullman Act), which prohibited the use of tax-exempt MRBs to finance single-family housing after December 31, 1983. The act also placed additional restrictions on uses of the proceeds of MRBs so as to target the subsidy more precisely to low-income housing, by requiring state and local HFAs that issue tax-exempt MRBs for multi-family housing projects to set aside 20 percent of each issue for low-income households.

In 1982, the Tax Equity and Fiscal Responsibility Act (TEFRA) clarified the types of multifamily projects qualifying for the bond financing and eased the restriction for eligible single-family housing. TEFRA reduced the period during which units had to be set aside for low-income households, and the Internal Revenue Service (IRS) agreed to allow single-family houses to be designated as housing "projects" and financed as rental housing. This provision allows builders to refinance with MRBs unsold subdivisions of single-family houses as if they were multifamily developments.

The Ullman Act's prohibition of tax-exempt MRBs for single-family housing after December 1983 sparked an intense political battle. By 1984, the Deficit Reduction Act reauthorized single-family MRBs for four years but limited the dollar volume for each state to the greater of $150 per resident or $200 million. Many states jumped to issue MRBs, selling bonds before President Ronald Reagan actually signed the legislation. The interest rates on the mortgages funded by MRBs should be about 200 to 350 basis points (2 to 3.5 percent) below conventional mortgage rates, presently a net reduction in the monthly cost borne by the ultimate housing consumer of 10 to 15 percent.

While reauthorizing single-family MRBs, the 1984 Deficit Reduction Act also offers state HFAs the opportunity to trade in some of their bond authority and issue mortgage credit certificates (MCC) instead. MCCs provide first-time buyers with tax credits for the purchase, improvement, or rehabilitation of principal residences that do not exceed 110 percent of the purchase price of the average house in the region. The home buyer obtains a nonsubsidized mortgage from any lender, then claims a federal tax credit for a specified percentage of his mortgage interest payments. The tax credit essentially "buys down" the interest rate on a market rate mortgage. The market for tax-exempt financing was hit hard in 1986, as tax-exempt yields rose above taxable treasury yields. The source of the problem was speculation regarding tax reform and the near certainty of reductions in marginal tax rates.

Tax reform of 1986 will limit the role of tax-exempt mortgage-revenue issues in the housing market. Dollar volume of mortgage revenue and private purpose bonds will generally be limited to $75 per capita through 1987, and then fall to $50 per capita. In addition, banks will no longer be allowed to deduct interest expense for funds used to purchase and carry tax-exempt bonds. Property and casualty companies will have to pay taxes on income from tax-exempt bonds, and other companies with tax-exempt bond income may have to pay some taxes on such earnings under new minimum tax provisions.

Channeling the Mortgage Revenue Bond Funds

There are a variety of ways in which state HFAs can channel mortgage revenue bond funds to assisted housing and any number of possible restrictions. The principal mechanism in about every case represents some form of a "loans-to-lender" program. The loans-to-lender device links the state HFA as the ultimate source of funds with two banks, one acting as trustee for the bondholders and one as lender to the ultimate mortgagor. To obtain the highest possible bond rating, the state HFA establishes a trust agreement with a commercial bank selected to act as trustee for the purchasers of HFA bonds. A lender bank (or banks) is authorized to enter into mortgage agreements with borrowers up to some specified lending limit. Next, the agency's bonds are sold and the proceeds deposited into the lender's account. Then the lender issues certificates of deposit to the trustee matching the terms of the bonds. Finally, the lender disburses the mortgage funds to the borrower. As the borrower repays the lender, the lender pays the trustee, who in turn pays the bondholders. The advantage of this web of transactions is an AAA rating that Standard and Poor's gives the HFA bonds. The high rating and tax-exempt status render the bonds extremely marketable and yield the interest rate discount that subsidizes the assisted housing. To secure the most favorable bond rating, state HFAs have incorporated various forms of guarantees in their loans-to-lenders programs. Most lender guarantees take one of the following forms: bonds are collateralized (by the trustee) with a bank letter of credit secured by the value of government securities or mortgages; bonds are secured by a first lien on the cash flow from the collateral securities or mortgages, which lowers the required collateral amount and makes a letter of credit unnecessary; bonds are secured by the mortgages issued under the program together with a letter of credit from the principal lender; or bonds are guaranteed by private bond insurance or other third-party guarantees.

After the source of funds is secured, the key policy determinations of the state HFA are allocation of the funds and deciding what types of mortgage instruments to offer. The funds may be randomly distributed to qualified borrowers, but usually they are targeted for specific projects or areas. For instance, in November 1983 the New York

City Housing Development Corporation inaugurated its loans-to-lenders program with a $125 million bond issue dedicated to financing twelve public housing turnkey projects containing two thousand apartments. They were subsequently sold to the New York City Housing Authority at predetermined prices.

In another example, the Massachusetts HFA in 1984 authorized a new program called SHARP, State Housing Assistance for Rental Production. The program used HFA bond proceeds to supplement federal and state subsidies for low-income private rental projects. The HFA subsidy takes the form of fifteen-year low-interest deferred-payment loans, funded by agency bond issues, to write down the interest rate on the permanent mortgage loan to as low as 5 percent.

Regardless of the future status of tax-exempt MRBs, state and local HFAs can always issue taxable bonds to finance single-family housing to avoid the restrictions placed on the proceeds of tax-exempt bonds. According to *Savings & Loan News* (March 1983), taxable bonds could be used in a loans-to-lenders network, with S&Ls functioning as bond issuer, trustee, lender, and investment banker. This approach does not furnish a very deep financing subsidy but would reduce interest rates somewhat and could be combined with other state subsidy programs. Several state HFAs already have the ability to issue taxable bonds for single or multifamily housing, but to date only Alaska has exercised this authority.

Developments in Secondary Markets

The third key component in the new environment of housing finance is the growing role of the secondary markets. A necessary companion to the deregulation of housing finance and the emergence of new investments in housing finance is the ability to make these investments liquid. The more viable and active the secondary mortgage markets, the greater the ability of bank and other financing instrumentalities to lend, and the more acceptable novel finance instruments become.

In effect, the three principal U.S. government secondary markets, Federal National Mortgage Association (Fannie Mae), Government National Mortgage Association (Ginnie Mae), and the Federal Home Loan Mortgage Corporation (Freddie Mac), have had to step up their activity and absorb a larger volume of both taxable and tax-exempt mortgage debt. These agencies have played a dual role in making more financing available for low-income housing. They have guaranteed the mortgages issued by state housing financing agencies and traditional lenders, and they have then repurchased these mortgages from the lending organizations. In their role as guarantor, the secondary markets have lowered the effective interest on low-cost housing mortgages (in addition to any discount related to the tax-exempt feature). In their role as purchaser, the secondary markets have made more funds available to finance developments of new or rehabilitated housing.

The coffers of Ginnie Mae are replenished with federal tax revenue, but the other secondary markets (Fannie Mae and Freddie Mac) are not explicitly subsidized. They are funded by bond issues at prevailing market rates of interest.

Fannie Mae and Freddie Mac are not exclusively in the business of underwriting mortgages for low-cost housing, but they are willing and able to direct as much of their activity in that direction as is justified by the activity of the originating state agencies and other lenders. They are also increasingly creative in the combination of their guarantee and repurchase functions. Some examples are as follows.

Fannie Mae has served as the guarantor for tax-exempt multifamily bonds issued by the city of San Jose. The proceeds of the bonds were used to make a loan to a major developer. The loan was originated by a mortgage banker according to Fannie Mae's underwriting standards for a twelve-year term. At the end of twelve years, the developer has the option of refinancing the loan with Fannie Mae at the prevailing market rate. In case of a default by the developer, the bond trustee can ask Fannie Mae to buy the project mortgage and repurchase its loans. The city also obtained a letter of credit for twenty months to secure the developer's loan during construction.

Fannie Mae also has several programs targeted for lower-income home buyers. In one program, Municipal Tri-party Participations, Fannie Mae, a local or state HFA, or a local lender each takes part of the mortgage loan. The HFA charges zero interest on its portion of the loan, and the local lender usually offers a rate slightly below the prevailing market rate. The blended result is an inexpensive mortgage loan.

In another program, the Rehabilitation Loan Program, Fannie Mae purchases the mortgage on a property slated for rehabilitation, based on the property's expected price after successful rehabilitation. This sale gives the borrower money for refinancing and rehabilitation under a single debt instrument. This program could be complemented with grants from a municipal agency, in Municipal Tri-party Participations, or through local tax abatements.

Another innovation in secondary markets is the creation of a new debt instrument: the Collateralized Mortgage Obligation (CMO), which attracts nontraditional sources of funds to the housing market by using existing mortgages as collateral for CMO issues. In effect, this device permits the major secondary markets to double the liquidity associated with a pool of existing mortgages—first by purchasing the mortgages (making the original lender liquid) and then by issuing CMOs with the same mortgages as collateral.

CMOs are attractive investment instruments for pension funds, insurance companies, commercial bank trust departments, and other entities that are unable or reluctant to invest directly in mortgages. Because the funding under all these rubrics originates with the secondary market agencies, the CMO device can be seen primarily as a way of justifying a larger volume of secondary market borrowing in the bond market. Thus these various creative devices are another way to channel a larger share of the nation's aggregate capital into housing.

An additional appeal of CMO financing is that it offers interest rates below that of more traditional secondary financing. Current evidence suggests that primary market rates have been lowered by 50 to 100 basis points (0.5 to 1.0 percentage point) by using this financing vehicle. This is a potentially powerful tool in the hands of credit agencies that have special charter obligation to finance low-income housing. As of June 1986, $51.1 billion in CMOs have been issued. That $51.1 billion consists of $8.0 billion in Freddie Mac CMOs, $12.5 billion in builder bonds, $6.5 billion in thrift CMOs, $2.4 billion in thrift private securities, $20.9 billion in other private securities, and $0.8 billion in other CMOs.

Secondary Markets for Partnership Shares

Debt financing for multifamily housing has been fairly easy to sell. The same cannot be said of equity interests. This is particularly inhibiting to investors in syndications to finance low-income housing because of the long-term nature of the investment. One of the effects of the long period of high mortgage interest rates on real estate markets has been a virtual inability of many sellers to implement transactions without taking part in the financing. As a result, it has become very difficult to finance multifamily housing developments through the use of public syndications. Many investors remain locked in their partnership participations even when the underlying properties have been sold. For example, to sell a housing development, it has become necessary to take back long-term paper (twelve to fifteen years) for any sale proceeds above the amount needed to pay off the short-term debt.

This lack of liquidity has resulted in two problems. First, it has prevented investors from recovering their funds from existing conventional housing partnerships and reinvesting them in new developments. Second, it probably has discouraged many potential investors from participating in rental housing developments.

An interesting response to the lack of liquidity in real estate partnership shares is the effort to develop a secondary market in these shares by a group of real estate syndicators, developers, and investment bankers. One example of a secondary market is being developed by MCO Equities, Inc., a publicly owned entity controlled by a Houston financial group. The objectives of MCO Equities is to provide a market for shares in real estate limited partnerships. It will achieve this objective by enabling partnerships to trade all or part of their otherwise illiquid holdings for stock in MCO Equities. MCO, in turn, will hold a large, nationally diversified real estate portfolio. An important advantage of such a secondary market to its participants is that exchanges can take place without adverse tax consequences because under certain circumstances, trading property for stock may be considered a tax-free exchange.

An attempt in 1982 to create a secondary market for real estate partnership holdings, on a much smaller scale than the MCO Equities plan, has apparently been successful. First Capital sponsored three real estate partnerships during the period 1978-80 that were supposed to dissolve within five to seven years. When market conditions made dissolution unwise, First Capital developed an exchange device whereby limited partners exchanged their holdings for corporate stock. Wall Street investment banking firms such as Merrill Lynch appear to be showing some interest in using a secondary real estate market in relation to the large conventional public limited partnerships.

Primary Market Developments

Numerous creative financing schemes have appeared in the primary market. These instruments improve the affordability of housing, permitting more middle-income families to purchase homes and reducing the cost of multifamily projects that are likely to house low-income families. The government has begun to include some of these creative financing methods in housing programs. Congress authorized the use of FHA-insured graduated payment mortgages (GPMs) and shared appreciation mortgages (SAMs) for multifamily housing in November 1983 in a section of the Housing and Urban-Rural Recovery Act of 1983. HUD has issued guidelines for these instruments, which will make multifamily housing units more afford-able and offer advantages for lenders.

GPMs are based on the assumption that most developers expect their total rental incomes to increase over the life of the mortgage loan. In a GPM, the payments are small at first and increase gradu-ally for the first five (or ten) years of the loan. Therefore, GPMs are attractive to developers of low-income housing who are limited by a shortage of liquid assets but expect this constraint to ease in the im-mediate future. GPMs should be attractive in the multifamily mar-ket because they enable developers to defer more of the property's cost to a period when the project should be operating at a profit.

GPMs for single-family housing have been available through FHA since 1977 and totaled more than $17 billion through September 1982. They are available with five different amortization plans, dif-fering in the length of graduated payment period and the rate of increase in monthly payments. The most common plan is a 7.5 percent increase in payments for the first five years of the thirty year term.

Although GPMs help borrowers, they do not protect the lender from unexpected changes in market interest rates. The President's Commission on Housing has recommended a hybrid of the GPM and adjustable rate mortgage (ARM) in which the lender could adjust the interest rate and payments after the graduated payment period. The new HUD authority did not include this type of instrument.

Shared appreciation mortgages (SAMs) reduce the developer's ini-tial costs and insulate lenders and borrowers from inflation's impact on the nominal value of the property. The lender offers to reduce the mortgage loan rate and/or the down payment in return for a share of the development's appreciated value, to be paid when the develop-ment is sold or the mortgage is terminated. SAMs make multifamily residential mortgages more affordable because the borrower defers payment of the mortgagee's share of the appreciated value. SAMs provide lenders with a hedge against inflation to the extent that the price of the property varies directly with inflation. In addition, this partial hedge renders the S&Ls' portfolios less vulnerable to unex-pected changes in interest rates so that the institutions can offer more indexed liabilities. SAMs have been offered since 1980 for single-family homes, but the same principles are applicable to multi-family projects. The developer and the lender share the risk associ-ated with changes in the nominal value of the property over the life of the loan. SAMs are safer than conventional mortgages in an infla-tionary environment and as safe as price level adjusted mortgages if the rate at which the property's value appreciates is the same as the inflation rate.

Conclusion

As the old cliché says, there is no "free lunch." This chapter has explored a variety of ever-changing tax subsidies and financing mechanisms that can be deployed to lower the price of housing, including housing for low-income families. Anything that makes a good cheaper is a subsidy, and all subsidies must be paid for somehow. Where do these housing subsidies come from? Overwhelmingly the various devices discussed here fall under the category of "tax expenditures," in other words, federal revenues forgone. Changes in national tax law in the early 1980s favored housing investment—and low-cost housing in particular—directly. The activities of state housing finance agencies represent indirect tax expenditures by way of state use of tax-exempt bond issues. In both cases, there can be no question that the value of the tax subsidy to the ultimate housing consumer is considerably less than the cost to the treasury. But as many housing analysts point out, it is Congress that has dictated such an "inefficient" policy by closing the direct budget subsidy front door as it opened the tax subsidy back door even further. In 1986, Congress began to swing the back door shut as well.

The other source of subsidies that these devices tap is the federal government's easier access to capital. A large part of the mortgage borrowing necessary to finance housing—taxable and tax-exempt alike—is in the end sold to federal secondary credit markets (such as Fannie Mae). As federal agencies, they have a favored position in the national credit market, a benefit they pass on to the lenders whose assets they guarantee and purchase. The true cost of the federal government's role as housing lender of last resort is hard to quantify, and it is certainly less than the cost of tax expenditures. But there is a cost, showing up primarily in higher interest rates associated with other unfavored public and private borrowing.

To point out that tax and finance subsidies are inefficient is not necessarily to indict them. Public housing agencies and nonprofit private sponsors of low-cost housing are entitled to seek any form of subsidy available to pursue their missions. This chapter attempted to present these indirect financing subsidies as viable tools in the repertoire of developers of low-cost housing, not necessarily as socially desirable public policies. Even from the standpoint of housing activists, however, reliance on these devices carries some risk because of Congress's unending tendency to change the rules. Even as this volume goes to press, some of the rules discussed here are undergoing change.

8

A Modest Proposal
Housing Vouchers
as Refundable
Tax Credits
Elizabeth A. Roistacher

Closing the Affordability Gap

The housing problems of low-income families are, for the most part, problems of income. This conclusion seems to be the consensus of the other contributors to this volume, and it has motivated the transformation of federal low-income housing programs from ones subsidizing new construction to ones offering payments to make up the difference between what low-income families can afford and what they must pay for housing.

Although cash grants are more efficient than in-kind subsidies in addressing problems of inadequate income, housing vouchers are the political compromise that ties the cash grant more closely to an acceptable and necessary expenditure than does a pure income-maintenance scheme.[1] Society seems more inclined to redistribute income if it has a strong say in how the money is used. Moreover, by linking the income transfer to housing rather than to a family's complete budgetary needs, the amount of redistribution can be limited.

Efficiency gains dominate the case of housing vouchers: a given group of households can be provided with adequate housing at a lower cost. There are two reasons for the increased efficiency of vouchers. First, costly subsidies for new construction are replaced by subsidies to existing housing. Second, the subsidy satisfies the household more completely because it is free to select its own dwelling unit, with the proviso that it meets certain minimum housing standards. (The argument assumes that the private rental market allows the household to exercise this freedom to spend, but this is not always the case. This problem is discussed below.)

The efficiency gain from the voucher has the potential of reducing the major inequity of our present low-income housing programs, which is that not all needy families are served. Given dollars would serve more households. This is a particularly important consideration given that Congress appropriates funds for low-income housing programs far below the amount needed to assist all eligible low-income families. Budget outlays in 1985 for subsidized housing programs totaled $10 billion and assisted an estimated 4 million households.[2] Another 9 million eligible renter households will not be served.[3] (But even if all eligible households could receive federal support, not all would choose to participate.[4]) Improving program efficiency is a start to reaching the rest of those households that need and desire federal assistance.

The shift away from new construction and toward housing payments has been in process for more than a decade. Congressional concern with high program costs, buttressed by economic theory and evidence from the Experimental Housing Allowance Program, led to the passage of Section 8 of the Housing and Community Development Act of 1974. There were two components to the Section 8 program. The innovative "existing housing" component introduced rent certificates, which a household could use to shop for housing in the private rental market. The other component was similar to older, production-oriented programs. The new construction programs generally cost twice as much as programs using the existing housing stock. In 1984 HUD estimated that a new unit required an annual subsidy of $5,000, compared with $2,500 for a household in the Section 8 Existing Housing Program.[5] Between 1974 and 1980, the U.S. Department of Housing and Urban Development continued to undertake a significant amount of costly new construction. In fact, Congress attempted to constrain HUD to a fifty-fifty mix between new and existing housing.[6]

The Reagan administration has gone further, proposing to replace all low-income housing programs with a voucher program introduced in 1983.[7] This program is basically similar to the Section 8 Existing Housing Program but introduces a few important changes. A household is permitted to spend more on housing than the amount of the subsidy. Theoretically, the household then can spend more to obtain better or more housing. If a household spends less on housing than is assumed in the calculation of the voucher, it is permitted to keep the difference. Under Section 8, a household can spend no more on housing than a "fair market rent" ceiling. Moreover, a household receives a smaller subsidy if it spends less than the fair market rent. These refinements increase efficiency by making the voucher more like a cash grant. But the voucher is still intrinsically a housing subsidy because the household must occupy a unit that meets certain standards. In 1985 vouchers were made "portable" so that, with the cooperation of local housing authorities, which administer the program, a household receiving a voucher in one jurisdiction can use it in another.

But perhaps the greatest difference between vouchers and Section

8 subsidies has to do with the proposed length of the commitment to be made by the federal government. Section 8 existing housing is supported by what have effectively been fifteen-year contracts (actually three, virtually automatically renewable, five-year contracts) with local housing authorities. Under the vouchers program, these contracts are limited to five years. As of August 1986, HUD had ninety-one thousand vouchers reserved in its budget, although only about forty thousand were actually under contract to local public housing authorities.[8] The 1987 executive budget proposes another fifty thousand vouchers.

Although the voucher scheme marginally promotes efficiency, the ability of households to benefit from these changes—or to benefit from Section 8—is severely constrained by other changes in the parameters of the low-income housing assistance system. First, households now must contribute a bigger share of their income to rent before the federal contribution begins. Under the old rule, a household had to contribute 25 percent of income, after some adjustment for family composition. Under the new rule the tenant contribution will rise to 30 percent. Second, the quality of housing to be supported under HUD programs has been lowered. For example, the fair market rent for a particular area is now defined as a lower percentile of the housing stock.[9] Although these changes make given federal dollars go farther, they do so not from improvements in efficiency but by reducing the degree of support to individual households.

Of course, these cost savings could be translated into equity gains if they were used to increase the number of beneficiaries. Unfortunately, that does not appear to be the purpose of these changes. Budget outlays and the number of households in HUD programs have continued to rise, but this reflects mostly existing program obligations rather than new commitments to households or housing.[10] Budget authority—representing long-run commitments—has been dramatically cut in recent years. For 1985, budget authority was $10.7 billion, 40 percent of its 1980 level.[11]

Can we accept the reduced commitments to low-income housing programs at a time when increased expenditures for the poor seem politically unacceptable? The answer might be yes if the efforts to date increased efficiency *and* did not increase inequities in the overall set of housing policies. But that is not the case. If housing policy as a whole is examined, it is apparent that recent and proposed changes in low-income housing policy dramatically increase inequities and leave unaddressed some major inefficiencies in government spending for housing. Changes in low-income housing policy can best be understood in the context of total federal housing policy. And that requires examining federal tax expenditures for home ownership. The largest part of federal housing policy is in the federal income tax code. The special tax treatment of homeownership has included the deductibility of mortgage interest and property taxes, capital gains deferrals, exclusions for the sale of a primary residence, and tax-exemption of state and local housing bonds. For 1986, the federal government estimated that these favorable treatments will cost $43 billion in forgone revenues, with homeowners' deductions accounting for $37 billion. And the treasury's simple reckoning of the cost of these deductions significantly underestimates their true cost.[12] The Tax Reform Act of 1986 will not eliminate tax preferences for homeowners, although lower tax rates will reduce their value.

Although all homeowners are entitled to mortgage and property tax deductions, only about 50 percent have taken advantage of these provisions.[13] Some homeowners may have no taxable income; others find that they fare better taking a standard deduction because they have low (or no) mortgage payments and/or because their incomes are low.[14] On a per household basis, the $37 billion in tax expenditures associated with these deductions comes to nearly $1,500—over $1,000 of which is associated with the mortgage interest deduction.[15]

Affluent homeowners are most likely to itemize, receive the largest deductions, and get the lion's share of tax benefits. For example, in 1981, taxpayers with adjusted gross incomes of $50,000 or more— the richest 4 percent of taxpayers—claimed 20 percent of the total value of deductions for mortgage interest; but because of their higher marginal tax brackets, they received about 36 percent of the tax benefits. Taxpayers with adjusted gross incomes above $30,000— the top 15 percent of taxpayers—claimed nearly 60 percent of the deductions and nearly 80 percent of the tax benefits. High incomes have translated into high housing expenses, high marginal tax brackets, and large benefits from itemizing.

If entitlements for owners are the political reality, how can we promote greater equity for renters? Why not create an entitlement program for low-income renters in the spirit of the one that currently exists for high-income owners? This chapter proposes a refundable tax credit for housing for low-income renter households that can be structured along the lines of the proposed voucher scheme.

The Proposal

The refundable tax credit for low-income renters would require that each family (or individual) eligible for the program and wanting to receive benefits fill out a tax form that includes the calculation of its housing tax credit. The housing tax credit would be based on income level and family size. It could be geographically specific, but not to the degree that fair market rents for HUD programs currently are. (There are some three thousand different fair market rents calculated for the Section 8 existing program.)

Many families who would qualify for the proposed housing tax credit are likely to have no federal income tax liability. But because this credit would be refundable, they would end up receiving a check from the government. There is already a federal precedent for refundable credits. Under the earned income tax credit for low-income households, a very low-income household can actually receive a payment from the federal government.[16] Certainly it would take a bit of effort to publicize a new refundable tax credit, especially for a target population with a large number of nonfilers.[17] Housing advocacy groups would help publicize the program and provide assistance. No doubt tax service companies would soon be marketing low-cost assistance to many households to apply for refunds.

The refundable tax credit would be very much like the voucher. Under the voucher program, a fair market rent is established for existing housing in a given location. Then the amount of support is determined by a formula based on family income and composition. (The 30 percent contribution that HUD is now requiring is after adjustments for family composition.) Under the voucher, a household can spend more or less than the scheduled amount. If a household spends less, it can keep the difference. Such would be the case with a refundable tax credit.

The cost of such a program depends on the level of support built into the program. It is estimated that the annual per household subsidy provided by the voucher program in 1986 is $3,500.[18] Assuming that all 9 million eligible, but as yet unassisted, renter households were to take advantage of the refundable tax credit, the cost to the treasury would be an additional $31.5 billion annually.

But even if the program were well-publicized, some households would choose not to participate. Estimated participation rates for the EHAP test group with no housing standard ran from 78 to 100 percent. If a housing standard is established in any new program, participation rates would be significantly lower because households not living in qualifying units would have to move to participate. Search costs and moving costs lower the net benefits from participating. Thus when a minimum housing standard was required under EHAP participation rates fell to the range of 40 to 60 percent.[19] A program without a housing standard that would have a 90 percent participation rate would cost an additional $28 billion to house an additional 8 million households. With a housing standard, the added cost would fall sharply to $16 billion for 4.5 million households, assuming a 50 percent participation rate.

But $16 billion more of federal housing subsidies in a time of high federal deficits is not likely to be forthcoming unless there is a cost saving somewhere else. Over time there would be some cost saving as HUD's existing commitments to construction programs are phased out. But these savings might produce housing for only an additional 1 million households. There is, however, another potential means of reallocating dollars that are currently part of the housing subsidy system.

Restructuring and Reducing Tax Benefits to Homeowners

The added cost to the treasury of a refundable tax credit program for low-income households could be offset by restructuring tax breaks to homeowners from deductions to credits. Shifting to credits, not to exceed a specified ceiling, would not only provide revenue to fund the program for low-income families but would also reduce—but not eliminate—the inequity in the distribution of housing tax benefits. If deductions of mortgage interest and property taxes were replaced by a 15 percent credit (worth 15 percent of the cost of these payments) forgone revenues (for 1986) would fall by approximately $15 billion—coming predominantly from the wealthiest 15 percent of taxpayers. The credit could further be capped to prevent it from being applied to mortgages in excess of, say, $150,000. This cap would not only serve an equity goal, but it would also reduce excessive investment in residential housing. Its revenue-raising potential, however, is probably limited.

Switching to a tax credit for owners would also bring benefits to those homeowners who are currently taking the standard deduction. This would reduce the revenue gain from the proposal, but it would also reduce the inequities across owner-occupiers. On net, restructuring the tax breaks for homeowners could generate significant revenues to fund a program for low-income renters.

As the Tax Reform Act of 1986 is phased in, lower tax rates will bring about part of the cost savings that would result from the shift to a 15 percent tax credit, but these additional revenues are not earmarked for increasing assistance to low-income families.

Anthony Downs also proposed funding an entitlement program

for low-income families with revenues saved by reducing tax benefits for homeowners.[20] He estimated that a 14 percent reduction in tax expenditures for homeowners, facilitated by moving to tax credits rather than deductions, could fund an entitlement program with a minimum housing standard. But his entitlement plan for low-income families, structured along the lines of the housing voucher scheme, did not operate through the tax code.

Should a Minimum Housing Standard Be Required?

Should eligibility for the refundable tax credit require that the household occupy housing of a minimum acceptable standard, and who would certify that the housing meets the standard? Certainly such a requirement would truly distinguish the refundable credit from a skimpy form of negative income tax. If housing markets were highly competitive and if the level of funding were adequate to provide revenues to cover the cost of the minimum standard, local code enforcement should be able to do the job. Furthermore, if tenants can pay enough rent to maintain housing, landlords should be able to comply with housing codes *provided* that there is an adequate supply of housing that does not require major rehabilitation to meet code standards. In such a happy world, a properly structured housing tax credit would also contribute to a reduction in tension between landlords and tenants. These optimistic assumptions will not be met in all housing markets, but evidence from EHAP suggests they are valid in a large number of markets for a broad range of eligible households. But in other instances, there will be a need for other housing interventions, as discussed below.

Arguments can be made to favor or oppose minimum standards. On one hand, the ability of many municipalities to enforce their housing codes may be limited by the availability of local revenues and an unwillingness fully to enforce their own codes, even if they have the resources, because this would eliminate housing opportunities for unassisted low-income families. A refundable housing tax credit would help alleviate such a dilemma. Imposing a housing standard enforced by the federal government also creates a great deal of bureaucracy and will lead to significantly lower participation rates (the former raising costs, the latter lowering them). Also, there is no housing standard applied to households receiving tax benefits through deduction of homeowners' expenses.

On the other hand, if a household is entitled to the tax credit regardless of whether it is occupying a dwelling of minimum standard, the proposal becomes a skimpy negative income tax. Also, in the short run, having no minimum standard would surely mean that many households would not be spending their credit for "adequate" housing because the amount of the refundable credit is based only on a calculation of the household's housing needs. For many low-income families, the 70 percent of income left for nonhousing goods will not be enough. But there are other support programs, such as food stamps, to help make up the difference.

In the past there has been greater political support for housing subsidies than for general income assistance, but, of course, part of this support has come from the construction industry. Because this proposal is not tied to new construction and is likely to have little impact—either positive or negative—on new construction,[21] the construction industry would be unlikely to lobby for such a housing program. Surely the effective lobbying by this group was one reason for the continuing high commitment to new construction in the late 1970s. Although such organizations as the National Association of Realtors would find the tax credit proposal attractive, they do not possess the same political clout as the construction industry, which until 1980 had a good deal of influence with HUD and Congress because of the macroeconomic importance of construction.[22]

Not All Housing Problems Are Income Problems

The refundable tax credit and the housing voucher both address the fundamental problem of inadequate income leading to housing difficulties. But there are problems in housing markets that cannot be immediately addressed by alleviating the deficiencies of tenant income. In housing markets lacking a sufficient supply of adequate housing, either because of outright shortages or because the available stock requires rehabilitation, there remains some need for other housing market interventions. Congress included in its 1983 legislation new rehabilitation and construction programs, which are administered with very limited funds and in a highly discretionary way. Such programs can address some of the particular needs of particular communities.

There also may remain a need to produce new units for certain household groups, in particular large families. New construction programs have been retained for the elderly, another group with special housing needs. But in addressing these supply problems, perhaps the appropriate strategy is to separate the income support from the construction or rehabilitation subsidy. Although income support comes through the refundable tax credit, imperfections in supply can be solved by other mechanisms, such as "up-front" development or rehabilitation grants or loans.

What about Homeowners?

The refundable tax credit for low-income renters plus some restructuring of tax subsidies to homeowners would move us toward a more equitable and efficient set of housing policies. But these measures hardly address all the inequities and inefficiencies associated with our housing policies.

Nonrefundable tax credits for mortgage interest and property taxes will help extend benefits to lower-income homeowners, but there are some 10 million homeowners who would be eligible for housing assistance on income grounds[23] and who would get little or no benefit from such a credit. Some of these are elderly people with no mortgage obligation but with relatively high property tax burdens. And although economists often argue that the "permanent income" or wealth position of the elderly is significantly higher than current income indicates, it is hard to meet expenses when the primary source of wealth is the value of the home. This has led to the creation of such interesting but as yet not highly popular financing devices as reverse annuity mortgages, and some jurisdictions allow deferral of property taxes for the low-income elderly. But for poor homeowners of all ages, elderly and nonelderly, the fundamental problem is an income shortage, which may have to be alleviated with other policies, such as a refundable tax credit, adding substantially to my earlier cost estimates.

A federal policy that favors homeownership may be a reasonable policy objective, which should be justified and explicitly implemented. If homeownership is a social good, then policy should encourage the tenure (for example, improve the efficiency of housing finance markets, guarantee/subsidize mortgages for lower-income families) without encouraging excessive investment in housing for higher-income households. But as yet, there are no articulate arguments for the intrinsic social preferability of homeownership. This issue, so often assumed away, needs some serious thought. The model on which consideration of the social desirability of owning versus renting should be based is a tax-neutral world in which problems of income distribution have been alleviated.

Conclusion

This chapter has proposed a refundable tax credit for low-income renters as a way of addressing the major housing problem for low-income families: inadequate income. The proposal would take housing subsidies for the poor out of the annual appropriations process and make them an entitlement, two characteristics of our current homeownership policy for the nonpoor. Moreover, a significant portion of the added cost could be derived from some restructuring and reducing homeowners' benefits for higher-income taxpayers.

In the 1986 environment of tax reform and fiscal conservatism, a refundable tax credit for low-income housing may not be a viable proposal, but political environments do change. Nor does the proposal address all the problems in housing markets or all the problems in our current set of housing policies. But it would be a big step toward increasing efficiency and equity in low-income housing programs and overall housing policy. The voucher scheme and other "reforms" of our low-income housing programs simply ignore the fundamental imbalances in government housing policies.

Notes

1. Economists also emphasize the efficiency of demand-side subsidies associated with greater household choice: a household derives greater satisfaction from a given amount of subsidy if it can select its own housing. The extreme argument is that the household receives even greater satisfaction if it has complete freedom to allocate a cash subsidy, hence the preference for unconstrained cash grants.

2. Executive Office of the President (1985a).

3. According to special analyses of the 1983 *Annual Housing Survey* data, 12.9 million renter households were eligible for HUD programs. The U.S. Department of Agriculture assists more than 1 million households through its housing programs, but it is estimated that only about 250,000 of these are low-income households according to HUD's definition (50 percent or less of area median income) (McGough, 1986).

4. Based on data from the Experimental Housing Allowance Program, participation rates under an unconstrained program, one that does not require a household to occupy housing of a minimum standard, are in the range of 80 to 100 percent. If a housing standard is required, as is the case under current HUD programs, then participation rates fall to the 40 to 60 percent range (Straszheim, 1981).

5. McGough (1984).

6. For fiscal year 1979, Section 8 reservations were as follows: new construc-

tion, 147,000; existing housing, 130,500; and substantial rehabilitation, 43,000. Cumulative reservations were respectively 614,000, 805,500, and 114,000. Occupancy figures, however, do not show the same new construction bias; these numbers were respectively 151,000, 583,000, and 19,000 (U.S. Department of Housing and Urban Development, 1979).

7. There are, of course, existing commitments to production-oriented housing programs that cannot be transferred to the voucher framework. Federal policies for low-income housing have been criticized for inequities among recipients, as well as between recipients and nonrecipients. There are a variety of different programs, including Section 8 new and existing, public housing, and older programs such as Section 236 under which low-income families still receive benefits. Because of the different subsidy mechanisms, households in similar economic circumstances will receive different amounts of subsidy. If all of these programs could eventually be replaced by a single program such as the voucher, this horizontal inequity among recipients would be eliminated (see Struyk, Mayer, and Tuccillo, 1983, and Roistacher, 1984, for assessments of housing policy under Reagan).

8. Office of Policy Development and Research (1986).

9. The administration had proposed that fair market rent be based on the fortieth percentile of an area's rent distribution after exclusion of substandard units and new built units (those built in the past two years). The previous rule had been the fiftieth percentile for recent movers (excluding units built in the past two years), the notion being that these rents reflect the current market. An administrative compromise resulted in the use of the forty-fifth percentile for recent movers in determining fair market rents (McGough, 1984).

10. Between 1980 and 1985, outlays increased from $4.5 billion to $10 billion. In 1980, the number of households in HUD's low-income housing programs was 3.3 million, and by the end of 1985 it reached 4 million. The 1986 executive budget proposed a two-year funding moratorium on additional assisted housing (Executive Office of the President [1980], [1984], and [1985a]; Struyk, Mayer, and Tuccillo, 1983:16).

11. Executive Office of the President [1985a].

12. Executive Office of the President [1985b]. Tax subsidy to homeownership can be more rigorously estimated as the difference between the special treatment and the cost to the treasury if owner-occupied housing was treated the same as rental housing. To make this calculation it is assumed that an owner-occupant takes on the role of tenant and landlord (to himself). Suppliers of rental housing are taxed on their net rental income, that is, the difference between rental income and expenses, including property taxes and mortgage interest, as well as maintenance, operating outlays, and depreciation. A homeowner, however, as a landlord renting to himself, receives an imputed rental income based on the housing services he consumes each year, and this income is not taxed. Thus the tax treatment of homeownership, as compared to rental housing, allows for fewer deductible expenses for greater untaxed income. It has been estimated that, for 1980, by not taxing imputed net rental income of homeowners, the treasury forgave some $14 to $17 billion in taxes beyond the $23 billion estimate based solely on deductions of mortgage interest and prop-

erty taxes (Simonson, 1981). Although it is often maintained that it is not possible to tax imputed income, several European countries still do this, and Britain taxed imputed income until 1965.

13. According to the *1981 Statistics of Income* (Internal Revenue Service, 1983), 23.5 million taxpayers itemized mortgage interest and 26.8 million itemized property taxes. If we assume that each taxpayer represents only one household (that is, that no two taxpayers are writing off the same mortgage), this suggests that 50 percent of the 54 million homeowning households were taking advantage of these tax benefits.

14. The *1981 Annual Housing Survey* (U.S. Department of Commerce, 1983) reports that 36 percent of single-family homeowners—who account for nearly 80 percent of all owners—have no mortgage outstanding. The median income of those with a mortgage was $27,600, as compared to $14,400 for those with no mortgage.

15. This calculation takes into account the fact that the number of taxpayers (and households) deducting property taxes is greater than the number deducting mortgage interest. See note 13.

16. A number of states have refundable credits as a part of "circuit-breaker" programs. See Advisory Commission on Intergovernmental Relations (1986: 110–16).

17. In 1980, the median income of HUD-assisted households was $4,978. For assisted families headed by a married couple, it was $9,507 (Dolbeare, 1983). Households with such incomes were not likely to have positive tax liabilities.

18. The $3,500 figure is calculated by me based on discussion with the Office of Policy Development and Research, U.S. Department of Housing and Urban Development (1986).

19. Straszheim (1981).

20. Downs (1983:11 and 170–71).

21. See Mills (1981) for impacts on new construction.

22. By the end of the Carter administration, it appeared that the construction industry had lost some of its clout. High interest rates in 1980 led to a dramatic downturn in housing starts, but Congress and the administration did not support a subsidy program to stimulate the construction industry because it would have aggravated inflation. Some observers have commented that it had become the "whipping boy" rather than the "handmaiden" of macroeconomic policy.

23. McGough (1986).

References

Advisory Commission on Intergovernmental Relations. 1986. *Significant Features of Fiscal Federalism, 1985–6 Edition.* Washington, D.C.

Clark, Timothy B. 1981. "The American Housing Industry: From 'Sacred Cow' to 'Sacrificial Lamb.'" *National Journal* 13, No. 49: 2157.

Dolbeare, Cushing N. 1983. "The Low-Income Housing Crisis," In Chester Hartman, ed., *America's Housing Crisis,* Boston: Routledge & Kegan Paul.

Downs, Anthony. 1980. "Too Much Capital for Housing?" *Brookings Bulletin* 17, no. 1:1–5.

———. 1983. *Rental Housing in the 1980s*. Washington, D.C.: Brookings Institution.

Executive Office of the President. [1980]. *Budget of the United States Government, Fiscal Year 1982*. Washington, D.C.: U.S. Government Printing Office.

———. [1984] *Budget of the United States Government, Fiscal Year 1986*. Washington, D.C.: U.S. Government Printing Office.

———. [1985a]. *Budget of the United States Government, Fiscal Year 1987*. Washington, D.C.: U.S. Government Printing Office.

———. [1985b]. *Special Analyses, Budget of the United States Government, Fiscal Year 1987*. Washington D.C.: U.S. Government Printing Office.

Internal Revenue Service. 1983. *1981 Statistics of Income. Individual Income Tax Returns*. U.S. Department of the Treasury. Washington, D.C.: U.S. Government Printing Office.

McGough, Duane. 1984. Telephone conversation with Duane McGough, Office of Policy Development and Research, U.S. Department of Housing and Urban Development. August 22.

———. 1986. Telephone conversation with Duane McGough, Office of Policy Development and Research, U.S. Department of Housing and Urban Development. October 1.

Mills, Edwin S., and Arthur Sullivan. 1981. "Market Effects." In Katharine L. Bradbury and Anthony Downs, eds., *Do Housing Allowances Work?* Washington D.C.: Brookings Institution.

Office of Policy Development and Research, U.S. Department of Housing and Urban Development. 1986. Information provided by telephone. October 2.

Roistacher, Elizabeth A. 1984. "A Tale of Two Conservatives: Housing Policy under Reagan and Thatcher." *Journal of the American Planning Association*, 50, no. 4:485–92.

Simonson, John. 1981. "Existing Tax Expenditures for Homeowners." Washington, D.C.: Office of Policy Development and Research, U.S. Department of Housing and Urban Development.

Straszheim, Mahlon R. 1981. "Participation." In Katharine L. Bradbury and Anthony Downs, eds., *Do Housing Allowances Work?* Washington, D.C.: Brookings Institution.

Struyk, Raymond J., Neil Mayer, and John A. Tuccillo. 1983. *Federal Housing Policy at President Reagan's Midterm*. Washington, D.C.: Urban Institute.

U.S. Department of Commerce, U.S. Bureau of the Census. 1983. *Annual Housing Survey 1981: Financial Characteristics of the Housing Inventory for the United States and Regions*. Part C. Current Housing Reports, Series H150-81. Washington, D.C.: U.S. Government Printing Office.

U.S. Department of Housing and Urban Development. 1979. *1979 Statistical Yearbook*. Washington, D.C.: U.S. Government Printing Office.

———. 1984. *Summary of HUD Budget for Fiscal Year 1985*. Washington, D.C.: U.S. Department of Housing and Urban Development.

Can We Ensure That All Americans Are Well Housed?

Peter D. Salins

In this chapter I wish to summarize the analyses, arguments, and conclusions of the contributing authors to this volume and suggest some tentative answers to the twin questions animating this project: what is the nature of the housing problem facing the nation's poor and what can be done about it? The eight contributors (excluding myself) deal with different aspects of housing policy and approach their subjects from differing points of view but nevertheless mesh in their analyses and agree in their conclusions to a remarkable degree. And the integration of their data, their arguments, and their insights goes a long way in clarifying the terms of the ongoing national housing policy debate—and reveals the extent to which we can hope to solve what I characterized in Chapter 1 as America's permanent housing problem.

The Historical Overview

Let me begin by taking us on a brief excursion through the preceding chapters. George Sternlieb and David Listokin in Chapter 2 review the design and effectiveness of U.S. housing initiatives (not all meant to help the poor) from World War I to the present, with particular emphasis on the post–New Deal period. They highlight certain persistent tendencies and certain notable shifts in policy focus. One striking finding, which should perhaps surprise only the naive, is that housing policy has been driven, over the years, not so much by the dilemma of the ill-housed as by the importunings of the homebuilding industry. In the political alliance between the builders and the housing reformers, it was usually the builders who won, although the justification for government-assisted housing programs was invariably on the basis of "need." Both the rhetoric and the programs in recent years have shifted in the direction of greater concern for the poor and less for the housing industry, yet even the most recent program, Section 8 (which subsidizes construction or rehabilitation of dwellings only for low-income families and limits their rent to 30 percent of family income), has been much more of a windfall for developers than for poor renters. Another consistent feature of federal housing policy, which was ended only during the civil rights revolution of the 1960s, was blatant racial discrimination. The FHA mortgage insurance program, which was responsible for so much of the new housing in the post–World War II period, discouraged loans for homes in racially mixed areas. The public housing developments ("projects") funded with deep federal capital subsidies were so located and tenanted as to be intentionally segregated. Small wonder, then, that federal programs—even under ostensibly "liberal" administrations—produced so little benefit for the poor and ill-housed when they were primarily designed to help the housing industry and to keep blacks "in their place."

Another aspect of post–New Deal housing policy which Sternlieb and Listokin discuss is the frailty of housing as a federal priority even in the best of times. Periodic attempts to make housing assistance an entitlement (like food stamps) were invariably beaten back (in spite of the "decent home" flourish of the preamble to the 1949 Housing Act). The level of funding has been highly variable from year to year, and only occasionally robust (as in the 1970s). Given the small slice of the federal pie that has usually been devoted to all housing assistance, the piece that reached the poor and ill-housed has always been especially meager. In view of this history, the current complaints about the Reagan administration's stony-hearted and, presumably atypical, dereliction on the housing front must be seen as being grounded in nostalgia for an elysian housing policy era that never was.

With regard to aspects of federal policy that have changed significantly over the years, Sternlieb and Listokin note two interesting phenomena. One is the gradual shift from producer, supply-oriented subsidies toward consumer, demand-oriented ones. If the quintessential supply subsidy was the public housing "project" built by a local housing agency with Washington picking up the entire construction cost, the quintessential demand subsidy is the housing voucher, as presently proposed by the Reagan administration. Demand-side subsidies are not new in conception. It has taken fifty years for them to gain public and congressional acceptance, and in their purest form they have not been implemented yet. Supply-side subsidies have been waning in appeal because they are costly on a unit basis, and by being so visible and site-specific they have too easily highlighted the failure of national housing policy. There are too many Pruitt-Igoes (a failed St. Louis project that was publicly leveled in 1974) for supply-side strategies to hold much appeal. Demand-side subsidies make Congress nervous, first, because they cry out for treatment as entitlements. It is easy to conceive of rationing a fixed stock of newly constructed dwellings (you cannot distribute what you have not built), but it is much harder to justify rationing dollars on any basis other than a strict eligibility criterion. Second, housing vouchers can so easily be seen as a fairly direct income transfer program at a time when income transfers are not very popular.

The other dynamic element in federal housing policy concerns the question of who is to be helped—what I referred to as broadening the target in Chapter 1. Federal policy has been profoundly ambivalent in choosing between approaches that help only the poor and ill-housed and those that help the deserving nonpoor: people of "moderate" income, especially the elderly. In the 1930s and the immediate postwar period, the number of inadequately housed was so large that the issue seemed unimportant. Later, periods of targeted assistance for the poor and near-poor were followed by periods when assistance was aimed primarily at the middle class. We appear to be on the verge of another pendulum swing back to wanting to help only the poor.

What conclusion can we draw from Sternlieb and Listokin's historical review? First, the devotion of the national government to finding a workable and fair solution to the housing condition of the poor and ill-housed has rarely been very deep or very sincere. Second, virtually every federal program that was aimed at helping the housing-disadvantaged suffered from one or another of the following defects: high cost per unit of assistance and ineffectiveness in actually improving housing conditions. Third, federal programs have been bizarrely inequitable in their distribution of benefits, by class, by income, by race, or by region. Finally, federal policy has been so volatile and unpredictable with regard to program changes and funding levels as to render it nearly useless in the calculations of either local governments or disadvantaged households. The overall conclusion, then, might be characterized as follows. In the absence of a revolutionary change in Washington's attitude toward housing, do not look to the federal government for a comprehensive or enduring solution to the housing problems of the poor.

The Rising Tide

The gloomy conclusions to be drawn from Chapter 2 are offset considerably by the data and arguments of John Weicher in Chapter 3. He maintains that, notwithstanding the failure of public efforts on the housing front, the private sector has been doing a great job, overall, during the post–World War II period in dramatically improving housing conditions for all Americans, including the poorest. The issues developed in Weicher's chapter go to the heart of the debate over housing policy. On one side is the notion that has animated virtually all public assistance programs in the housing field, namely, that the poor and ill-housed can be helped only by publicly funded efforts that deliver dwelling units directly to them. On the other side is the proposition that a high level of housing production in the private sector—even if it is aimed initially at the middle- and upper-income end of the market—will improve the quality of housing across the board. In other words, a "rising tide" of private construction will raise the quality of even low-income housing "boats." As Weicher points out, choosing between these hypotheses is not as easy as it might superficially appear. Yet informing such a choice is critically important in setting the direction of American housing policy.

Weicher tackles the two competing hypotheses from a theoretical (what *should* happen) as well as empirical (what *did* happen) vantage point. On theoretical grounds the "rising tide" or "filtering" hypothesis gets only marginal approbation, much as aerodynamic theory suggests that bees are really too heavy, relative to their wing size, to fly. The eminent theorists whom Weicher cites maintain that overall housing quality can improve only if the relative price falls and that construction of new housing will not reduce housing prices. As rapidly as new housing is built, the older stock will deteriorate to the point that its quality-adjusted price remains constant. But pointing to the empirical evidence, Weicher demonstrates that, just as bees do fly (my metaphor, not his), housing quality has improved steadily over the entire post–World War II period and for all economic and ethnic classes. The rising tide does appear to be lifting all boats. More specifically, for every three new housing units built, regardless for which income group, one inadequate dwelling will disappear from the stock.

On the other hand, publicly subsidized housing seems to fail the test on theoretical and empirical grounds. The theory suggests that publicly assisted housing units merely replace ones that the private sector might have built. Looking at publicly assisted housing empirically, Weicher finds that though tenants in these projects obviously receive a direct benefit, the rest of the eligible poor or ill-housed population has not even benefited indirectly. In aggregate terms, there is no evidence from any of the studies that Weicher reviews to indicate that public housing efforts have made any net contribution to the incremental housing quality improvements seen in the postwar period. If Weicher's analysis is correct, it suggests that even well-designed federal housing efforts will not reduce the residuum of housing disadvantage. Sternlieb and Listokin succeeded in demonstrating that federal housing programs have not worked; Weicher points out that they cannot work.

An important aspect of the rising tide hypothesis is the issue of what makes the tide rise. Most housing analysts attribute high levels of private housing production in the postwar period to the preferential treatment accorded to housing in credit markets and the federal income tax code. Weicher argues that these preferences have not made as much of a difference as is commonly thought and that a more important factor has been the sustained growth in real incomes over the last four decades. This is an important issue as the nation is about to embark on its experiment in tax reform, which promises to reduce these preferences significantly. One comes away from Weicher's chapter convinced that a vigorous unsubsidized private sector is the key to improving housing for all classes, but somewhat uncertain as to what measures are needed to maintain the vigor.

The Residuum of Housing Disadvantage

In Chapter 4, William Apgar appears to refute the optimistic conclusion of Weicher's chapter, namely that we can rely on the private sector to improve the housing stock without help from government. Apgar does not deny the general level of housing improvement that has taken place to date. Rather, he asks us to attend to two problematical facts blighting the otherwise bright picture. First, he notes that the pace of housing improvement has stalled in recent years. Second, he shows that the positive aggregate housing quality statistics hide serious deprivation in certain places for certain groups and mask two growing concerns: neighborhood deterioration and the problem of housing affordability. Much of the difference between Apgar's and Weicher's analysis can be traced to differences in perspective rather than disagreement on the facts. Whereas Weicher takes a broad and macroscopic view, Apgar is concerned with the details of housing disadvantage as they affect specific groups. Whereas Weicher rates housing improvement strictly according to objective measures of quality, Apgar notes the more subjective deficiencies associated with neighborhood quality. Whereas Weicher sees victory in the decline in the number of deficient housing units, Apgar is concerned that poor people must pay more for their housing today. On several counts, then, Apgar's analysis is a prime example of the "moving target" problem I discussed in Chapter 1.

Apgar makes an important contribution, however, in raising the issues that he does. He puts his finger on what is troubling students of the housing problem today. Like other analysts and housing reformers, he suggests that we can draw little comfort from aggregate improvement when we visit or read about the wretched neighborhoods that remain the home environment for millions of minority households, for tens of millions of children in female-headed families, even for millions of lower-middle-income white families and many of the elderly. Nor should our discomfort be much assuaged by noting that many of the indicators of neighborhood inadequacy reflect population rather than housing characteristics. And though "affordability" (meaning a high rent-to-income ratio) is a slippery concept, certainly rent-to-income ratios averaging 40 percent spell clear-cut hardship. Apgar's chapter leaves one with a rationale for reading the rest of the book—yes, there is a housing problem for low-income people—without necessarily convincing us that the previous chapters have been wrong in casting doubt on the efficacy of public housing efforts.

Locating the Poor

In chapter 5, Ira Lowry goes one step further in disaggregating the housing problem of the poor by looking at its spatial implications. Lowry recognizes that the public efforts at housing assistance require making locational choices. Although the rhetorical question, "Where should the poor live?" is rarely asked publicly, it looms in the background as one of the most crucial operational issues that must be resolved. In attempting to arrive at a satisfactory answer to his rhetorical question, Lowry takes us through the history of postwar housing and development policies. He traverses the same terrain as Sternlieb and Listokin in Chapter 2. But he does so with a keen eye for the locational dynamics of these programs and their rationale of improving the physical environment of American cities, rather than viewing them merely as a means to upgrade the living conditions of their immediate beneficiaries.

Lowry notes the contradictory nature of the agendas animating housing location policies. On one hand, the majority of urban citizens would rather not have the poor as neighbors. On the other hand, the neighborhood improvement objectives of housing policy, which as Apgar suggests are becoming increasingly important, would require a dispersal of the poor. Lowry notes that the contradiction has never been resolved. Instead, policies have alternated between one or another of the objectives, or tried (often unsuccessfully) to accomplish both at once.

His most useful insight is that the poor are not a monolithic group. The more upwardly mobile among them, those attached to middle-class values and cohesive ethnic or other communities, need only some help in paying for shelter but will make their own locational choices, which will be optimal for the larger community as well as themselves. The disorganized or socially deviant poor, however, will constitute the primary manifestation of neighborhood deterioration in any area in which they live. Thus, Lowry concludes, any attempt to integrate them into middle-class areas will be destructive and ultimately self-defeating. Left to their own choices, he implies, the deviant poor would segregate themselves away from the mainstream to everyone's benefit. They would pay less for housing, and the rest of the community would be more secure in their own neighborhoods. So Lowry's answer to the rhetorical question, "Where should the poor live?" is wherever they *want* to live, and public agencies should not try to modify the choices.

Lowry also makes one other important observation. He maintains that the dramatic improvement in housing conditions of the last forty years owes much to the forced demolition of slums occasioned by federally funded central-city redevelopment efforts which impelled many of the poor to find better housing elsewhere. Because this clearly was a location-oriented policy, Lowry's approbation of urban redevelopment seems somewhat at odds with his otherwise free-market locational choice orientation.

Solutions: Fixing Up the Housing We Have

The first chapters deal essentially with a definition of the housing problems facing poor families. The second half of the book is concerned with solutions. In Chapter 6, Howard Sumka reviews our experience with the increasingly popular strategy of fixing up our older dwellings and neighborhoods rather than building new ones. Policies for using existing stock are attractive today for several reasons. They are obviously much cheaper on a unit basis than new construction. They can mesh very well with the consumer housing subsidies that Sternlieb and Listokin as well as Lowry see as replacing subsidies to producers. They suit the prevailing winds of architectural preservation and grass-roots community activism. And in a policy environment of constrained resources and modest expectations, strategies for using existing stock are appropriate in scale. Sumka outlines the major strategic objectives of such policies: to ensure that adequate and continuing funds flow into the maintenance and preservation of older dwelling units and to reverse the processes of neighborhood social instability and physical disinvestment. Specifying the objectives is easier than seeing them achieved.

Of the four operational programs that Sumka reviews, none stand out as successful and replicable paradigms for a comprehensive national approach aimed at upgrading older housing and reversing neighborhood decline. Sumka looks at areas that are targets of "neighborhood preservation partnerships," subject to a coordinated investment by lenders and local governments (using federal funds) to upgrade neighborhoods of moderate-income, owner-occupied housing through a combination of low-interest-rate loans and public improvements. He finds that such neighborhoods appeared to improve but no more so than other areas with similar profiles not subject to "neighborhood preservation partnerships" attention. Another policy called "homesteading" refers to the policy whereby local governments give away dwellings or sell them at a very low price to families that promise to fix them up and live in them. Sumka finds that where it has been used as a neighborhood improvement strategy in areas of predominantly one-to-three-family houses it has proven effective, but usually because it attracts a new kind of resident to the target area. Thus it is unlikely that the strategy can work in areas of limited market appeal, or where the prospective residents might be the hard-core disadvantaged. Sumka also reviews what he calls "multifamily homesteading." This involves turning over publicly owned, tax-defaulted apartment houses to their tenants (or other poor people) to own and operate as housing cooperatives. Basing his evaluation primarily on experience in New York City, Sumka finds that this approach can be successful, as well as cost-effective, if the tenant cooperators are highly motivated and have the appropriate organizational skills, and if the buildings are in reasonably good repair. Where these conditions are not met, as they were not in many of the instances outside of New York, the failure rate is high. Another program reviewed by Sumka, called "neighborhood strategy areas," allowed local governments to target their Section 8 rehabilitation allocations to specific, high-priority, deteriorated neighborhoods. These areas would also receive federally funded community development and other assistance, the notion being that a heavy infusion of resources from a variety of programs would be able to turn things around in areas where a scattered approach would undoubtedly fail. This program, affecting 150 neighborhoods, was launched in 1979 and evaluated in 1981. Sumka concludes that the neighborhood strategy areas approach, where it was fully implemented, was successful in upgrading housing and improving physical and social conditions in neighborhoods. It is an expensive approach, however, and hard to replicate on a large scale.

The last of the strategies for existing stock that Sumka examines is a combined producer-consumer subsidy approach currently going under the name of the Rental Rehabilitation Program. The concept entails a no-strings rehabilitation grant to owners of low-cost housing in conjunction with rent vouchers to their tenants to help them afford the newly remodeled apartments. The program appears plausible and in its limited experimental implementation was popular with local officials. But because owners, under RRP, may charge market rents, or even sell their remodeled buildings, and because tenants may use their vouchers to move or spend on nonhousing goods, the subsidies seem to be very slippery and may not have an impact on the problem of housing disadvantage.

One may conclude from Sumka's thorough review of just about every trick in the existing stock repertoire that all approaches suffer from one or several of the following defects. Such programs either succeed by running with the obvious winners—that is, repairing the "unbroken" as it were—or they are very costly in dollars and bureaucratic energy for each dwelling helped, or they cannot be replicated on a large scale. That said, however, among the programs reviewed, the most cost-effective and potentially most extensive approach appears to be homesteading—especially if coupled with better tenant training and a greater potential for tenants to gain meaningful equity in their homesteads.

The End-Run Approach to Housing Finance

One of the discernible trends shaping U.S. housing policy since the end of World War II is the increasingly circuitous route by which federal funds reach their targets. Rather than bemoan this fact, Kevin Villani in Chapter 7 counsels us on how such indirect subsidies can be effectively deployed by local or nonprofit agencies determined to sponsor low-cost housing. He stresses that in the near-term federal housing policy environment these oblique funding sources will also be the only ones. Villani identifies three important devices available to finance low-cost housing: tax shelter provisions under current laws, state mortgage revenue bonds, and new private market mortgage instruments. The greatest potential leverage lies in the former two. The present tax law, even as recently modified, can make each private housing investment dollar stretch considerably further, a fact that has been turned to advantage primarily to wrest high returns from luxury housing. Villani shows how the same tax provisions could make privately owned low-cost housing affordable.

Villani's other major back-door low-cost housing funding source is proceeds from state-issued mortgage revenue bonds. At present, states are permitted to issue tax-free bonds under rules that permit them to turn the proceeds over to private parties to advance local welfare objectives. Villani discusses how, under this rubric, state agencies that finance housing have been raising funds with tax-exempt, relatively low-interest bond issues to underwrite a secondary market in cut-rate housing mortgages for eligible low- and moderate-income families. The bonds are collateralized (backed) by packages of outstanding mortgages. Villani also discusses how the major national secondary markets can feed the stream of low-cost housing finance directly, but usually at market rates of interest.

Although Villani's discussion is mainly a technical description of ways that potential sponsors of low-cost housing can find funds to finance their projects, it does suggest both the opportunities and limitations associated with this oblique approach. On the opportunity side, Villani demonstrates that one need not rely on explicit federal budget outlays to finance housing. Indeed, Villani points out, as have many others before him, that tax expenditures have long contributed the largest of federal housing subsidies and have been primarily exploited by the owners and tenants of middle- and high-cost housing. It follows naturally that we tap this rich vein of underground federal largesse on behalf of the poor.

But the limitations of the approach, suggested not so much by Villani but naturally springing off the page, should give one pause. The most troublesome of these is the volatility of national tax policy. In 1981, Congress significantly liberalized depreciation allowances (making housing cheaper) and then in 1983 curtailed them. The new round of tax reform has significantly scaled back the depreciation subsidy. Throughout the 1970s Congress ignored the "abuse" of the state mortgage revenue bond approach to back-door federal mortgage subsidies, but after 1980 it began to scrutinize this mechanism and legislated a scaling back. Again, the tax reform of 1986 restrains the use of state mortgage finance.

A persuasive counter argument to such concerns is that direct housing subsidies have been no less volatile. If local or nonprofit sponsors want federal financing of low-cost housing, direct or oblique, they must learn to swim with the tide, make hay while the sun shines, and so on. In other words, they should take advantage of whatever programmatic format exists and be prepared to shift course on short notice.

Simply a Matter of Money

Our volume concludes with a chapter by Elizabeth Roistacher, which returns to the book's prevailing view that there is nothing especially wrong with our private-market housing system that a little more purchasing power for the poor cannot cure. Roistacher argues not only for a system of cash vouchers for the eligible poor, to close the gap between the cost of adequate but modest market housing (most of it undoubtedly drawn from the older existing stock), and what the poor can afford but also that the subsidy be channeled through the tax system. Her arguments in favor of the tax approach rest on two points: the resistance of tax preferences to the annual tinkering and funding variability that characterize explicit budgetary allocations and the symmetrical elegance of an approach that balances the massive tax subsidies of the middle class with modest ones for the poor. Naturally, to be effective, housing tax credits for the poor must be refundable (meaning that if your tax liability is negative, the government sends you a check), which does make them different from the prevailing middle-class tax benefits. Roistacher departs from all other proposals in this book in one important respect. She would make the tax-based housing vouchers a universal entitlement for all eligible households, much like the food stamp program. According to Roistacher's calculations (for 1986), we would need to assist at least 4.5 million households, at approximately $3,500 each, adding $16 billion dollars to the total federal housing bill. She would recapture some of these funds by restricting the tax benefits of the middle class. Assuming such a change is politically viable, even the remaining cut looks like a great deal of money at a time of fiscal austerity. Nevertheless, the expenditure would represent a real bargain if it ended housing disadvantage in this country once and for all. Roistacher herself, however, doubts that her plan would indeed eliminate substandard housing without a minimum housing standard as a condition of participation. But then she also worries that a minimum housing standard is unenforceable (dependent as it would be on local action) or inequitable (some eligible families might not be able to find qualifying dwellings).

As a comprehensive, simple, and elegant solution to the housing problem, Roistacher's proposal looks very appealing and makes an appropriate conclusion to the seven-chapter housing policy dialectic that precedes it. Of course, for those who do not believe that the housing problems of the poor are primarily a matter of money, or for the die-hard pragmatists who refuse to believe that the nation will ever commit an additional $16 billion to housing, hers remains, as Roistacher dubs it, a "modest" proposal.

Summing Up

The essays, analyses, and proposals that make up this volume raise virtually all the issues worth addressing on the subject of housing for the poor. Just about every policy that could be tried to ameliorate the problem of housing disadvantage, as well as every policy that has been tried, is reviewed here. The authors of the previous chapters make us aware of the pitfalls of each potential remedy as well as its promise. We are also treated to varying opinions as to what constitutes the problem and how much of a problem there actually is. Yet this rich and varied tapestry of research and recommendation on housing will bring us no closer to a resolution of the problem of housing disadvantage in America unless we ask ourselves, and answer honestly, some hard questions. Until we stop believing, in the words of the Red Queen in *Alice in Wonderland*, "six impossible things before breakfast," housing for the poor will indeed remain America's permanent problem.

First, let us be honest about the source of funding for the improvement of housing conditions. There are only three possibilities. The resources can come from one or another component of the housing industry, from the beneficiaries, or from all of us collectively, drawing directly or indirectly on tax levies. This list can be narrowed further. We can forget about the real estate industry or any of its parts (owners, developers, banks, and the like) because its members cannot be compelled to swallow a housing subsidy that lowers their rate of return uncompetitively with other investment opportunities. The beneficiaries, the families occupying the improved housing, can be, and often are, asked to bear a substantial part of the burden, as is the case whenever we mandate higher housing construction or maintenance standards than many households really want. But because these higher standards must be paid for with higher rents, we are then confronted with the dilemma of affordability. So, unless we can disregard those who, like Apgar, find high rent-to-income ratios unacceptable, we are left with only one housing funding resource and that, however it may be disguised, is taxes.

I have no doubt that housing reformers will be neither surprised nor dismayed by this insight. But because a somewhat larger cohort than housing reformers must pay these taxes, a fudging of the real source of funding for housing improvement will result only in futile and ineffective measures that, as our authors testify, inevitably breed cynicism, disillusion, and reaction. To elicit an effective and lasting commitment to housing improvement, we (meaning the people who think, write about, and implement housing policy) must be clear, consistent, and brutally honest about what we can and should try to achieve.

The Question of Quality

The issue of housing quality is one example. The housing standards built into the conventional housing improvement agenda reveal its authors as guilty of, at best, unrealistic naivete, or, at worst, cynical disregard of their stated objectives. Because of the moving target of ever-rising standards, to escape a label of inadequacy (or whatever the current sobriquet happens to be), housing must be considerably more than "decent or safe." It must be built and maintained to middle-class standards. This self-imposed constraint places most housing policies and programs for low-income groups on the horns of a dilemma. A large-scale effort that permitted a great many disadvantaged families to enjoy the program benefits would not only entail an enormous expense but would create a politically unviable situation, causing many of the subsidizing taxpayers to live less well than the newly subsidized beneficiaries. Yet a modest, inexpensive, and politically palatable program would assist only a few randomly selected households. In the jargon of welfare economics, unrealistic housing standards must result in an unacceptable level of either horizontal or vertical inequity. This suggests to me that a sensible agenda of housing reform must set a consistent fixed target of housing quality, at a level above "indecent" and "unsafe" but well below that enjoyed by the majority of unsubsidized taxpayers, unless, of course, we ask the beneficiaries to pick up part of the tab, even if this imposes a rent-to-income burden that exceeds the affordability criterion.

Another aspect of the quality issue that demands an honest confrontation with reality is the criterion of neighborhood quality, which Apgar and other housing reformers decry as the major contemporary locus of housing inadequacy. The "inadequacy" of neighborhoods today is manifest, in the last analysis, in only three objective conditions. The most egregious of these is the randomly interspersed pattern of extreme physical deterioration occasioned by housing abandonment. Almost as important, and figuring prominently in the

Annual Housing Survey's list of neighborhood deficiencies, are the antisocial behavioral manifestations of the neighborhood's own residents. These include crime, litter, graffiti, noise, and a variety of other common practices that are unsanitary, unaesthetic, or disturb the peace. The third is an evident deficiency in the provision of normal municipal services such as garbage collection, street lighting, street repair, or other items of civic amenity.

If these three manifestations indeed constitute the major part of neighborhood inadequacy, how can we remedy them? Upgrading municipal services to the standard of other local neighborhoods is simple to contemplate, and it is only fair. Would that this were really a serious cause of neighborhood squalor because it would be easy to fix without requiring any general national subsidy. In many instances, however, it is a specious issue. Very often what appears to be municipal neglect is just another sign of vandalism and abuse by residents. But whether this self-imposed neighborhood destruction is directed toward civic or private property, little public support will be forthcoming for the proposition that it is something the rest of the community is obligated to curtail or repair.

That leaves abandonment. Abandonment is the result of market forces. The properties involved command so little market demand that their tax and finance debts exceed their resale value. Because abandonment cannot be stopped, all that can be done is to eliminate its physical evidence. Enlightened local policies can ensure that tax-foreclosed properties are speedily demolished or sold to more viable entrepreneurs. But such policies are often criticized as callous measures of "planned shrinkage" or "gentrification." It is often demanded in the name of neighborhood improvement that public funds be used to repair abandoned housing and lease it at a loss. So we are back to contemplating a set of dwelling unit subsidies. Thus an honest assessment of the causes of "neighborhood inadequacy" must lead us to conclude that much of it defies public solution, except at a great public expense. To advocate incurring this expense raises the political issue addressed earlier. To suggest achieving the same objective without the expense is to fool oneself and breed disappointment among the residents of blighted neighborhoods, as well as the general public.

The Question of Efficiency

Although a review of prevailing attitudes regarding housing quality reveals considerable confusion and intellectual inconsistency, on the issue of the efficiency of housing reform efforts, realism and common sense seem to be gaining ground. The work of our contributors reflects the convergence of views and attitudes among housing reformers generally that we must seek more efficient ways of reducing housing disadvantage. The current orthodoxy maintains that new dwellings for the poor are to be eschewed in favor of existing ones. Public development and ownership are not to be preferred to private efforts. Expensive subsidies to producers are to be replaced by lower-cost assistance to consumers. Untargeted help lavished indiscriminately on low- and moderate-income households is to give way to assistance targeted precisely on the "truly needy." The early analytical chapters of this book (Sternlieb and Listokin, Weicher, Lowry) document or reflect the degree to which the pro-efficiency bias has come to dominate thinking about housing policy. The later solution-oriented chapters (Sumka, Villani, Roistacher) all make the efficiency criterion a central aspect of their search for viable policies and programs. The reason for efficiency's ascendancy in housing reform is not hard to deduce. It is a natural adaptation to straitened fiscal resources in general and a hardening of the public heart toward housing assistance in particular.

A general drift toward efficient solutions must at some point cohere around specific programmatic measures. What are the most efficient housing policies? The answer depends very much on the level of housing quality we mean to assure. Quality and efficiency are linked. A high and consistent standard would move us toward a prototypical housing assistance package with a nonprofit sponsor, modest rehabilitation of the cheapest available existing dwelling units that are currently substandard, using tax-sheltered financing (to the extent permitted) raised in limited partnership syndications, restricting tenancy to households with incomes 50 percent below the median (depending on household size), who would be required to devote, say, 35 percent of their income (exclusive of utilities) to rent. A lower standard would modify this package by including a large component of homesteading—low and high density—coupled with small rehabilitation grants (probably drawn from state mortgage revenue bond proceeds or federal Community Development Block Grants). The homesteaded stock would be owner-occupied, with no restrictions regarding profits accruing to the beneficiary households if they resell their homesteads, other than repayment of the rehabilitation grant. The lower qualitative standard would justify a policy of housing stipends, available to all income-eligible families, just large enough to make up the average difference between market rents charged for the most modest but "adequate" housing and 35 percent of the household income. For the stipends to be most efficient, the recipient households must not be required to spend the entire stipend, or even a major part of it, on housing. They must merely be able to demonstrate that they are occupying dwellings that meet our qualitative standard.

Obviously, this rather breezy summary does not constitute a program. Apart from the considerable political and fiscal obstacles attending even such an "efficient" choice of approaches, any specific program must take into account the condition of the existing stock in various regions, the characteristics and predispositions of the putative beneficiaries, effects on neighborhoods of the nonpoor, among many other factors. I offer these paradigms only to make us think somewhat more comprehensively and operationally about an efficient and effective housing reform agenda.

The Question of Equity

However inefficient or ineffective the government-sponsored housing policies of the past may have been, their most egregious failing, as noted at a number of points in this volume, has been their inequity. This inequity has resulted from the intersection of three factors. The principal one is the small amount of aggregate public funding available for housing. With too few dollars chasing too many eligible families, most are bound to be left out. The impact of this resource constraint has been much exacerbated by the broad and diffuse criteria for eligibility—too few dollars chasing too varied an eligible population, as it were. Finally, the excessively high and variable standards for the housing quality to be achieved have assured that the meager dollar allocations would reach the smallest rather than the largest number of eligible households. The natural result is that housing assistance has been a lottery—one with relatively few winners and very unequal prizes.

Seen from the vantage point of the potentially eligible population, the inequity of the housing assistance lottery is manifest in one or another of the following circumstances. The vast majority of families that can be characterized as housing disadvantaged at any given time receive no assistance. But because the excluded are aware of the existence of housing assistance programs—and may even know families who have benefited—they are likely to find their condition even more intolerable than under a situation in which no housing assistance is available for anyone. Even the beneficiaries of one or another assistance program may be unhappy because the level of assistance is so variable. Such households are bound to know others who have gained access to better apartments or who are paying lower rents. Finally, the inequity is apparent to the ineligible. Both the broadened target and the high standards associated with previous housing assistance programs have assured that the issue of equity touched many who are not housing disadvantaged in two ways. The least well housed of this group have been put in a position of seeing their taxes support better housing for others than they themselves enjoy. The unassisted not so badly housed see their economic peers benefiting from access to situations that lower the cost of their housing—again, invariably at general taxpayer expense.

Although no serious analyst of housing policy will challenge the assertion that housing assistance has been random and unfair, many fail to acknowledge how corrosive and counterproductive are the effects of this inequity. The prevailing view has been that "something is better than nothing," "half a loaf is better than none," and so on. There has been an entirely inaccurate perception of the housing problem as one of relatively stable dimensions, with incremental programs gradually, but surely, chipping away at the mountain of housing deprivation until none is left. But because existing housing continues to deteriorate and new cohorts of disadvantaged families continually enter the housing stream, this approach cannot result in a long-term aggregate improvement of housing conditions. Housing conditions have, indeed, been getting better because of rising incomes and high levels of private housing production, but that has only disguised the failure of the policies of direct housing assistance. It is time for us to acknowledge that the lottery approach to housing assistance is not acceptable—that half a loaf (actually one-sixth of a loaf) is worse than none. We would consider an attitude toward elementary and secondary education that was satisfied with scattering benefits haphazardly among a fraction of the nation's school-age population as irresponsible and frivolous; such an attitude is no less frivolous when applied to housing assistance.

What, then, can be done to make housing assistance equitable? First, let me suggest that we limit the dimensions of the problem by recognizing the private housing market as the provider of the first resort. We should not exaggerate the intensity of housing disadvantage that results from private-market forces, nor should we exaggerate the number of people who need help. For a start, we should look very warily at such concepts as "neighborhood inadequacy" or "affordability." The task of housing assistance should be to assure only that all Americans have access to decent—but perhaps minimal—shelter. To the extent that many families may prefer better than decent but minimal, they may indeed have to allocate a higher than typical share of their budget to housing. Also, to the extent that some families with the means to secure good housing are indifferent to housing quality, they should be permitted to indulge their budgetary preferences. Equity, as well as efficiency, demands that we design criteria that restrict eligibility for assistance to those most likely to be living in substandard housing. This may be difficult to do explicitly, but a very low income threshold might accomplish it just as well. Equity also demands that housing assistance programs deliver the same level of benefit to all the eligible—in proportion to their need, preferably. If we collectively wish to devote only meager resources to housing, or if we decide on a high income eligibility threshold, an equitable policy will yield very small benefits per household. Unit benefits could rise as we spent more in the aggregate or as we tightened the eligibility criteria. An equitable policy should assure only that the dollar value of the benefit be uniform. Whether this policy yielded equal housing outcomes would depend on individual household preferences and trade-offs, as well as the prices and housing available in local housing markets.

These criteria suggest that a uniform national housing program of some sort would be optimal. But to the extent that states or localities wish to implement housing assistance programs independently of Washington (perhaps because they understandably despair of Washington acting soon enough or generously enough), the criteria for an equitable housing assistance program could still be applied within the constrained jurisdictional boundaries. Even an equitable housing assistance program limited to residents of Minnesota or Chicago would be preferable to the present unfair hodgepodge.

Conclusion

The title of this chapter is a rhetorical question: "Can we ensure that all Americans are well housed?" The chapter should conclude with an answer—and that answer is a qualified yes. The contributors to this volume, including myself, have expressed a great deal of skepticism as to the wisdom of present and past housing policies. This is not to be mistaken for cynicism, however. We can ensure that almost all Americans are well housed if we take an honest view of the problem and a realistic approach to the solution. First, we should bear in mind that our task is made much easier because most Americans are already well housed, with their housing getting better in each succeeding decade. Second, because "well housed" is a subjective concept, we can go a long way toward meeting our housing objectives by setting a sensible—low but decent—housing standard as the criterion. Third, we can ensure that all Americans are well housed, even with the allocation of modest resources, if we do not squander our funds on the already well housed. Finally, we can ensure that Americans—of all income levels—will feel good about such housing assistance as we are willing or able to provide if we take pains to distribute it equitably. I will not conclude with any particular policy "magic bullet." The contributors to this book have outlined as clearly as anyone the pros and cons of the various available approaches, both the old and new supply-oriented ones and that ultimate demand-side solution—the housing voucher. Rather than close with a prescription of my own, I wish merely to propose that we evaluate the problem of housing disadvantage with intellectual honesty and set out to solve it with a clear but imaginative view of our objectives.

Contributors

William C. Apgar, Jr., is associate professor of city and regional planning at Harvard University's Kennedy School of Government and serves as associate director of the Harvard-MIT Joint Center for Housing Studies. He is author of *Housing and Neighborhood Dynamics* and coauthor of *Housing Outlook: 1980–1990; Assessment of the Likely Impacts of the President's Tax Proposals on Rental Housing Markets;* and *Microeconomics and Public Policy.*

David Listokin is a professor at the Center for Urban Policy Research. He holds a Ph.D. in urban planning from Rutgers University and has written numerous monographs and articles on housing, land use, and public finance.

Ira S. Lowry is an economist specializing in housing and urban development issues. Associated for many years with the Rand Corporation, he is now an independent consultant based in Pacific Palisades, California.

Elizabeth A. Roistacher is associate professor of economics at Queens College of the City University of New York. She served as deputy assistant secretary for economic affairs of the U.S. Department of Housing and Urban Development from 1979 until 1981. She is coauthor of *Tax Subsidies and Housing Investment* and coeditor of *Rental Housing: Is There a Crisis?*

Peter D. Salins is chairman of the Department of Urban Affairs of Hunter College of the City University of New York. He is a senior research fellow of the Manhattan Institute, associate editor of *New York Affairs,* and book review editor of the *Journal of the American Planning Association.* He is also author of *The Ecology of Housing Destruction* as well as other monographs and articles on housing policy, land use patterns, and economic development.

George Sternlieb is director of the Center for Urban Policy Research and professor of urban planning and policy development at Rutgers University. He is a member of the Census Advisory Committee on Population Statistics and a trustee of the Urban Land Institute and has served on a number of presidential task forces on urban development. He has written over twenty-five books on housing and urban development issues.

Howard J. Sumka is director of the Division of Community Planning and Neighborhood Studies at the U.S. Department of Housing and Urban Development, currently on assignment in the Office of Housing and Urban Programs at the U.S. Agency for International Development. He is the author of many articles and monographs on housing and urban development and has taught at the Universities of Kansas, Maryland, and Virginia.

Kevin Villani is executive vice president and chief financial officer of Imperial Corporation of America. Previously he has been senior vice president for financial and economic analysis and chief economist at the Federal Home Loan Mortgage Corporation.

John C. Weicher holds the F. K. Weyerhaeuser Chair at the American Enterprise Institute. He was deputy staff director of the President's Commission on Housing and deputy assistant secretary of the U.S. Department of Housing and Urban Development. He has been affiliated with the Urban Institute, Ohio State University, and the University of California at Irvine. He has authored four books and many articles on housing and recently edited *Maintaining the Safety Net: Income Redistribution Programs in the Reagan Administration.*

Index